Agayuliyararput

Our Way of Making Prayer

Felicia...

January 1996

Agayuliyararput
Kegginaqut, Kangiit-llu

Our Way of Making Prayer
Yup'ik Masks and the Stories They Tell

Transcribed and translated by Marie Meade
Edited by Ann Fienup-Riordan

Published by the Anchorage Museum of History and Art
in association with the University of Washington Press
Seattle and London

Funded by:
The National Endowment for the Humanities
The Coastal-Yukon Mayors' Association

Library of Congress Cataloging-in-Publication Data
Agayuliyararput : kegginaqut kangiit-llu = Our way of making prayer : masks and the stories they tell / transcribed and translated by Marie Meade ; edited by Ann Fienup-Riordan.
    p.   cm.
   Includes bibliographical references.
   ISBN 0-295-97509-1 (alk. paper)
   1. Yupik masks.   2. Yupik dance.   3. Yupik Eskimos—Rites and ceremonies. I. Meade, Marie.   II. Fienup-Riordan, Ann.   III. Anchorage Museum of History and Art.
E99.E7A38   1995
391'.434'089971—dc20   95-25849
                                                  CIP

Cover illustration: John McIntyre (left) from Eek dances with Joe Chief, Jr., from Bethel. Photo by James H. Barker

Qaneryarangqerrsaaqut-am taukut.
Carrait qaneryarangqerlaryaaqut.

There are stories behind those [masks].
There is something of significance to say about every little thing about them.

— Mary Mike, February 1994

Ukut kalikat umyuaqut kaput Nick Ayaginaar Charles-aam atranun
canritlermini kegginaqulitullermun cingumaillermun-llu
yuraryaramek. Cali-llu ukut kalikat umyuaqutkaput imkunun
ayagyuanun niiteksailngurnun ukuni kalikarni igaucimaltianek
ciulirneret qanemciitnek quliraitnek-llu.

To Nick Charles, Sr., a great teacher and mask-maker, and
to the younger generation, who have not heard these stories.

Ukut Kalikat Imait

Contents

Quyavikluki Ikayuutellret

Quyaviksuganka cakneq ciulirneret tamalkuita ikayuutellret makut ak'allaat kegginaqut akmaken maavet iluvautellerkaat upyutlemteggu. Angukaraat arnarkaraat-llu nunacuarnun ayagaurallemni kangingengnaquurlua kegginaqulallratnek tamarmeng ciuniurturallruatnga cakneq ilaliurlua, nerevkarlua nunakegcivkarlua-llu. Nunacuarni makut tegganret yuk'egtaraat tengruluteng qalaruqurallruatnga imumi anguvilqerluki tangllermeggnek kegginaqurluteng agayulallratnek. Tamarmeng piyugteqluteng, imucetun kasnguyulriacetun pivkenateng qanrutkurallruit imkut ciuliamta piciryarallrit. Caperrsulriacetun-llu wall' alingelriacetun pivkenateng qanerturallruut makut tuaten angalkut apaaluki caliarat-llu kanaraluku.

Ukut tungaunaki qalarutellrenka caknerpak quyaviksuganka, maa-i cali uitaluteng ilagarluta: Negeqlirmek, Mary Mike, Justina Mike, Jasper Louise, Johnny Thompson-aaq-llu; Qerrulligmek, Alma Keyes, Cecilia Foxie, Pauline Akaran, Willie Kamkoff-aq-llu; Mamterillermek, Kay Hendrickson, Dick Andrew, Fannie Wasky-llu; Nunapicuarmek, Nickolai Berlin, Natalia White-aq-llu; Kangirnarmek, Martha Mann, Julia Azean, Charlie David, Elena Phillip-aq-llu; Napaskiarmek-llu, Joseph Evan; Mikuryamek Harry Wesley, Robert and Edna Kolerak; Cev'armek Joseph Tuluk, Angelina Ulroan, Mary Friday-llu; Kuigilngurmek Frank Andrew; Nuigtarmek-llu, Elsie Tommy. Ukut-llu qalarutraanemnek ak'a catairutellret cali quyaviksuganka, Negeqlirmek Andy Kinzy, Kangirnarmek Mary Worm, Anchorage-aamek-llu William Tyson.

Ann Fienup-Riodan-aaq-llu quyviksugaqa cali. Ellii-llu ikayuqlunuk man'a caliaq akikangrraanranek caliaqurallruarpuk. Elliin-llu cali kalikarugarnek imiriquluni akikaa mat'um unakengnaqellrua piciurrvianun. Watnacillerkarput-llu elliin umyuangutkelqaa ukut-llu, Fr. Astruc, Andy Paukan, Tim Troll-aq-llu ikayuqluki Anchorage Histori-cal Museum-aami calilriit qalarutellruit ellait ikayuqluki man'a caliaqsugluku. Museum-aam-llu calistain piyullrat ciuniullruat. Anchor-age-aami-llu museum-aam angayuqra Pat Wolf-aq quyaviksugarput

Acknowledgments

I want to thank all the elders who helped in their special way to prepare for the brief return of old masks from museums in this country and abroad. In my travels to various villages in the Yukon-Kuskokwim delta searching for information on traditional mask use and ceremony, old men and women welcomed me into their homes with kindness, food, and shelter. As I listened to these wonderful and gentle elders tell of their brief experience with mask ceremonies and their work among the Yupiit in depth, I knew they were expressing traditional paradigms. The ways of their ancestors were expressed freely, without shame or remorse, as evident in their tales of the *angalkut* [shamans] who were candidly spoken about.

At this time I want to thank the elders I spoke with directly: Mary Mike, Justina Mike, Jasper Louise, and Johnny Thompson from St. Marys; Alma Keyes, Cecilia Foxie, Pauline Akaran, and Willie Kamkoff from Kotlik; Kay Hendrickson, Dick Andrew, and Fannie Wasky from Bethel; Nickolia Berlin and Natalia White from Nunapitchuk; Martha Mann, Julia Azean, Charlie David, and Elena Phillip from Kongiganak; Joseph Evan from Napaskiak; Harry Wesley, and Robert and Edna Kolerak from Mekoryuk; Joseph Tulik, Angelina Ulroan, and Mary Friday from Chevak; Frank Andrew from Kwigillingok; and Elsie Tommy from Newtok. I also want to thank those elders who have passed on since I talked with them, including Andy Kinzy from St. Marys, Mary Worm from Kongiganak, and William Tyson from Anchorage.

I also want to thank Ann Fienup-Riordan. Since the beginning of this project she and I wholeheartedly and continuously worked together. She worked assiduously, even before funding was granted, to make this book and exhibit possible. With the support of Andy Paukan, Tim Troll, and Fr. Astruc, she approached the Anchorage Museum of History and Art to explore the possibility of putting together such an exhibit. The idea was accepted by the museum staff. We would like to thank museum director Pat Wolf for supporting the exhibit. We also thank them for

kegginaqut ciuniullranek yugnun tangercetnaluki. Nunakauyarmun-llu ciumek ayaulluki pillrat, tuamtell' kinguakun Mamterillermun, tamana quyatekarput ellaitnun. Nunakauyarmiuni-llu quyavikamceci ciuniullerpecenek kegginaqut nunavceñun, yugnun-llu tailrianun tangercelluki. Mamterillermiuni-ll' cali tuaten pillerci quyakarput.

Quyumta-llu Irene Reed-aq, Anna Jacobson-aaq-llu [Fairbanks-aarmiunguuk] ukut kalikat imarkait Yugtun igausngalriit naaqurluki yuvrinqegcaarturallruaput, alangqalriit kitugtaqluki. Kass'atun-llu ak'a mugigtellrenka cali ikayuqluta kitugqurallruaput assirikanirluki naaqsunariluki. Taũgaam cali nallunailngurmek Kass'atun pimallrit ilait alangqaciqut cukangnaqluta pillruamta. Elkek caknerpakayak qayvikqapqapqapiararagka akingutkamegnek qanerpek'natek ikayuutellragnek ukut kalikat imarkaitnek caliurallemni. Nurnamek tengrupiarlutek elkenka ikayullruagnga sass'at amllepiat aturluki.

Ciulirneret qalarutkurallrit amllepiaryaaqut, taũgaam qanrukurallrita ilarrait ukuni kalikarni igausngaut. Ukaniku piyunarqekumta cali ukucetun naaqerkarpecenek igauciyugyaaqukut.

Cupluar, June 1995

allowing the exhibit to begin in Toksook Bay and Bethel. We thank the Toksook Bay people for welcoming the masks and exhibiting them to the people. We thank the Bethel community for doing that also.

In preparation for this publication Anna Jacobson of the Alaska Native Language Center and Irene Reed of Fairbanks helped me in proofreading and editing the Yup'ik transcriptions and gave invaluable assistance with the English translations. They volunteered many hours to this project, and for this I am deeply grateful. However, I am responsible for any errors that are undoubtedly still present due to shortage of time allowed for a thorough editing.

The elders recounted many fascinating things from their knowledge and wisdom, but only a fraction of what they said is printed in this book. We would like to continue our work to provide materials such as this to the general public.

Marie Meade, June 1995

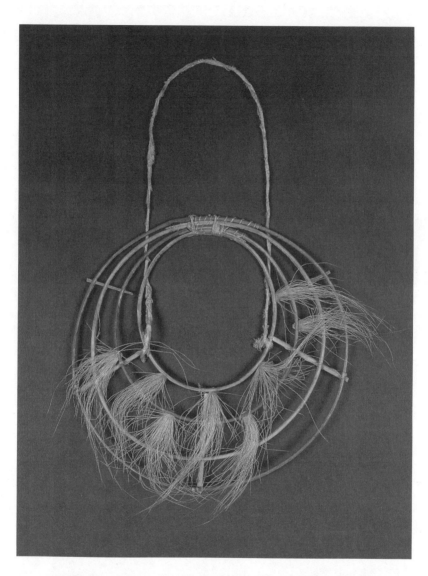

Arnat atutukiit kegginaquq A. H Twitchell-aam pillra Kusquqvamek 1900s-aani.
Uivenqellriit tamarmeng ellanguaruluteng. National Museum of the American
Indian, New York

Woman's mask collected by A. H. Twitchell from the Kuskokwim, early 1900s.
Each hoop is designated *ellanguaq* (pretend universe). National Museum of the
American Indian, New York, 9/3437 (66 cm)

Kalikaliyararput: Our Way of Making a Book

From 1993 to 1995 an anthropologist, representatives of the Yup'ik community, and museum professionals worked together to create a unique exhibit of Yup'ik masks. The *Agayuliyararput* exhibit—opening in the village of Toksook Bay in January 1996, moving to the regional center of Bethel for a two-month stay, in May traveling to Anchorage for five months, and then moving on to several Lower Forty-Eight venues—celebrates not only masks but the unique view of the world of the Yup'ik people who created them.

The idea for the exhibit was born in 1989. That year I had the opportunity to visit several museums on the East Coast containing Yup'ik collections. I came away amazed by what I found. Brick and glass buildings thousands of miles from Alaska contained masks unlike any I had seen, including masks in pairs and masks made to be worn by women. I knew that what I had found would interest friends and colleagues in Alaska. When I returned I shared my excitement with Pat Wolf, director of the Anchorage Museum. I asked her if we could bring the masks home for an exhibit, and she answered enthusiastically, "Sure, why not?"

At the same time I was discovering Yup'ik masks in museum collections, Andy Paukan and Tim Troll were uncovering treasures closer to home, specifically the things Sheldon Jackson had collected at Andreafski in the 1890s and deposited at the museum in Sitka bearing his name. Tim Troll and Andy Paukan went to Sitka with Yukon elders Willie Beans and Wassilie Evan to choose one hundred objects to bring to the Yukon River community of Mountain Village, where they would be exhibited during a four-day dance festival. Their interest in the masks and other artifacts in the Jackson collection was far from academic. For Andy Paukan and the Yukon village elders, these things were the tangible remains of a fragile heritage, much of which younger generations had all but forgotten. Their hope was to use these "objects of myth and memory" as part of a grassroots effort to foster pride and self-awareness among the descendants of their makers. The Mountain Village exhibit did this, and much more.

Andy Paukan's and Tim Troll's interest in bringing home "captured heritage" and my excitement over buried treasures in museums might have remained discrete had it not been for a mutual friend, Father René Astruc. Father Astruc has worked in southwestern Alaska for more than thirty years, first as a village priest and more recently as head of the Jesuit Native Deacon Program. Father Astruc's own life mirrors the Native Deacon Program's efforts to bring the best of the Yup'ik past into the modern Catholic Church: he is a priest as well as an experienced Yup'ik dancer. Father Astruc attended the Mountain Village festival and exhibit. Several years later he heard me describe the masks I had seen during my travels and invited me to the Jesuit House to meet Andy Paukan and Tim Troll. Within a week we met again with Pat Wolf, and a joint exhibit was born. We would bring Yup'ik masks back to Alaska, exhibiting them first in the Yukon-Kuskokwim villages in which they were made and then in Anchorage for all Alaskans to appreciate.

The depth of feeling that the return of the masks evokes for the Yup'ik community is apparent in the title they gave the exhibit: *Agayuliyararput: Our Way of Making Prayer.* On Nunivak Island *agayu* originally meant "mask," and the verb phrase *agayuliluteng* meant "they making masks" to request that animals and plants be plentiful in the coming year. As Christian missionaries' suppression of masked dancing began at the end of the nineteenth century, the verb base *agayu-* evolved to mean "to pray" or "to worship." *Agayuliyararput,* as applied to the return of the masks, evokes both the old and new meanings of the word in a single phrase.

Unlike past American exhibits, *Agayuliyararput* opens in a village and ends in a cosmopolitan center. The exhibit's opening at a large dance festival recalls the social context in which Yup'ik masks were originally shown. Also unlike previous exhibits, *Agayuliyararput* frames the presentation of the masks in Yup'ik terms, drawing on the detailed remembrances of Yup'ik elders born in the first decades of the 1900s, who saw the last masked dances before missionary efforts forced their decline. Few remain who can describe these events, and their remembrances have rarely been recorded. Thus, the exhibit has involved a great deal of research—work that had to be done now or never.

In February 1993 Marie Meade and I met with elders at the annual St. Marys Potlatch. We interviewed half a dozen people there and several more the following January in Bethel. After that, Marie carried out interviews on her own. My job was to visit museums and photograph what I found. Marie visited elders and showed them pictures, asking specific questions about the masks and what they meant. Marie and I shared what we learned. I encouraged her to pursue specific questions, and she determined which directions to follow. None of what follows would ever have been recorded without Marie's dedication to this work and her sensitive listening, hour after hour, to what older Yup'ik men and women had to say.

The results of Marie's research have gone beyond our highest hopes, culminating in more than thirty hours of taped interviews with elders from all over southwestern Alaska. She carefully transcribed and translated that material, producing several thousand pages of transcripts in Yup'ik and English. I studied the transcripts, quoting from them extensively in *The Living Tradition of Yup'ik Masks* (University of Washington Press, 1996), the book I wrote to accompany the *Agayuliyararput* exhibit.

Marie-Meade-am erinairturqii Angelina Ulroan-aaq, Cev'ami, March 1995-aami. James H. Barker

Marie Meade interviewing Angelina Ulroan, Chevak, March 1995. James H. Barker

In December 1994 I submitted a six-hundred page manuscript to the Press, including one-hundred pages of stories describing masks and masked dancing in both Yup'ik and English.

As I wrote *The Living Tradition,* I kept a running file in Yup'ik and English of all statements I quoted from the transcripts. I knew that the long passages in my original manuscript would require editing so as not to interrupt the literary flow for the English catalog's intended audience—the general public—and I wanted to retain a complete, uncut, record of what the elders had said.[1]

Even after I edited the manuscript, the catalog remained long, and it became clear that Marie and I had written not one but two books. My rendering, emphasizing the masks' visual component, communicated the elders' personal statements in an abbreviated fashion. But the longer accounts and stories had value in their own right, emphasizing the masks' verbal component. Together, the elders had authored their own book about maskmaking and masked dancing, and many readers will find it more compelling than the translated, summary accounts.

At first we called this second book our "Yup'ik catalog." Certainly it will interest the Yup'ik audience who visits the mask exhibit, especially the many younger men and women who have never heard these stories. But like *The Living Tradition of Yup'ik Masks,* it, too, is aimed at a national audience, including linguists, folklorists, anthropologists, historians, and other scholars concerned with Native American oral tradition. Art historians and specialists interested in Yup'ik and Inupiat art and ceremony also will appreciate the full accounts of the masks' meanings and the stories they tell. This book is written for those interested in not only what the elders have to say, but also how they say it.

Dividing a single book into two was not an ideal solution, as the original unity made an essential point: we base what we know on the elders' narratives. The separation did, however, offer advantages. The quoted material could be presented uncut. Ironically, the editorial need to rid the English text of repetition has a parallel in the masks' own history. The most famous example is the pairs of masks Kuskokwim trader A. H. Twitchell collected and sold to George Heye in the early 1900s. Heye viewed the pairs as redundant and deaccessioned the extras.

---

[1] In fact, repetitions, common to all oral literature and used to enhance memory, are a standard feature of Yup'ik oratory and often occur in threes.

Unlike the lost pairs, however, this book provides a safe harbor for the special information jettisoned in the interests of communication to a wider audience.

This is the first time anywhere in the world that an exhibit of Alaska Native material has been accompanied by a book written, essentially, by Native elders. As editor, I helped Marie choose the stories and accounts that best described masks and masked dancing, but beyond this introduction, readers will learn what they learn from the elders' descriptions.

Few exhibits in the continental United States, and none in Alaska, have begun in a village and closed in New York. This bilingual book is equally innovative, providing Yup'ik oratory and first-person accounts by Yup'ik elders instead of anthropological analysis of Yup'ik art and ceremony by a non-Native. I am a non-Native anthropologist, and my writing has its time and place. This is not one of them.

Two of the *Agayuliyararput* exhibit's three primary venues are Yup'ik communities whose members speak Yup'ik as a first language. Yup'ik is the second most commonly spoken Native language in the United States and the third most common in North America north of Mexico, following Navajo and Inuktitut. More than twenty thousand people live in southwestern Alaska, and more than half speak Yup'ik as their first language. In a fourth of the seventy Yup'ik villages, Yup'ik is the first language of everyone, from the eldest to the youngest. Producing this book is not an academic exercise—it is a matter of respect. The men, women, and children who attend the exhibit in Toksook Bay and Bethel will be much more interested in what their elders have to say about masks than in my summary accounts, and this book has been designed with their interests in mind.

Paul John, Andy Paukan, and other members of the Yup'ik steering committee that guided this exhibit from its inception adamantly stated the importance to them of their language being front and center along with their masks. In the English-first world of Anchorage, they are made to feel like second-class citizens at every turn. The *Agayuliyararput* exhibit is an expression of Yup'ik pride, a gift to Native and non-Native viewers alike. Their ancestors made the masks, their elders explained their meaning, and this book makes these gifts available to those interested in a uniquely Yup'ik form.

Yup'ik students and non-Native students of Yup'ik language and culture can enjoy this book for what it is—remembrances of masks and masked dancing by the last people to view and participate in them. We have tried to let these men and women speak for themselves. Turn to the words of the experts, and they will explain how masks came to be *agayuliyararput,* "our way of making prayer."

Ann Fienup-Riordan
May 1995

Ciulirneret Ikayuutellret
Yup'ik Elder Contributors

Atra Name	Nunii Residence	Yuurtellran nunii Birthplace	Yuurtellra allrakua Birthdate
William Tyson	Anchorage	Pastuli River	1916
Andy Kinzy	St. Marys	Qissunaq River	1911
Mary Mike	St. Marys	Uksuqalleq	1912
Justina Mike	St. Marys	Caniliaq	1912
Jasper Louise	St. Marys	Anagciq	1916
Johnny Thompson	St. Marys	Tuutalgaq	1923
Pauline Akaran	Emmonak		
Cecilia Foxie	Emmonak	Penguq	1912
Alma Keyes	Emmonak	Pastuli River	1922
Willie Kamkoff	Emmonak	Nunapiggluugaq	1923
Paul John	Toksook Bay	Cevv'arneq	1929
Martha Mann	Kwigillingok	Qipneq	1910
Julia Azean	Kongiganak	Urutuq	1918
Charlie David	Kongiganak	Anuuraaq	1915
Elena Phillip	Kongiganak	Esriq	
Mary Worm	Kongiganak	Cevv'arneq	1898
Joseph Evan	Napaskiak	Paingaq	1906
Nickolai Berlin	Nunapitchuk	Qikertaq, Eek Island	1912
Dick Andrew	Bethel	Kayalivik	1909
Kay Hendrickson	Bethel	Ciguralek, Nunivak Island	1910
Elsie Tommy	Newtok		1922

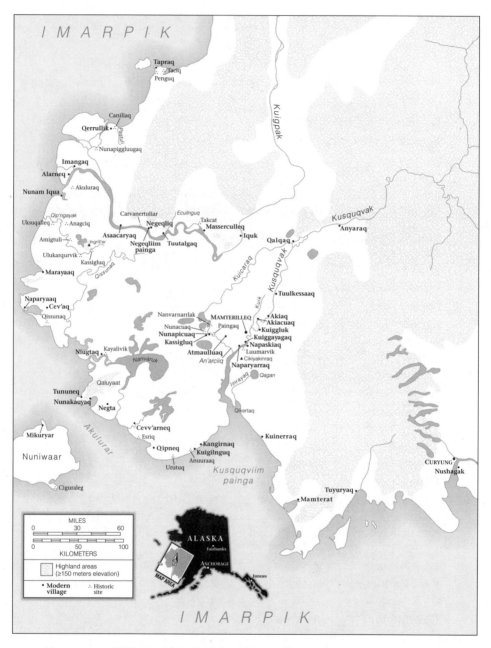

Nunanguaq, 1990. Patrick Jankanish and Matt O'Leary

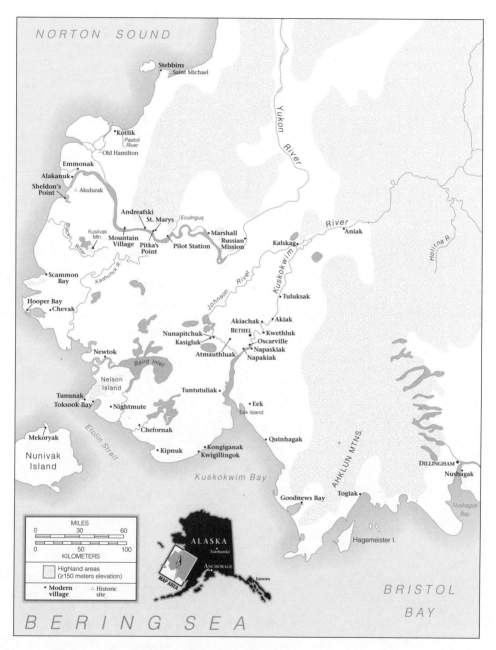

Yukon-Kuskokwim Delta region, 1990. Patrick Jankanish and Matt O'Leary

Agayuliyararput
Our Way of Making Prayer

Paul John-aq yuralria 1987-aami Mamterillermi. Paul John-aq piuq, "Ak'a tamaaken ayagluteng Yupiit kegginaqurluteng yura'arqameng agayuyaramek aptullruat. Kegginaqirluteng kaigalallruut pitarkat paivngasqumaluki pissuquneng." James H. Barker

Paul John dancing at a Bethel dance festival, 1987. According to Paul John, "From a long time past when they used masks in ceremony they called it *agayuyaraq*. . . . They did wear masks. It was a way of praying so the animals would come when they hunted them." James H. Barker

1. Kalikat Ikirrluki

Paul John-ankuk Andy Paukan-aaq-llu qalartellrak kegginaqut taicimallratnek Asaacaryamun Sheldon Jackson Museum-aamek 1989-aami.

Paul John, Nunakauyaq, April 1994

Cali-llu tuatnamacimcetun, piciryararkiumacimcetun, man'a maa-i kiingan nutemllarmun tangrruteksaguskevvut yuraq umyuaqelriani, ellarpallraam yui tamaq'apiarmeng yuraucirluteng ellmeng pimeggnek. Tamaani-llu ellarpall'er man'a kassugluku eglertellriartaitellruyaaquq, tengssuutetaitellrani, phone-artaitellrani, satellite-artaitellrani-llu. Qaillun nunarraminek tuaken cayarani aperturyarturciigatellruyaaqaa yuum yaaqsilrianun. Tuaten pisciigatellrung'ermi Agayutem tua-i piciryararkirluta cakuciungramta yuurcetellruyaaqelliniakut tuaten cayarangqelliniluta. Maa-i mat'um nalliini tangrrutngurtuq kiimi nutemllarmun mat'umun yuraq man'a.

Andy Paukan, Negeqliq, April 1994

Tamana pitekluku makut teggnerraat tua-i ikayuqluki qanertekluki makut maani ciuliamta aũgkut piliallrit atullrit ataam makunun ayagyuanun tangercelluki. Ellaita iingitgun tangercelluki teggnernun makunun nalqigucelluki qayuw' atutullrit, qayuwa-ll' piliaqetullrit. Tua-i nalqigcesqumaluki taumek ayagnillruukuk Tim Troll-aq-llu.

Tua-llu ayagniqatallratni yuarluta naken tamakunek yugtarnek pilianek ut'ruciyuumallemtenek. Tua Sheldon Jackson-aamek uumek niilluta tamaani yugtaat amllerrniluki. Tua-i 1989 Mountain Village-ami festival potlatch-aqataata tuani tamakut yugtaat nasvagyugluki kinguliamtenun makunun. Waniwa-ll' una wani [Paul John] tuani

"Opening the Book": The 1989 Mountain Village Dance Festival

Paul John and Andy Paukan's words about the masks that were brought to Mountain Village from the Sheldon Jackson Museum in 1989.

Paul John, Toksook Bay, April 1994

Each cultural group in this world has its own way of dancing, and considering our dancing, it is the only ceremonial tradition remaining in our culture. In those days when there were no airplanes, telephones, or satellites, people did not travel around the world and could not go to far-off places to share their ways. Though we were unable to do that, God created us all with our own traditions. At the present time dancing is the only custom remaining from our traditional ceremonial ways.

Andy Paukan, St. Marys, April 1994

Let us make our ancestors' ways known to our younger generation, allowing them to see through the eyes of our few remaining elders as they explain the use and construction of these cultural materials. Tim Troll and I began the project because of our intense wish to have the elders explain and talk about these things.

When we began, we searched for a place that had museum pieces we could bring home. We heard that there were a lot of things in the Sheldon Jackson Museum. We decided we wanted to show them to our younger generation at the 1989 Mountain Village Festival. He [Paul John] attended the festival when they were exhibited. And he will know

uitallruuq tamakut nasvallratni. Nallunriciiqaa kingunermini camani tamakut taikata qaill' auluklerkait.

Ukugnek taũgaam teggenregnek Wassilie Evan—tayima allragni yuunriũrlullruuq taun' angun—una-llu Willie Beans Mountain Village-armiu, teggenruagnek, Kuigpagmi-llu piliallrit tamakut kegginaqut atutullrit, cat piliallrit nallunrilagneki tua-i maliklukek Sitka-mun atraullukek. Tuan' atraqatállemteni camek nalluyaaqukut qayuwa eglertellerkamteñek. Taũgaam Peter Corey-m ciuniurluta, Tim Troll-aq malikluku, ciunerluta museum-aamun atraulluta. Tua-i itramta imumun Sheldon Jackson Museum-aamun narrlullagyaaqua, taũgaam-qaa makut maani maa-i tangrrarkaput. Cunawa elliviatni camani, storage room, nutaan amlleq yugtaq, Yupiit aũgkut ciuliamta piliarit uitalriit nalluluki nurcillagyaaqlua.

Nutaan tua-i malrugni erenregni tuani taumi storage room-ami yuvrillruukut tamakunek yugtarnek Kuigpagmiutarnek ceñamiutarnek-llu yuarluta. Taukuk tuani Wassillie Evan-am Willie Beans-am-llu tangerrluki tamakut elitaqnaurakek, una-gguq uum piklinia aterpaggluku-llu ciuliaq tauna. Uum-gguq una piliaqellinia elitaqaa-gguq. Tuaten malrugni ernerrluta, piyulkegnek taũgaam elkenka tua-i ut'rutarkaurrluta Mt. Village-amun. Qayutun, hundred cipluku canek pilinguanek kegginaqunek ciuliamta-ll' aũgkunek atutullritnek ut'rutellruukut tuani.

Malruk taũgaam ut'rucullerput Peter Corey-m pillruakut ut'rucesciigatnilukek. Tamaaken nuniitnek anesciigatnilukek. Uum wani Irurpiim, niitnaulalria Kuigpagmi, angalkullrem tamaani, cauyaanek ut'rucugyaaqluta, tua-i kingunranun tamaavet kinguvrinun-llu tangercecugyaaqluku taun' cauyaq, pisqellrunritaa. Navriuteklermegteggu ecia qagertellrulliniatgu. Cimingnaqsaaqluku-llu tua elluamek cimirpek'naku. Tua-i tauna pitekluku ayaucetellrunritaa. Uum-llu cali Wassilie Evan-am, Anguyagpiim, elitaqluku taum tangtullruniluku Irurpiim cauyaa. Cauyaq tauna angellrunrituq. Angssiyaagpek'nani. Epukegciqapiarluni taũgken yugmek, nasqurluni, tallirluni, irurluni-llu qukamikun taũgaam qupumaluni. Kegguteruarluni-llu avatek tamarmek. Tauna elitaqellrua Irurpagmun cauyaqniluku.

Aũgna cali egan, Tuutalgarmi egaciarat qikumek piliaruluni. Ecuilngurmek qikumek piluteng egacitullrulliniluteng tamaani. Ang'uq egalvall'er. Tauna cali ut'rucugyaaqluku, tua-i ut'rutesqevkenaku navegciqniluku eglerrnginanrani. Tamakut-gguq qikut, qikumek tangerqerluni tua-i pililaagyunaituq. Taũgaam-gguq cat qikut ilait tua-i

how to care for them when they come to his home down there [at Toksook Bay].

We took Wassilie Evan [from Pilot Station]—the poor guy died last year—and Willie Beans from Mountain Village to Sitka with us since both of them were elders who knew about the use, construction, and some of the makers of Yukon masks from the past. Before we went down we did not know how it was going to work. Peter Corey [museum director] met and welcomed us, including Tim Troll, and took us down to the museum. When we first went into the Sheldon Jackson Museum I became disappointed thinking, "Is this all we are going to see?" It turned out that there were many, many more things down in storage. Not knowing that, I was disappointed at first.

We examined Yup'ik things in the storage room for two days, searching for Yukon and coastal things. Wassillie Evan and Willie Beans would recognize some of the objects and even give the name of the person from the past who had made each one. They actually named the person. After those two days the decision was made to take back to Mountain Village only the items selected by the two elders. So at that time we brought back more than one hundred Yup'ik artifacts and masks.

Peter Corey told us we couldn't take two things among those that we wanted to take home. He said they could not leave their place there. We wanted to take back the Yukon shaman Irurpak's drum so his descendants could see it, but he wouldn't allow it. He said that once before when they loaned it out, the drumhead got split. They tried to replace it, but they could not find a good replacement. That was why they would not release it. Wassilie Evan, Anguyagpak, recognized it as well, saying that he used to see Irurpak's drum. The drum was not large. It wasn't too big. It had a beautiful handle comprised of a human figure with head, arms, and legs, but it was cracked in the middle. The back of the drum had teeth placed around inside the rim. He recognized it as a drum belonging to Irurpak.

He also didn't want us to take a clay pot made in Tuutalgaq [Pilot Station]. Apparently they used to make pots out of clay they got from Ecuilnguq River. It was a huge pot. He didn't want us to take it. He said it would break in transit. They say you can't make a pot like that with just any kind of clay. They used a certain kind that would last a long time.

Kuigpagmiullrem angalkum Irurpagmek pilallrata cauyaallran ayuqii. Cauyam teguyaraa yuguaruluni qilui alaunateng, aqsiigken-llu ukimallran avatek ungungssim keggutainek kapusvikumalutek. Cauyam-llu qamani iluan avatiini ciissiruartarluni paralucetun ayuqellrianek tamaa-i-gguq taum angalkum tuunrai. Willie Beans-aaq-llu piuq elliin tangvallruniluku tauna angalkuq tuunrillrani una cauyaq aturluku. Beans-aaq-llu piluni, "Caqerluta eglerrnginanemteñi angyakun Kuigglualegmi niitellruaqa cauyallrani. Niitellruarput cauyallrani aturluni tuaten. Kuigpiim akiani akma uitallruuq ellii wangkuta-llu ukalirnerani, taũgken qastuluni niitnaqluni. Taq'aqami atunermek nepliraqluni." Jackson-aam una cauyaq pilqaa Qaluyaanek. Heye-aq-llu cali ayuqiinek pillruluni Kusquqvagmek 1900-aam ayagnengaarallran nalliini. Tamarmek Jacobsen-aankuk Nelson-aaq-llu waten aqsamegnegun qanrualegnek keggutelirlutek pilianek pillruuk, Nelson-aaq-llu qanlliniluni uum canguam yua waten keggutelilrianek qanengqerrarkauniluku. Sheldon Jackson Museum, Sitka

Drum like that belonging to the Yukon *angalkuq* Irurpak (Long Legs). The handle is a human figure with the body cut open to expose the internal organs, and the opening is lined with animal teeth. Inside the rim are wormlike figures said to represent the *angalkuq's* helpers. Willie Beans remembered Irurpak's using a similar drum in a healing session. He also recalled, "At one time when we were traveling with a boat, at Kuigglualek I heard him drumming. We could hear his drum and him singing. He was on one side of the Yukon River, and we were on the other, but we heard him very clearly. When he finished a song he would make a sound." Sheldon Jackson Museum, Sitka, IIS171 (49.5 cm diameter)

ak'anun piutulit, tamakut-gguq taũgaam nakmikluki tamaa-i egacitullruut tuaten. Tuani Ecuilnguum iluani tamakucirtangqelliniluni. Taumek picirluta ut'rucullruyaaqerput tauna ut'rutesqellrunritaa.

Tua-i akwaugarpak, ernerpak, unuaqu-llu tuaten umyuarteqluta uum wani kingunrani (Paul John) 1996 Yup'ik Festival-aaqata tamakut ut'rutarkat kegginaqut kinguliamteñun tangrresqelluki, makunun-llu teggnernun cali kangiit qanrutkesqelluki kinguliamteñun, taun' umyuaqluku tauna tuani ataam tuani Tuksugmi piyugyaaqluta. Tua-i una ciuliqagtekluku piyullrinek pikumta assinruciquq. Ayuqluku Kuigpagmek Kusquqvagmek-llu caliarit tamakut quyurrluki nasvagyugyaaqluki. Tamaa-i paivngarilliniut. Naken pillerkait nallunrircetai uum [Ann Fienup-Riordan]. Tamakunek akwaugarpak select-aararluta atrautarkanek piniartukut. Taumek taũgaam qanrutamci.

Paul John

Makut maani wangkuungramta mikelnguaraput taringesqumaaput ciuliat catullritnek. Tua-i-wa maa-i watua wangkuungramta irniaput, tutgaraput, kinguqlirkait-llu ciuliameng callritnek, tua-i-w' nallullrat man'a elpekesqumayaaqngamegteggu, wangkuta waten pitarilriani makut maa-i ak'a ciuliamta atullrit tangrresqumaaput. Cali-llu man'a yuraryaraq arulairesqumavkenaku cali nutem avaken ciuliamteñek pikngamteggu, imutun tua angelriaruluku cakneq yuraryaraq man'a avaken ciuliamteñek atulriaruan.

Cali man' yuraq pitekluku yuut waten quyurtaalallrat nunanun, tuani tua-i yurarvigkaatni waten ullagaluki naken quyurtaalallrat ikayuurpalliniuq. Ilakuyucim imutun nallunriutekelriatun ayuqluku. Tua-i ilakuyutnguqapiaralliniluni yugnun avaken ayagluta ciuliamteñek. Cali-llu ilakuyutnguami tungayiit, ilakutat nalluyaaqerraarluk' waten yuraq pitekluk' quyurtaqata nallunriraqluki. Tua-i ilakuyutngulliniami man' yuraq avaken ayagluni, pimiutauluni, kenkutauluni.

Quliriqaqernaurtua ilakutellrata yuut tua-i-w' ayagneqelriatun ayuqiitnek. Tamaani yuut ayagassuutaicaaqellruut makunek cukaluteng ayagalrianek. Una-ll' cali waten ciuliamteñek ayagluni qaneryaraq: Ella-gguq allamek yuituq. Tamakut ella allamek yuitnilallermeggni, man'a maa-i nunateng imutun direct-arluku pilriatun qantullrulliniut.

Evidently that kind of clay could be found in Ecuilnguq river. That was the reason why we wanted to take it home, but he didn't allow it.

As we meet today and tomorrow let's keep in mind our goal to display these masks while our elders explain them to the younger generations when they have the Toksook 1996 Yup'ik Festival at Paul John's village. It would be good if we accommodate Paul John and bring the selections he has made when we do this again there in Toksook Bay. We would like to put together the work of the Yukon and the Kuskokwim people in this showing. Evidently those works are obtainable at this time. Ann Riordan has made known to us where to get them now. Today and tomorrow we can make a selection of what to bring down there. I'm suggesting that to you.

Paul John

We are eager to have our children learn and understand the ways of our ancestors. We elders would like our children and our grandchildren to become aware of their lack of knowledge about the ways of our ancestors, and we would like them to see what our ancestors used so they can pass it on to their descendants. Also, because Yup'ik dancing has been passed down to us through our ancestors since time immemorial, unchanged from its original form and as important to us now as it was to our ancestors, we do not want to see it discontinued.

The tradition of *yuraq* [dance] in its many forms was a uniting force in bringing people from villages together in the larger Yup'ik community. It was supportive of the extended kinship system of the people. When they gathered for any *yuraq,* it gave an opportunity for extended family members to meet each other for the first time in many cases. So, this tradition has been a system for perpetuating kinship ties for a long time, based on our long-standing value system of compassion and love for each other.

Let me give you an example from the past that illustrates the beginning of why people maintained the old kinship system. At that time the people did not have fast modes of transportation. There is an adage that has been around since the time of our ancestors: Humankind populates the world and all people are one. Those who follow the

Ayagassuutaileng'ermeng waten imumek, angutem ilii naken yaaqvaarnek tekillun' arnamek tegullun' ayautaqluni, wagg'uq nuliqsagulluku. Cali-llu angun naken tekilluni tuavet nunanun tekitaqami utertevkenani arnamek cali aipangluni taukumiungurtaqluni.

Taumek waniw' Yupiit yuuyaraacetun ayuqelria una. Tua-i ilumun ilakutlinilriit tamaaggun tamaa-i waten avaken ciuliamteñek tuatnallratgun. Wiinga-llu tan'gurraulua tuaten qanraqata ella allamek yuitniluku umyuarteqtullruyaaqua yaaqvanelnguut cakumanricukluki. Maa-i watua ayagalqa murilkelluku pingrraanemnek tan'gurraunriama, una nani nunani yaaqvaarni uitang'ermi imumek apqemteñek kangirqaqami ciuliani auğkut kangirqelluki, apaaluki, niicugniurallra cali wangkuta kingunemteñi qanlallrat ciuliamta umyuaqluku piaqamteggu elitaqnaurput, tauna ima-tanem tamaavet ayallrani tamaaken utertenritnilaqiit. Wall'u tuaten pinrilkuni, tauna ima-tam' tamaaken tekitaulriarullrunilaqiit. Cunaw' tamaa-i ilumun waten ilakut'luugtellinilriit ataucimek taqestengqengramta imutun cagingayaaqellemteñek tuarpiaq ilaksagulluta waten tua-i pillemteggun.

Akwaugaq cakneq wii ucuryullruunga, iillayuglua-llu, waniw' apa'urluurteng'erma ellangyugnaunii yuurcugnaunii-ll' atulallrita ilait tangaallemni camani [Anchorage Museum of History and Art]. Tua-i iillayullruunga ilumuñ cakneq qanemciullrit tangrruarluki tegglitangvailgan, arcaqerlua auğkunek uluallernek teggalquñek tangllemni. Cali-ll' auğkunek, cavig-nurnallrani canassuutellernek tangllemni. Auğkut iillakengramki tua-i taukugnek malrugnek akwaugaq iillayullruunga cakneq.

Cali tamakunek tangllemni teggalqunek uluanek arcaqerlua cali auğna qanemciq umyuamni uitallruuq; kass'am aklua caitqapik maani tangrruuyugnaunaku. Tauna scientist-alqellinikiit ciuliamta unuakumek-gguq waten ayaglun' maktellerminek cauyangaqami atakullranun yaavet, taq'aqami qanernaurtuq-gguq, kinguliat-gguq uka-i ak'aku akluit qevlerillrat tekiteqerluku taq'uq. Tauna tuani scientist-allrat ciuliamta man'a maa-i tegglinek aklungllerkarput qang'a-llu qevlertelngurnek makunek, tekilluku tamana tangtullrullra akwaugaq umyuamni uitallruuq cali.

principle behind the adage conduct their lives accordingly, that is, showing respect for all people. Though our people did not have fast modes of transportation back then, a man would come from a distant place in pursuit of a wife and would take her back with him. And sometimes a man could go to any place to get married and settle down, becoming a member of that community.

This example illustrates a practice of the Yup'ik people. By following this practice, people are connected since the time of our ancestors. When I first heard people saying the aforementioned adage, I thought people who lived far away were not connected to me in any way. Now that I'm older I pay more attention when I travel. During my travels when I meet people and they begin to talk about their genealogies, and when a person mentions one of his relatives, we find ourselves recognizing names that our elders mentioned. When a certain person was mentioned, suddenly we would remember that it was one who had left and not returned home. Or you might recognize the name of someone who came from far away to live in your village. And since we all come from one Creator, we are related even though we are widely dispersed.

Even though I am a grandfather, I was filled with pride and awe yesterday when I saw down at the Anchorage Museum the things they had used before I was born. I was totally amazed seeing what I had imagined in old stories I had heard, being especially struck with fascination when I saw the stone *uluaq* [woman's knife] and stone carving knife that they used before metal was introduced. Though it was fascinating to see the other items, I was especially awe-struck seeing those two.

When I saw the stone *uluaq,* what came to my mind was a story set long before the arrival of white people's manufactured goods to this area. The character in the story was a scientist of our ancestors who they say would get up in the morning and drum all day long. He would travel through future time while drumming, and when he stopped drumming, he would say he had reached a time when shiny material [metal] was beginning to be used by future generations. Yesterday I was reminded of that ancestral scientist who was able to foresee the time we would be using metal and other shiny material.

2. Kegginaqut Nutemllaat-llu Yuut Quyurrluteng Caciryarallrit

Mary Mike, Negeqliq, February 1994

Yuramek ciumek pilartut uksuarmi, aug'umi cauyarvigmi-gguq atungluteng. Cauyarluteng-w' tua-i atungluteng. Ukut-llu tua-i taqngameng, mat'umi [February] tua-i ayagnirlaryugnarqut taukut Amigtulirmiullret, arulamek. Tua-i taūgken arulamaluteng, tuar wangni arulamalalriit, caliluteng-llu-w' tuaten muragnek pilaameng, kegginaqululuteng. Ak'anun tua-i arulamanaurtut. Unuaquaqan tua-i atakumi arulaurnaurtut.

Tua-i waten nangniiqatarmiaqameng imkut ingluteng tuqlurluk' taisqelluki. Piciatun-am piyulriit anglaniyarluteng tekiqluteng yugyagluteng, waten tua-i makucetun tuqluuſmanrilngermeng tailuteng.

Kegginaqulgiyuunateng. Taukut taūgaam nunalget kegginaqurluteng arulaaqluteng apalluqluki tamakut kegginaqut. Canguat pinguat yuarutnun apalliutaqluki.

Kay Hendrickson, Nuniwaar, January 1995

Makut kegginaqut cugnginam uum pikenritai. Angalkuneg kangingqertut. Angalkut makut pikait. Kwaten kevgirluteng kwagg'ur kevgirluteng nunaneg allaneg aqvataqameng allanerkameggneg, tamakut tamaa-i kevgag kinguagni, nunaneg allaneg cugneg aqvatellriim kinguani, angalkut tamakut taqutetullruut pilivkarluki kegginaquneg tekiskata imkut yuraqata aturkaitneg. Ellait angalkut atuyuitait, pisqumaketeng tamakuneg pimeggneg aturtelluki pivkatulqait.

14

Masks and the Traditional Ceremonial Cycle

Mary Mike, St. Marys, February 1994

In the fall during what they said was "the time for drumming" they would begin singing, doing the *yuraq* dancing first. They would drum and start singing. After that part of the dance cycle was over, probably around February, at Amigtulirmiut they would start *arulat* [motion dances accompanied by songs with verses]. This dancing period extended for a long time, it seemed, because they would also be making masks. They would dance for a long time. Every day they would dance in the evening.

Before the final dancing session, they would summon the people to come over from their counter-village. They would come in great numbers to watch, just as they have come today [to St. Marys], invited or not.

The guests never brought masks with them. Only the host village would dance with masks, which had songs composed specifically about them. Appropriate lyrics would reflect what the masks depicted.

Kay Hendrickson, Nunivak Island, January 1995

These masks didn't belong to just ordinary people. They come from *angalkut*. They belong to the *angalkut*. In preparation for *Kevgiryaraq* [the Messenger Feast] messengers were sent out to invite people from another village, and while they were gone the *angalkut* would have the carvers make masks which would be used in performances when the invited guests arrived. The *angalkut* didn't use the masks during presentations but would appoint people of their choice to do that.

15

Kegginaquq at'lek negeqvamek. "Negeqvam yua assililartuq ella nenglliraqan ellarrlugaqan-llu. Una kegginaquq pikestiin alaillrua March-aami nivurpaumanguarluni qanra up'nerkarniaraan." Mamterillerni uitaluni kiputetulleq A. H. Twitchell-aaq malrugnek kegginaqugnek negeqvamek atelgegnek pillrulliniuq tamaani 1900-aam nalliini. 1944-aami aipaa kia imum piksagutellrullinia tayima-llu nanluciirulluni. Aipaa taũgaam una waniw' cali uitaluni. National Museum of American Indian, New York

Mask representing Negeqvaq, the North Wind. "This spirit likes cold and stormy weather. It is used in the dances in March and has a sad expression on account of the approach of spring." Bethel trader A. H. Twitchell collected two pairs of "Negakfok" masks in the early 1900s. One pair was deaccessioned from the Museum of the American Indian in 1944, while this mask remains in the collection. National Museum of the American Indian, New York, 9/3430 (91 cm)

Makut kegginaqut piciatun piciinateng aturturaqsaitellruit. Piciinaki aturturayuitelqait. Taũgg'am kwagg'ur kevgiraqameng nunaneg aqvalluteng, cug una, ataucir-llu yuukuni aqvaciiqur, angu-llu malruuluteg. Kinguagni tawa, taum nalliini tekiskata imkut atu'urkaitneg taqutetullruut tamakut angalkut, allat piliyuunateng angalkut kiimeng.

Ivarucirluki taum cali angalkum tawaten. Apallug ukug allauluku aapaa, cali allauluku aapaa. Pingayuneg-llu apalliryukuniu pingayuneg apallirluku. Ayuqevkenateng ukut apallut.

Paul John, April 1994

Ullaulluteng-wa piaqameng apqiitnek curukarluteng, curukamek kevgimek pilallermeggni, tuani tua-i ullakengameggni piarkaugaqameng tamakut atutukteng ang'aqluki. Wall'u kelgem nalkenrilengraaku tamakut pilitulit angalkut apeqmeggnek agayuliluteng kegginaqiaqameng agayuliniluteng. Tua-i-llu kegginaqurluteng tamakut yuraquneng agayuniluteng. Agayuluteng-gguq.

Allanun nunanun ayangermeng malikluki, ciunguluku piarkaugaqameng. Waten qaneryarartangqertuq tauna. Taukut-gguq imkut kelegteteng ullakengateng utertevkenateng mumigaruciiqngamegteki, tua-i utertevkenateng tuani egmian iqukliskata ellait pikuneng wagg'uq mumigarulluteng ellait tuani yurarluteng. Taũgken tuani pivkenateng pikuneng uterrluteng ataam ellaita cali upqaarluteng piyungekunegteki wagg'uq kelegluki ataam taivkarluki.

Jasper Louise, Negeqliq, February 1994

Cellangvimni tangvatullruanka. Ilait-llu tekilluteng kelellrit tua kegginaquteng malikluki akinaurarkaugaqameng-gguq. Akinaumek yuralriit taukut cimiq'erluki akinaumek atengqertuq. Yurar-man'a wangkuta anglanitekengnaqluku pilaamta.

These masks were not worn casually without respect and honor. They had a purpose. When they sent messengers to invite the other village, they would send either one or two people. After [the messengers] left, the *angalkut* alone would have the masks prepared by people they appointed for the task.

The *angalkuq* would compose a song/dance for each mask. The lyrics for the two verses of the song would be different. And if he wanted to make a third verse he would do so. All verses to the song would be different.

Paul John, April 1994

When the invited village comes to the host village during *Kevgiryaraq*, they would bring any masks that they planned to present at that time, or for noninvitational occasions the shaman mask-makers would say that they were creating *Agayu* [ceremony in which prayers are offered using masks]. And they would say they were praying when they danced with the masks. They were worshipping.

They would bring them to the host village having planned to use them in a presentation there. There is a word for that which is *mumigaruciyaraq* [immediate reciprocation], in other words, instead of returning to their village and inviting their host village to come to them, they choose to remain and reciprocate immediately after the day's events in the host village are over, making presentations, dancing, and performing for them. Or they may choose instead to return to their own village and invite them later.

Jasper Louise, St. Marys, February 1994

I observed them in the village where I became aware of things around me. Some guests would bring their masks if they are planning to reciprocate immediately. If the guests danced we [on the Yukon] called it *akinauryaraq* [reciprocating, way of paying them back]. Dancing was our way of entertaining ourselves.

3. Ca Pitekluku Kegginaqulilallrat

Mary Mike, February 1994

Ikayurteteng alairlarngatait kegginaqruluki.

Paul John, February 1994

Wii tau͡gaam kingunemni tanglallruunga ayuqevkenateng caunguaraqluteng. Cat tua-i imumek, iciw' kegginaqut ayuqevkenateng, iliit kaviarunguarluni, iliit imarpigmiutaunguarluni, iliit-llu caunguarluni. Tuarpiaq tamakut tamaa-i au͡gkut ciuliamta ellaita piyugngakmeggnek qaralilitullrulliniit. Imarpigmiutaat taum kegginaqum taqestiita tua-i piyugngakminek imarpigmiutaunguarluku taqluku, cali-llu makut allat ungungssiaraat piyugngastaita taungunguarluku taqluku.

Au͡gkut agayumanritellrunilaryaaqait ciuliaput, Agayutmek-llu nallullrunilaryaaqluki. Tau͡gaam wii maa-i ayagyuanriama yuucillrat-llu tangrruarqamku, man'a-ll' watua erneput makut, nutaan agayumapialriarullrulliniut. Camek ellaita pikenrilkemeggnek ayuqenrilngurnek tangerkengaunateng, ellaita una piciryararteng umyuamegteggun qavarraarluteng tupakuneng ernerpak ellaita elitnaurumallermegteggun umyuaqutmegteggun aturturluku erniaqameng, piicagturalriacetun ayuqetullrulliniut tamakut yullret. Watua tau͡gken maa-i wangkuta makeskumta tangerkengaput makut ayuqenripakaata camek umyugaunata tua-i camun-llu ellinguaravkenaki agayuvkenata, piicagpek'nata. Nutaan tamakut ciuliat agayumapialriarullrullinilriit Agayutmek nallunilangraiceteng. Tuaten wii tanglaranka ciuliat umyuaqaqamki.

The Reasons Masks Were Made

Mary Mike, February 1994

It appears to me that they would reveal their helping spirits in the form of masks.

Paul John, February 1994

I do not know about the ones that belong to others and I do not know what they represent, because I only saw some at my village. There was a variety of masks, one representing a fox, another representing a sea mammal, or ones representing other things. It seems that our ancestors chose designs that represented things that were desirable to acquire. The person who made that particular mask made it to represent something from the ocean that he was able to pursue in the hunt. Others made different animal designs depending on what represented desirable acquisitions for them.

They say our ancestors did not live a religious life and that they knew nothing about God. But now that I am no longer young, as I look back and see how they lived compared to the way things are at the present time, I have come to understand that they were really quite religious. Unburdened by the presence of negative influences and modern-day clutter, they began each day from the moment they woke up conscious of the teachings of their forefathers, and they conducted each day of their lives dedicated to those principles. But nowadays, each day when we get up we are bombarded by an array of purposeless activity because nobody is disciplined by the ancients' teachings or communing spiritually. So those ancestors of ours were indeed very religious, despite the fact that, as they say, they did not know God. Having given some thought to it, that is how I see our ancestors.

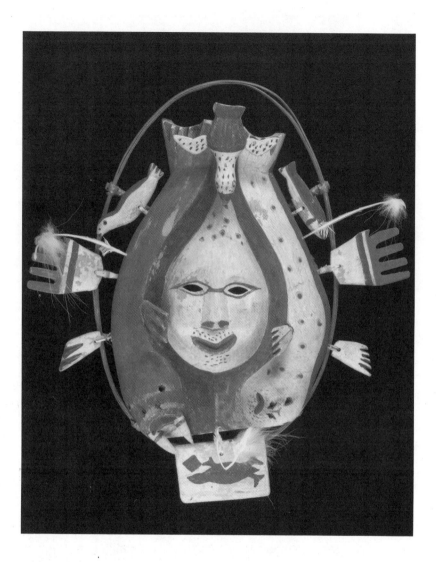

Una kegginaquq Billy Smith-am piliaqaa Naparyaarmium [Hooper Bay] John Smith-am-llu yurarluni atullruluku 1946-aami. Qukami kegginam mengliini taqukartarluni asvermek-llu. Milotte-am pillra, Alaska State Museum, Juneau

Billy Smith of Hooper Bay carved this mask, and John Smith presented it during a dance in 1946. A seal curves around one side of a central face and a walrus around the other. Milotte Collection, Alaska State Museum, Juneau, IIA5399 (50.8 cm long)

Andy Paukan, February 1994

Aūg'um-ll' avani Justina Mike-am nalqiguartellerminiki nangercecillermini tutgaraagminek, tamakunek kegginaqunek atutullritnek nalqigciqallruuq. Una-gguq angalkuq kegginaqumek aturluni aturarkauluni agayuliaqami tua-i yuarutem apalluinek kangingqerrluku kegginaqulivkarlarai. Elliin-ll' allamun taūgaam yugmun piliaqevkarluku qanruqu'urluku qayuw' ayuqellerkaanek. Tua-i taum piliaqestiin taqngaku tua-i elliin tauna kegginaquq aturluku yuraqata yurarluni. Agayuliaqameng-gguq tamaani una wani yuut nerengnaqutekaat amlleqaasqumaluku yugnun tamalkuitnun pissurtaitnun agayulitullruut tuaten nangerceciaqameng. Tua-i tauna umyuaqluku kegginaquq taun' piliaruluni. Camun iqlumun assiilngurmun tusngavkenani, taūgaam Yupiit makut tamalkuita natmun unavet ceñamun ayakata wall'u nunamiut makut yuilqumun ayakata, nunatarnek pissuqata, paivngatesqumaqeryaaqluki tamakunek pissullritnek. Tamakunek-gguq kangingqerrlartut tamakut kegginaqut aturaqamegteki tuaten, assiilngurmek kangingqerpek'nateng.

Paul John

Pinguarpek'nateng tua kaigaluteng.

Andy Paukan

Kaigaluteng. Agayuluteng.

Elsie Mather, Mamterilleq

Taūgaam ap'laraat un'gani pinguarluteng-gguq yura'arqameng ca imna piciurtesqelluku. Tua-i iciw' ca imna apaaluku-ll' yuarutmegteggun pinguartelluku ca imna.

Andy Paukan, February 1994

When Justina Mike presented her grandchildren to the audience, she lectured a little about masks they used in the past. When a shaman had conceived the idea for a mask and composed a song for it, he would then instruct a carver to make the mask according to the song. When the carver was finished, he [in this case the *angalkuq*] would put the mask on and dance. She said that when they were presenting young people before the audience, they would perform *Agayu,* honoring the spirits, beseeching them to insure the presence of game animals that the people needed for survival. That was the reason the mask was made. It was not based on anything evil. It was a prayerful petition that these animals be made available to the people when they hunted out on the ocean or on the land. That was the purpose for the masks they presented. The practice was not rooted in evil.

Paul John

They were not playing, they were praying.

Andy Paukan

They were praying. They were worshipping.

Elsie Mather, Bethel

But they said down on the coast that when they danced they would be representing something they hoped would come true. The lyrics of their songs would name the thing that was desired.

Paul John

Maa-i-w' tua-i piyuumirtacini yuk niilluku piicalalria. Tua-i kaigaluni cakneq piicagluni. Tamatuuguq tamaa-i.

Andy Paukan

Kegginaquq taman' tamatumek kangingqerrnilaraat.

Paul John

Ii-i. Cali-ll'-am agayulirtetailengraan tamaani agayumek atengqellra un' umyuaqela'arqa, amta-ll' agayulirtetaitellrulun' avan' ciuqvani.

Man'a-w' tua-i kegginaqum atra avanirpak tua-i agayuuguq. Agayulirtet makut agayumaciq igvaupailgatnek ayagluni qanemciugaqami tua-i agayullratnek qanernaurtut; ak'a-gguq agayullratni. Tua-i tamaa-i kegginaqu'urqata agayuniaqluki.

Justina Mike, Negeqliq, March 1994

Tuarpiaq akaarnun-ll' pilalriit. Canrirqameng ayanrirqameng pilarsukluki waten up'nerkangaqan, mat'um tuar nalliini. Tuani taũgaam kevgirqameng nutaan taivkarilartut. Tuani taũgken agasuniaqameng ellramegteggun piureluteng tamakunek yurarluteng. kaigaurluteng cat kegginaitnek kegginirluteng. Tavani imumi kiugumi capkutam iluani uitaaqluteng, ikirutaqluki tua-i kegginaqurlutek kankuk imutun. Agayuniluteng qanernaurtut. Ellaita apersaraqluku tauna. Taukut nunat apersaraqluku. Tua-llu ataam maavet piameng tava agayuninaurtut tua-i kaigaurturluteng, nutaan Agayucetangqellra-llu nallunrirluku.

Paul John

Nowadays people pray when they are inspired to do so. They would make an intense plea to God. That's what that was.

Andy Paukan

They say that masks originated with that intention.

Paul John

Yes. I've thought about the fact that it was referred to as *Agayu* back then even though Western clergy had not yet arrived. And yet we had no *agayulirtet* [priests] back then.

Throughout that period in the past, they called a ceremonial mask an *agayu*. Before the missionaries brought Christianity, when people told stories they would mention the *Agayu* religious ceremony that had been practiced by the people; they would say *agayullratni*. When they made a presentation with a mask they would say that they were practicing the custom of *Agayu*.

Justina Mike, St. Marys, March 1994

It seemed as if [the event] lasted quite a few days. It appears that they had these gatherings during the spring once they had stopped their winter subsistence activities. I think it may have been during this time [March]. They would invite another village only when they had the *Kevgiryaraq* [Messenger Feast]. But when they did the *Agayu*, only the village people would participate. They would dance using the masks representing desired things while they would beseech the spirits for animal and plant productivity. Two people wearing the masks were behind a curtain, and when it opened they would present them. They would say they were doing the *Agayu*. That was their term for it. It was the term that the village used. Then when they moved here [to St. Marys] they began going to church and praying, realizing at last God as known today.

Paul John, February 1994

Nauwa maa-i canek imkunek scientist-anek qanlalriit. Tamaa-i tamakut [angalkut] scientist-aqellrulliniit ciuliamta. Ciunerkamek waten nalluvkenateng. Ellaita uuggun alairumanrilngermeng ellangqellermegteggun ilameng ciunerkaa taringaqluku.

Cali-llu maa-i Kass'at biologist-anek qanlalriit, neqet murilkestaitnek. Tamakut cali ilait angalkut wagg'uq neqem tumyaraa tua-i caliaqaqluku pitullrulliniut. Kiaggauskaki-gguq yut'eng neqmek nuqlitevkenaki pillerkait caliaqluku, tuunriluteng neqet kiaku tagkata tumkait carrirluki, wagg'uq neqem tumyaraa kituggluku. Cali-llu unkut imarpigmiutaat ungungssit pitarkat seal-at pitekluki waten uksumi piyugngalriit, wagg'uq imarrluteng, imarpigmun ayagluteng cali tamakut up'nerkaqu pissungekata pitarkait mikurcetaaraqluki, paivngavkangnaqluki.

Paul John, February 1994

You know, they talk about scientists nowadays. Those [*angalkut*] were the scientists of our ancestors. They could foresee the future. With their extra-sensory perception they could tell what the future held for others.

And white people mention biologists nowadays, the ones that keep records on fish. Some shamans worked on the path of the fish the people were going to use. Wanting to insure a plentiful supply of fish for people when summer arrived, they would use their *tuunrat* [animals or extraordinary beings that help the *angalkuq*] to assist them in performing rituals that would remove all obstacles from the path the fish were going to use while coming up during the summer. It is said they were clearing the path for the fish. And then the [*angalkut*] who are able to would go down into the ocean during the winter to make a request for plenty of seals or other sea mammals, so that springtime would bring an abundance when men went out sea-mammal hunting.

Qissunami 1946-aami up'nerkami kegginaqurluteng yuralriit qasgimi. Qacarnermi keluatni yuralriit can'get tupigat tangerrnaqluteng cauyaata-wa teguyaraa canguaruluni piliaq. Tuani yurarraarcelluki asveruat kegginaqut iliitnek Frank Waskey kiputellrulliniuq tauna-llu kiputellra maa-irpak uitaaqluni University of Alaska Museum-aami Fairbanks-aami. Una tarenraq Alfred Milotte-am pilqaa, Alaska State Museum, Juneau

Masked dancers performing in the *qasgiq* in Qissunaq during spring, 1946. Note the *tupigat* (grass mats) covering the back wall and the carved drum handle. After the performance Frank Waskey purchased one of the walrus masks worn by the dancers. It is presently in the University of Alaska Museum, Fairbanks. Alfred Milotte, Milotte Collection, Alaska State Museum, Juneau, Neg. no. 1103

Alairiyaraq Kegginaqumek:
Kangia Qanrutekluku, Qalrialluku, Aturluku Yuarucetaa

Jasper Louise, Negeqliq, May 1993

Kegginaqilallruut qalrialluki-ll' ellaita qalriuciitnek. Unimaanka taũgaam watua cat tangerrluku taũgaam una qanruteksuumayaaqaqa kegginaquq. Yuarutait taũgaam maa-i nallunritanka ilait kegginaqut.

Kegginaqilartut tua taungunguarcelluku. Angalkut yuarutait, kangiit tamakunek pingqerrlartut. Angalkuuvkenani taringumanarqenritut wangkutnguulriani. Angalkut pililartut canek tangllermeggnek; alairilartut, alairinilarait waten tangellritnek canguanek.

Mary Mike, February 1994

[Ellanguat] akagenqeggluteng uum kegginaqum elatiinlluteng. Canguaneg-am makut pingqerrluteng akulait melqunek, akulait-ll' makut canguanek, muraggarnek canguaruluteng. Waten tua qaalriuciaqameng waten all'uku, kavcagpak tamakut pinaurtut. Qalriuciitnek qalriucelirluteng qalrialuteng. Nalqigqurluki caullrat pillrat angalkum pikestiita.

Jasper Louise, February 1994

Makut kegginaqut ciulia'urlumta yugmek-llu anirtuiqallerkarteng pitekluku waten pilartut. Anirtuutngungalnguut ciuniurlarait angalkuulriani. Angalkuuvkenani tangssunaitut, makut taũgaam kegginaqurtait wangkuulriani elitaqnaqluteng. Kangiit angalkut nalluvkenaki yura'arqameng-ll' aperturtura'aqluki qasgimi, waten una cayarauniluku.

Presenting the Mask:
Telling Its Story, Providing Its Call, Singing Its Song

Jasper Louise, St. Marys, May 1993

They would put on the masks representing certain animals and mimic their cries. At this moment I cannot recollect stories behind any masks, although I can look at a mask and can talk about it. I do know songs that accompanied some of the masks.

They made masks depicting things. The songs composed by the *angalkut* would illustrate the things being depicted. We ordinary people cannot truly understand the essence of the mask the way an *angalkuq* does. They say that the *angalkut* made likenesses of things they had seen. Their masks depicted those images during presentations, revealing to the people what they had seen.

Mary Mike, February 1994

Ellanguat [representations of the universe] are made of rings [usually bentwood strips] surrounding the mask, separated from it with some sort of pegs. Various appendages made of wood and feathers were attached to or through the *ellanguaq* pieces. Those pieces would rattle loudly when they wore the masks and cried out imitating the sounds of birds or animals represented. The owner of the mask, the *angalkuq*, would explain to the people present what it represented.

Jasper Louise, February 1994

Our dear old ancestors used masks to help others. The *angalkuq* accepts *tuunrat* that would be used to help others. An ordinary person cannot see what an *angalkuq* can, although one is able to recognize what is depicted on a mask. The *angalkuq* knew the source and deeper significance of the mask and would explain it to others in the *qasgiq* [men's communal house] during his presentation.

Dick Andrew, Mamterilleq, January 1995

Ii-i, tangvalallruunga, tamakut angullruanka. Kaŭgpagnek-llu kegginaqurluteng piaqluteng. Kaŭgpagualria tauna imarniteg-uitermeg-imumek kavirutmek minguglutek, tua-i-ll' kegginaqurluni kaŭgpaguamek. Kaŭgpaunguarluteng tang qalriagaqluteng yurainanermeggni. Qavciugat? Pingayuuyugnarqut waten yuralriit. Qalriagaqluteng kaŭgpagtun. Tua-i-llu up'nerkaqan-llu kaŭgpaguallruaqata-ll' kaŭgpiit amllepiaraqluteng.

Tua-i-w' tuaten pilalriit tangvallemni. Tua-i tauna neqnguaq tuaten piniluku, tua-i naspaaniluku tua-i unaknayukluku-llu, wall'u-llu seal-ar-unaknayukluku. Tua-i tuaten tauna kegginaquq ayuqniluku, kegginaquliaqellni qanrutekluku. Tuaten pitullruut. Ii-i, tuunrameggnek aturluteng tamakunek kegginaqiluteng, yurarluteng tua-i tamakut aturluki. Taqkuneng-llu tua-i tamakut cali peggluki. Waten mikelngurnun naanguarutkevkarluki wall' egcarturluki ilait.

Taŭgaam pinguarturluteng canek-wa tua-i unangengnaqluteng pitullruut yullret imkut, neqa kiingan yuutekellruamegteggu kass'artartaitellrani man'a.

Dick Andrew, Bethel, January 1995

Yes, I observed them, having had the chance to see them before they were discontinued. They would perform using walrus masks. One with a walrus mask would have on a seal-gut rain parka painted with red ocher. While dancing they would mimic the sounds walrus make. Let's see, how many were dancing? Perhaps three. They would call out like walruses. There would be many walrus available during the spring if they had presented these walrus masks.

That's what they did when I saw them. During a presentation, one would show a fish mask or a seal mask revealing what he was hoping to get in abundance. While presenting the mask he had created, he would explain the meaning behind it. That's what they used to do. Yes, they would use their *tuunrat,* depicting them in masks, wearing them while they danced. And when they were done with them they would release them. They allowed the children to play with some, and they would leave others out [on the tundra or in the wilderness].

Our ancestors made representations of things they wanted to acquire, since fish and game provided their main source of food during the time before the introduction of store-bought foods.

Kegginaquq Mamterarmiunek [Goodnews Bay] pillra Ellis Allen-aam 1912-aami. Yaqulek cilulria yuan-wa kegginaa qukaani unalviik nengingalutek yaqulgem yaqugcetun. Kegginaquq uqamaitepiarluni yuralriim-llu atuquniu nayumiqascirluku yurautarkauluku. Uucetun ayuqellriit kegginaqut alaitetullrulliniut ceñarmiuni Naparyaarmiut ngelkarrluki. Thomas Burke Memorial Museum, Seattle

Goodnews Bay mask collected by Ellis Allen in 1912, simultaneously a bird in flight and its powerful *yua.* The back of the bird reveals a human face, with its wings the outstretched hands of the *yua.* The large mask is too heavy for a performer to use without external support. Masks of this type were made along the coast as far north as Hooper Bay. Thomas Burke Memorial Museum, Seattle, 4539 (62.5 cm wide)

Tuunralek

Jasper Louise, February 1994

Maani anerteqnginanemteni caput tamarmeng kegginaqruut, carayaguat-llu. Keglunret tamakut pirpaugut apalluqellrat angalkuulriami. Pirpaklaraat, kalivqinailata-gguq. Keglunret maa-i kalivqinaicugnarqut, caprunateng kalivqinaunateng. Akultuut taũgaam, caqapiaraat pitullruat, pitarkall'er carayak. Caqapiaraat kegginaquqetullruat. Pirpaggaat yuarutkait, imna-llu tuullek. Angalkurpaggaat tamakunek apallungqerrlartut. Angalkurpaggaat tua-i nalluvkenaki nunalgutaita maaggun callratgun. Ik'iq-llu nalluvkenaku iigken'gun.

Makut nallunritelput tamarmeng kegginaqurtangqertut pitarkat yuguaruaqluni-llu ilii. Nunat ukut nallunritellrit, maaniunrilengraan-llu, angalkuita kegginaqiryuumait tuunraqliuskunegteggu. Yuarun niiskunegteggu, ukugnek-ll' apallurluni, tangerciqai-gguq angalkuulriani. Ilii angalkum keneklaraat ciulia'urluut. Umyuacuunrituq-gguq. Anirturingnaqellriit pitacirramegtun nallunritaqluki. Ayuqenrilmilliniameng-am angalkut. Imumek watua qanllemtun, iingit iciw' qurrasqitaralrianek qanelrianga.

Tamarmeng kegginaqut angalkut piliaqait. Tuunrateng tangerrluki kegginaqilartut. Yuungraata-ll' ilait tuunrangqerraqluteng tuqullernek—angalkuuluteng tuqullernek. Tuunraq tauna ikayuqellriatun pikaqluku, kiingan anirtuutekluku tamaani, yuungcaristetaunani-llu cellangeqarraallemni.

One with Tuunraq

Jasper Louise, February 1994

While we are alive, anything we have that can inspire us has the potential of becoming a mask. When the *angalkuq* used the wolf in the lyrics of his song, it would be powerful. The wolf is highly regarded because it is bold and capable of easily capturing whatever it pursues. But [bear masks] were scarce. On rare occasions, an *angalkuq* would present a bear mask. Another highly regarded mask was that of the common loon. The more powerful *angalkut* were known to everyone in the village by the way they performed. They knew by his eyes if an *angalkuq* was not to be trusted.

There are masks for every animal we know that is potential game, and some of the masks are even images of humans. The *angalkut* could have masks made of animals known to the people in the village if the animal had become the *tuunraq* of that particular *angalkuq*. When the people heard the song with these *apalluk* [two verses], an *angalkuq* could actually see [the animals]. Our dear ancestors revered some of the *angalkut*. They knew if the shamans had good intentions, and if they worked to the best of their abilities to heal others. Apparently all *angalkut* were not alike. As I just said, the shifty-eyed ones were not to be trusted.

Angalkut made all the masks. They created masks in the images of their *tuunrat*. Some *angalkut* even had deceased humans as their *tuunrat*—deceased *angalkut*. The shaman used the *tuunraq* for healing purposes, and it was the only source used for healing. When I first became cognizant and aware of my surroundings, there were no medical doctors from outside.

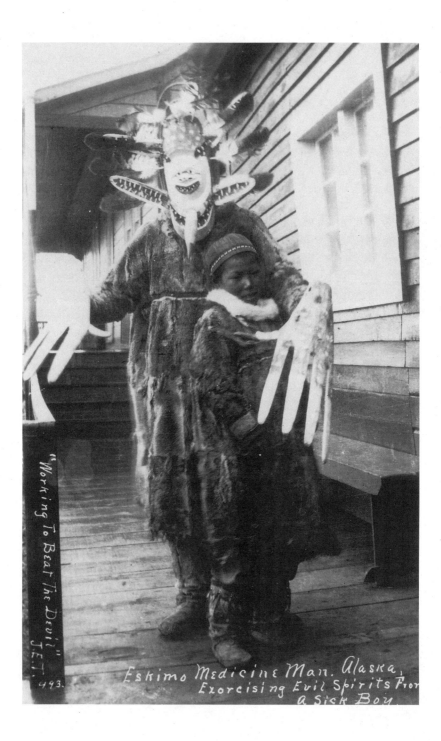

"Working To Beat The Devil" J.E.T. 493.

Eskimo Medicine Man. Alaska, Exorcising Evil Spirits From a Sick Boy.

36

"Tuunrangayak Callukii Cirliqevkarluku: Angalkuq Alaskarmiu, Angalkum Tuunriskii Nangteqellria Tan'gurraq." John E. Thwaites-aam Tuyuryarmiu [Togiak] angun tarenraillra nangengqaluni enem ciuqerrani Nushagak-ami 1906–08 nuniigni. Thwaites-aam pillra, Alaska State Library, Juneau

"Working to Beat the Devil: Eskimo Medicine Man, Alaska, Exorcising Evil Spirits from a Sick Boy." Photograph taken by John E. Thwaites of a Togiak man posing on the steps of a frame building at Nushagak between 1906 and 1908. Thwaites Collection, Alaska State Library, Juneau, Neg. PCA 18-497

Yua

Pauline Akaran, Qerrullik, February 1993

Tamakut-wa univkarat, imkut ak'a, ciuliameng aturlallritnek univkarinilalriit. Wii-ll' niicugniaqama tamaani univkaranek canek iquklicarturqamegteggu, yaani iquani, una yuk itellruaqan tuavet enemun, taum yuum anqata'arqan alerqurlaaraa, "Kiteg-at' waniwa ankuvet keggavet, ayakarluten, qavcinek amlliqerluten, kingutmun kingsarniartuten causuklua, yuusuklua paqnakekuvnga. Kingutmun cauqerniartuten ingna anvikellren amiik paqnakekuvgu." Tuaten-gguq alerqurnauraa anqata'arqan. Tua-i-gguq an'aqameng tua-i cayaqlirluteng kingunerteng takuyarnauraat unguvalriim igtiinun itellrullinilriit.

Alma Keyes, Qerrullik, February 1993

Yuut tamaani caurtaarluteng, unguvalriarurtaqluteng-llu pituameng. Man'a-gguq nuna man'a can'egtellrani waten cat alailluteng-llu pilallrulriit. Tua-gguq cat alaillallruut nuna can'egtellrani watuacetun ayuqenritellrani. Tua alaicuiruciiqniluki tamakut unguvalriit-llu pilallrulriit nuna can'urikan, yuut-llu ayuqenrirluteng. Una kaviaq wani yug'ullruusaaqelliniuq. Tua-am waten wani up'nerkami, urukatami, kaingengluni neqkaicungluni. Kuicungaq man' asguqacia maaggun ceñiikun pekluni. Qanerluni, "Qayuwa tayima pikuma neqkamnek-llu nalaquciiqsaaqellilrianga." Makut-gguq kuicungaat carvengluteng. Kiarrluni-gguq piqertuq ilaqcuugaq imkuciq.

Asguraralria-gguq una-i unani kuimarluni. Unaviaraa-gguq, qayuwa-llu tegusciigalamiu qalutekailami. Qayu-gguq pek'artaqan ayakarnaurtuq tayima. Caqerluni-gguq mianiqluni ullagluku tua pia, "Ilaraarrlugaaq unsuuq, ilaten qaluurait. Ilaten qaluurait." Tua-gguq kiungaicuknermi kat'um mikellriim im'um ilaqcuugaam kiugaa ciugarrluni, "Ii-i. Ilanka qaluurlitki." Tua-i-llu-gguq tayim' anglluqerluni ayagluni tuaten elliurluku. Tua-i-gguq caqerluni pissursaaqekii-gguq taum kaviarem, tua-i-llu-ggur-am pugngan iliitni pia taum wani kaviarem, "Ilaraarrlugaaq unsuuq, ilaten qaluurait. Ilaten qaluurait." Ciugcami-gguq taum ilaqcuugaam pia, "Ii-i. Qaluurliki-kin. Elpet terr'en cuigcuigninarquq." Tua-i-llu-gguq kasnguyulliimi, tauna kaviaq ayagtuq

Its Person

Pauline Akaran, Kotlik, February 1993

They say the stories they tell are accounts of what our ancestors experienced long ago. I, too, heard stories in those days, and if any person came into the house while the narration was about to end, when the story ended and the late arrival was leaving, they would tell him, "When you go outside, look back a few steps away from the house if you are curious to see whether or not I am a person." When they left and finally looked back, they would see that they had been in an animal's den.

Alma Keyes, Kotlik, February 1993

Back then people used to transform into animals. Many things were visible when the earth was thin. Things were distinct when the land was thin, not the way it is today. They predicted that animals and other things that were visible at that time would no longer be visible, and they said there would be many people of different races. The fox was once a human being. He ran out of food and was getting hungry during the spring just before the thaw. As he was going along the side of a river, he said, "If I looked around perhaps I would find something to eat." The little river was beginning to flow. He scanned the area and saw an *ilaqcuugaq* [needlefish].

The needlefish was swimming up the river. When he couldn't find anything to scoop it up with, he called down to it. If he made a slight movement it would swim away. Trying to be absolutely quiet, he moved up to it and said, "*Ilaraarrlugaaq*, down there, they are dipnetting your relatives. They are dipnetting your relatives." He didn't think it would respond, being so little, but it lifted up its nose and said, "Fine. Let them dipnet my relatives." Then it dove deeper and swam away. The fox kept pursuing it, and when it came up again he said to the needlefish, "*Ilaraarrlugaaq*, down there, they are dipnetting your relatives. They are dipnetting your relatives." When the needlefish lifted its head up it said, "Yes. I wish I could dipnet them. Your anal area stinks." And then the fox

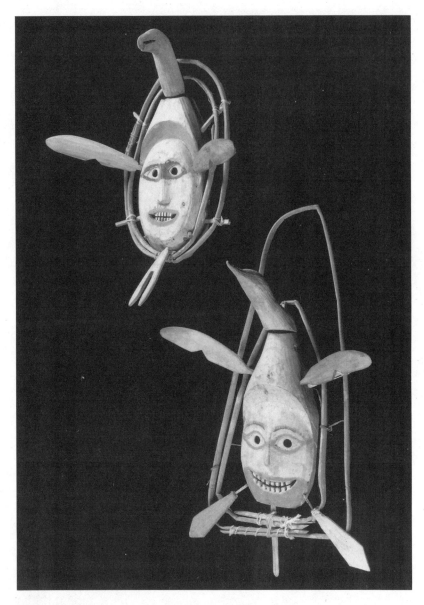

Ilagket qavcin inglukellriit kegginaqut pillrin Robert Geirke-m Kusquqvagmiunek 1920-m nalliini. Thomas Burke Memorial Museum, Seattle

One of the dozen paired masks collected by the trader Robert Gierke on the Kuskokwim in the 1920s. Thomas Burke Memorial Museum, Seattle, 1.2E651 (45 cm) and 1.2E652 (31.5 cm)

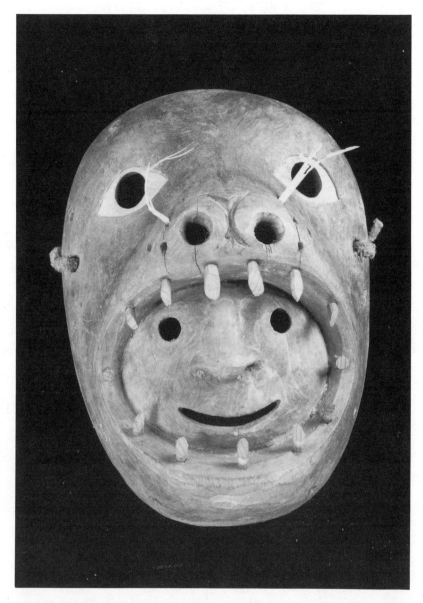

Taqenqeggluni taqukaruaq kegginaquq yuan kegginaa qanrakun uyangqaluni. Ukinerluni qula pingayunek cipluku avatii kegginaqum aipaagni melqunek ellivikumallrunganani wall' tuntum melqurranek. Ellis Allen-am pillra Mamteranek 1912-aami. Thomas Burke Memorial Museum, Seattle

Finely carved seal mask, its *yua* peering out from its mouth. Thirteen small holes around the rim indicate that feathers or a caribou ruff framed the face. Collected by Ellis Allen from Goodnews Bay in 1912. Thomas Burke Memorial Museum, Seattle, 4516 (14.5 cm)

qaini kiartaqluku. Kavingiriinarluni, imkucirluni qayuwa piluni kavingluni. Kaviririinartuq qainga man'. Man'a-llu-gguq maani pektengluni man' qainga. Kiartaa-gguq melqut makut. Eglertuq tua-i. "Yuugua-ggem wanirpak. Kasnguyugpakaama yuilqumi uitanalua piunga."

Tua-ll'-am ayagluni, ayangluni, eglertengluni. Yuum wani kenillranun cami tayima—cami tayim kenillrulliniluni yuk—cuputet tamakut. Tua-i-ggur-am piqersaaqlun' piuq, "Arenqiapaa-ll'! wangni kavircepakarlua assiiciiqngatuq' qaika." Tua-i-gguq piqersaaqluni, cuputmek tegucami qengagni minguglukek una-llu-gguq ciutmi qulii. Unavet atrarluni tarenriurluni mermun, ellakeggan-llu, "Waten ayuqekuma kinguliaraat wani tangrraqamegtenga assikeciqaatnga." Piqersaaqluni-gguq, tamana araq ilii-gguq qatercecan piuq, "Arenqiapaa-ll'! pamsungqerrlua-ll' mat'umek." Ingna-gguq iqua wani nuqluku uivluni pisaaqaqani nurluku, keggengnaqluku-llu pingraani nurluku. Qayuw' piqerlun' aqumqerluni pilriim tava tegucami-gguq aramek tamatumek mingugaa, minguglukuu qat'ringluni una. Tua-gguq nangercami taun' pamsuni qayuwa piluku, tangerrluku yaavet piuq, "Iicillra! qangvarpak kinguliaraat, waniwa waten unguvalriarurtelliniunga, pissuqunegtenga tangnikciqaatnga." Tavatelluteng-gguq makut kaviaret kavircellartut, cuputmek-llu-gguq mingungqerrluteng.

Alma Keyes, May 1993

Inerquutnguqapigtuq. Atairutma inerqutuakut [taqukanek]. Wii tam' niiculriarullrunrilama kiirrarma-llu ayaglua pitengnaqlalrianga unataryarlua-llu kiirrarma. Yuilqumi ernerpak kiirrarma, qanrutaqluki-llu. Yaaqsing'ermeng-gguq qanrutellriani niillartut. Ngel'aqacitkesqevkenaki-llu, ngel'aratekesqevkenaki maani kingunemteñi uitangramta. Niillartut-gguq, nunam-gguq aciakun niillartut.

Atam cali-gguq—pinguarlallikiitnga-llu wii. Ukvekluaqerlanricaaqaqa. Waten uksurlalria carayiit-ll' imkut tamarluteng. Atairutka pila'arqa carayagcurlaan, "Ciin-mi tamakut uksumi alaircuirullartat nani niitnauriluteng?" Atam-gguq igtemeggni nani enliluteng uitalartut uksumi. Atam-gguq pikgun egalengqerrlartut. Cali-llu-gguq yuum iliin wani neqkai aglumaaqamiki, nersugaqamiki, kaingaqami, yuvrirluki

got extremely embarrassed. He walked away examining his body now and then. He was turning red from being embarrassed. The fox walked away looking at himself. His body was turning red. And he began to feel some movements on the surface of his skin. When he looked, he was covered with fur. Continuing on, he thought to himself, "I was a human a while ago. I am so embarrassed, I should be living in the wilderness."

Then he began to travel. He came upon a place where someone had cooked at one time, and there were some charcoal pieces among the ashes. After contemplating the situation he said, "*Arenqiapaa!* [expression, see glossary] If my body is plain red, I don't think it will look very good." Then after more contemplation, he took a piece of charcoal and painted his nose and the tips of his ears. Then he went down to the water, and he saw his reflection in the calm water because the weather was nice. "If my appearance is going to be like this, the people in the future will think I look nice." Back at the firepit he saw that some of the ash was white, and he said, "Gosh! I shouldn't ignore my tail." He tried to reach the tip of his tail but couldn't; then he tried unsuccessfully to hold it with his teeth. After a while he sat down, and there his tail was! So he took some ash and painted it until it turned light. "*Iicillra!* [expression] Since I've become this animal, all those who hunt me in times to come will think I look fine and beautiful." So that is why the red foxes are that color today with black on them.

Alma Keyes, May 1993

This is a very important rule. My late father used to caution us about them [bears]. And since I wasn't always cautious and timid, I would go hunting and berry picking by myself. I would be out there by myself all day and would talk to them. And they say that if you talk to them they will hear you even though they are out in the distance. They would tell us not to make fun of them out there or in our homes. They say they can hear you, saying they can hear you through the ground.

And also, they would say—maybe they were joshing me—something I don't entirely believe myself. Winter would come, and the bears would disappear. Since my late father hunted bears, I asked him, "Why are bears no longer seen or heard during the winter?" He said they wintered in dens that had skylights at the top. And he said that if a bear became hungry, it would look around and examine the people and their cache to

kiarrluki yuut neqkait-llu kiarrluki. Atam-gguq yuum ilii qanerniartuq, "Imna-tanem wani pilqa cukamek tayima nang'a! Qang'a-llu neqerrluut ak'a nangqatarluteng. Cukavakartat?" Tua-gguq tamakut piyullermeggnek assikurallermeggnek yaggluteng tegulluteng nerlartut.

Tua-gguq yuusaaqlartut. Atam asguranairluku pillrukegka nangteqlua cakneq, yugni-llu uitayunrirlua pillemni. Cellaka nalluqertaqluku—qiini. Ekviggarpagmek pilaraat. Tangllemni kuicungaam akiani—qeckuni-llu tua-i pita'arkarkaulua. Cellangarrlua. Aarpautnauraanga ikavet, keggutai-ll' alaunateng.

Atam picirciitekluki yuum pinrilkani, qanrutellriani pipigglalliniut. Qanrutaqami ciutek peknaurtuk. Peklutek tuar-llu niicugnillaqiinga. Atam picirciiteksunaitut. Takarnarqut. Wii takarsuglartua qavcirqunek tangerrlartua yaaqvanun pivkenii.

Yugmun tangercecukuni tangerceciiqelliniuq. Tangerrsukani tangerceciiquq. Qanruqu'ureluku pilriani niillartut. Tua-gguq yuk ayuquciatun pituat. Pinerrlugatukan-llu ellaita-llu pinerrlugaluteng.

Justina Mike, February 1994

Kauturyaraat-am yugnun tukituluteng. Tamakut cali caqaasqenritnaurait, ilalkesqevkenaki. Camek-kiq tayim kangilirluki pilartatki? Tua-ll' cam' iliitni tangerqilii arnam qetunraan yaqruirtellia tamakuciq. Taum aaniin teguluku qanaaquraqiliu yaa-i yaani. Tauna cellangqenrilan waniwa akngirrniluku pivkenaku pisqelluku; akinauresqevkenaku. Akinaurutengqelarngatut. Tamaa ayagluku mamengciraraasqelluku tauna tengmiacuaraq qanaaquraqiliu yaa-i yaan'. Cellangqenrilan tauna pitsaqa'artevkenaku piniluku. Qayuw' pivkenaku mamciraraasqelluku ayagluku. Ayagteskiliu.

see if the food in it was desirable. He told me that they would stay in the den in the winter. And he said that they had a skylight up on top of their dens. And it checked out the person and their food when it wished to take someone's food. Then somebody would begin looking for food he had cached, looking for dried fish, he would say, "I wonder why my food supply is going so fast! And my dried fish is almost gone. Why are they going so fast?" They say the bears reached out and took whatever they wished to eat.

They say they are humans. Down at the coast when I was ill and became depressed, isolated myself, and at times became unaware, it became plausible to me. They called the place Ekviggarpak. I saw [a bear] across from the little slough; if it had jumped over, it could easily have killed me. At that moment I became fully aware. It growled at me from the other side, showing its teeth.

If a person doesn't assume the bear has bad characteristics and talks to it in a normal tone, it could understand. Its ears moved when I talked to it. They would move, and it appeared to be listening to me. They are not to be criticized. I've seen them at close range a few times, and I've always given them the utmost respect.

Evidently, the bear can reveal itself to a person if it wants to. If a person wanted to see it, it will come to that person. It will reciprocate according to how people treat it. If a person mistreats it, it will mistreat that person.

Justina Mike, February 1994

Swallows apparently like to stay with people. [People] would always tell us never to bother them. They told us never to mistreat them. I don't know why they warned us about them. One time a woman's son injured a swallow's wing. The boy's mother took the bird and talked to it as I watched. She told the swallow that the boy had hurt it since he wasn't aware of his action. She asked it not to take revenge on him. It appears that they have ways of reciprocating. She told the little bird to go on and recover. She told it that the boy didn't mean to hurt it and not to retaliate this time. Then she released it. They also talked about robins in the same manner. They mentioned them too.

Ircit

Kay Hendrickson, January 1994

Ircinrram tar tawa tumaineg tangllemni—unuakuayaarmi akerta pugqataartelluku tagellrullinilria cenqur una tungekluku. Una ayagnginanemteni ataka nep'gaartur tumet-ggur tar makut. Maavet tangekerluki qanertur ircim-ggur tar tumeklinikai. Murilkanka tumet makut ikamraan—ak'akika uweryulria taw' ukatmun ikamraa. Man'a tallirpian tungii qanikcami maani qap'illuni pillinilria. Man'a-wa cali iqsuan tungii qanikcaam qaangani cetruteksuartuarallinilria maa-i. Cali-wa ukut cuum tumai tukullgi murualriit maani qanikcami, ingluit murilkanka terikaninraat makut qanikcaam qaangani murumavkenateng enliulluteng taũgg'am. Atama taũgken kwaten uikaqai, ngelqauluteng tamakut ukuni kwa-i. Pavani, akertem pugqatallrani, qemimi mayullinil' qayutun uciarluni augmeg kucirturluni, pitamineg. Illiit kucirtullret—nenglliryaaqur kenegteqiyaqemni qunuteksaunani. Qemini piini mayulliniyalriim pii, ukatmun yuurrngiinarluteg qemimi tumai. Tumlicungremiangam irukegcinrilami. Tamaaken uyangeskumegnug camun tayim uyangciqlilriakug qemimeg.

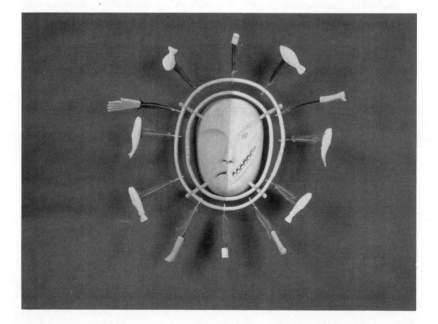

Extraordinary Persons Appearing as Humans or Animals

Kay Hendrickson, January 1994

When I saw a trail left by an *ircinrrar* early in the morning as the sun started to rise, it looked like it went up toward a hill. As we traveled along, my father exclaimed that they looked like tracks. As he looked down at them he said they were the tracks of an *ircir*. When I examined the sled tracks, one side of the track was deeper than the other as if the sled were leaning to one side. The right sled runner had sunk in as the sled was moving, and the left sled runner had been riding on the snow without sinking. Then I noticed footprints on the snow, and one side, which was a human footprint, was deeper. When I looked at the other footprints, I noticed they were of a fox [or other small land animal], barely making an impression on the snow. When my father placed his foot in one of the human footprints, it was the exact size. It appeared that as the sun was coming up, it had been going up hill with a big load and with its catch dripping blood. It was cold, but when I touched one of the blood drops it wasn't frozen. When we examined the further tracks, they were becoming more and more like those of a human.

Nunivaami Kevgiryaram nalliini iliita piliallrat kegginaquq avga yuum kegginaqluku avga-llu kaviam. Amllermi qanemcilriit makucit kegginaqut irciuniluki pilartut. Uumi kegginaqumi kavircetellria yuum kegginaqluku qiugliq-llu kaviam. Thomas Burke Memorial Museum, Seattle

Human/fox mask made for a Messenger Feast, Nunivak, 1946. Many accounts depict *ircenrrat* or *ircit* as half human and half animal. Dance masks representing *ircenrrat* often have human features on one side of the face and animal features on the other. The red half of this mask depicts a man and the blue half a fox. Thomas Burke Memorial Museum, Seattle, 2-2128 (31.8 cm)

Tawa-wa cuum kegginaatun ayuqsuitelliniut. Ingluit ayuqengremeng ingluit ayuqevkenateng, pipiaret cull'erraaraunrilnguut.

Nepcetat

Andy Kinzy, Negeqliq, February 1993

Una wani atauciq kegginaquq nepcetamek pitullrat, kegginaquni maani quyilriaruuq. Quyinruluni kegginaquuguq nepcetaq-ggur-una. Atam, imkut ak'a temainaunelnguut makut nepcetatullermeggni iliini nepcetar-una wani tallimanek-ll' atkugnek patuluku pusvikaqani neptelartuq.

Paul John, February 1994

Atam yuungcaristet kayutatkenrilnguut umyuaqeqaqernauput. Yuungcaristem yuk ilii piyugngalaraa. Uum taũgken yuungcaristengungermi capeqluku. Tua-i tamakut kegginaqut qanemciugaqameng tuaten ayuqut. Canguaq taun' pikestiin tua-i aturyugngaluku. Allam-llu pikenritestiin elliin pileryagyung'ermiu, tuarpiaq doctor-aam piyugngak'ngaa, elliin artuamiu pisciiganaku.

Tamakut tamaa-i angalkut pilarait nepcecitulit-gguq kegginameggnun kegginaqumek nepceciiyugnalriit-llu amllerpek'nateng; amlleq-llu pisciiganani. Tua-i taum uskurailengraan maaggun nepcecitulim ellikani tua-i waten nepingalriacetun igcugpek'nani, put'engraan-ll' iggngaunani. Wagg'uq neqcetarluni.

Mary Mike, May 1993

Nepcetaq tauna tangvaglallruaqa, yaatiinek taũgaam waten ullagpek'nak', Amigtulimi naskuggalleraulua. Tuani-ll' uitalanrilamta,

Although he wanted to continue, my father did not have strong legs. We might have seen something if we had looked on the other side of the hill.

They never look like a normal person's face. One side looks like a human face, but the other half does not.

The Ones that Stick to the Face

Andy Kinzy, St. Marys, February 1993

In all the classes of masks, the *nepcetaq* is ranked highest, being the most powerful mask. You see, long ago when the *temainaunelnguut* [ones disembodied in some sense] used these *nepcetat,* sometimes the mask [resting on the floor] would fuse with a shaman's face and adhere to it after he bent his head to bring his face down into it, even though five parkas had been placed on top of the mask.

Paul John, February 1994

For instance, doctors specialize in different areas of medical care. One doctor, depending on his/her specialty, can help a person get well. However, another doctor wouldn't be able to. The power behind the masks was like that. A certain mask could only be used by its owner, and another person could not just take it and use it as effectively.

They call those *nepcetat,* the masks they say the *angalkut* fused to their faces, and not many of them were able to do that. Although the *angalkuq* placed the mask on his face without a string to hold it there, it would adhere to his face and not fall off even though he would bow down.

Mary Mike, May 1993

When I was a girl at Amigtuli, I used to see a *nepcetaq* from a distance but never approached it for a closer look. We didn't live at Amigtuli, but

Andy Kinzy-m yuullgutni qularuskai Mountain Village-ami 1989-aami, ciuqerratniwa kettinaqut ak'allaat Andreafski-rmiutaat. James H. Barker

Andy Kinzy speaking to fellow villagers in Mountain Village, 1989, with masks collected at Andreafski spread before him. James H. Barker

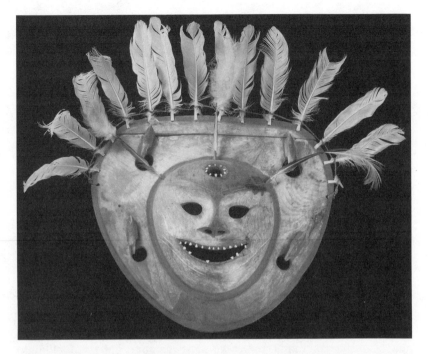

Sheldon Jackson-aam pillra *nepcetaq* Andreafski-mek 1893-aami. *Nepcetat* tamarmeng uucetun ayuqelartut kegginaruam avatiini murak ellanguaruluni, mer'unguarluni, wall' nungaunguarluni, ukinret-wa cali, aipaagni qilagmi ukinret wall' elakat cikumi imkut pitarkat tumyarait pissurteteng ullagaqamegteki. Sheldon Jackson Museum, Sitka

Nepcetaq mask collected at Andreafski by Sheldon Jackson in 1893. The plaque backboard typical of *nepcetat* masks represents variously the universe, water, air, and land, and the holes in the mask's surface represent the passages (sky holes or ice holes) through which the animals move in their journey toward the human hunter. Sheldon Jackson Museum, Sitka, IIB8 (32.7 cm high)

waten taū͡gaam yaaqsinrirqan nangniillerkaat aqvaaqatkut, elpengcarqatkek-w' angayuqaagka, taglalriakut tuavet.

Tauna ussukcausngaluni amaterluni muragmek ak'ak' ellegluni, kapusnganganani-ll' nunamun qasgim elatiini. Tua-i-gguq yuum taum [Teggalquq] nepcetaqlallra. Tua-i-wa kankut, ug'um Sophie Beans-am apa'urluin aū͡gkut apa'urluat. Kegginaminun nepculluku takuyartaarutlallrua. Atkugmek-gguq tunglilirluku, yuum atkuanek, nepcetatuuq tauna angalkuq. All'uku-gguq tua-i nepcetarlaraa.

Cali-llu-gguq qayaq-gguq canirrluku nepcetaqellrua, painganun elliluk' tauna. Ak'ak' uqamaipagtuq-kiq. Tuunraryaramikun taū͡gaam arturpek'anku pilarngataa. Takuyallagatnauraa-gguq qalrialuni tuaten. Angalkurpaunilallruyaaqekiit-wa tauna Teggalqumek pilallrat. Teggalqumek atengqerrluni.

Jasper Louise, February 1994

Nepcetanek pilallrit iillanarqut. Nepcetauguq-gguq una. Kitaki-gguq piqerliu nepcetaq. Tua-ll' imna waniw' kegginaquq natermun elliluku. Waten piaqami taigartellartuq natermelngermi, mayurluni kegginaanun. Tua-llu kan'a mayuan ilasqaat. Atkugmek saggluku patuat. Iliini atkuk waten pingraatni mayuyuituq. Ciin mayuyuita? Tauna atkukestii ngelmirqerkaunritaqan, tuquarkaugaqan mayuyuituq. Anerteqerkamek-llu piatni tua-i mayu'urrluni. Ataam-gguq. Atkuuk malruurtuk. Uqiggetlanricaaqellilriit tayim atkuuluteng. Ataam puc'an mak'niitungluni tuunralgem kegginaqrua. Melugyulriit-wa tua-i mak'niituullilriit. Pingayuurtaqan waten ilasciigatait. Uqamaitut angalkuulriani murilkellat kankut.

Tua-llu nep'arcata, waten piluteng atraqercetlaraat, unatmeggnek waten. Pinritaqan-llu inglugtun waten atkuum elatiikun. Tangvagluki wii, taū͡gaam pikestait tayim akaurtut tangerrnaunriuciat. Tua-i tangvalqa iquklituq.

when they invited my parents for the last dance performance [of a cycle] we would go there.

That mask was nailed to a large wooden post outside the *qasgiq*. It once belonged to a person now deceased. He was Sophie Beans' great-grandfather. He stuck it on his face and swung his face from left to right during a presentation. The *angalkuq* put a parka over the mask. He fused it with his face that way.

And I heard that he used a kayak as a *nepcetaq*, placing the mask on the kayak hole. My gosh, it must have been heavy. But with his powerful *tuunraq* it must have been weightless for him. Making animal sounds, he would turn his face from side to side. They said he was a very powerful *angalkuq*. Teggalquq was his name.

Jasper Louise, February 1994

The ones that were called *nepcetat* were amazing. He said that the mask he was presenting was a *nepcetaq*. Then people told him to go ahead with it. The mask was placed on the floor in front of him. When he bowed, the mask rose up to his face. If the performance was a success, someone would suggest that a parka be placed over the mask, and a parka would be placed on it. At times the mask would not rise after the parka had been placed there. Why wouldn't it rise? If the owner of the parka was destined not to live very long, it would not rise. And if they placed the parka of a person who was not going to die soon, it would rise. Then they put down a second parka. Being parkas, they probably were heavy. When he bowed again, his mask would begin to rise. Perhaps the masks that adhere by suction are *mak'niituut* [from *makete-* "to rise, get up"]. They could not add any more after the third parka. They're obviously heavy even for an *angalkuq*.

Once they adhere to the face, they use their hands to remove them like this [pushing down and away from the face]. And if that doesn't remove the mask they use both hands like this on the outside of the parka and pull it away from the face. I observed those performances, but the people who owned those kinds of masks have been gone a long time now. That is all I observed.

Alma Keyes, May 1993

Ataucirqumi aūg'umek tuunrilrianek tangertua. Alingelqa tauna avausuitaqa. Tauna anaanairutka wani malikluku, maligtesqenganga-am aanama, paqnayugngama, malikluku qasgilunuk tuunriqatallratni. Tua tuani ik'um wani Aqaran atairutii, tauna pingegglermiami, una wani yuk-llu anirtungnaqluku pinricaaqlartuq, taūgaam ucurnarqengnaqluni pilallilria.

Amik-llu umegturluku, kan'a-llu kenirlallrat maqilriit umgumaluni. Maqinerraraam kinguani nengllirpek'nani-llu tamana qasgiq. Imarnitegnek naken yuut piatnek, all'uni, elliin-ll' piminek pivkenani tukuunrilmiami, piculiunrilami. Avangcamek tang aūg'umek atellria tangkuraqallemni. Alingqercaaqlua murilkaqa. Cetamaungatut aūgkut ukinret pikani. Avangcarpall'er. Nangercami tua enuursaaqekii aūg'asciigalluni. Wagg'uq tamakut acirnaurait nepcetanek. Wagg'uq neplartut aūg'asciigalluteng.

Avangcarpallraat aūgkut tangerrlallruanka, tavaten-am taum yuut iliita alutekellrani, nuviskaangqerrami-ll' tauna enii, wagg'uq nepcetat. Kegginaquusaaqut taūgaam ugg'un ukinengqerrluteng. Qayuwa tayima kegginaa tauna avangcausaaquq, kegginaquusaaquq. Uiteranek tamakunek paint-aumaluni. Cali-llu naken' cungaglinek pilartat.

Canguaruciitaqa arnaralleraulua alinglua tuaten tangkellemni. Waten taūgaam qanruteknaurait nepcetaruniluku. Aūg'asciigalluni-am tua enuungraani. Qayuwa-llu-am piqerluni aūg'arqani tua ak'a kiirtevkaq'apiggluni, kiirsukapiggluni. Nepengluni. Nepeng'an-am tuar ca enem acianek itellria. Qanersaaqlallriami kangingnaqevkenani cauga. Taumek tang alingqertellrulrianga cakneq. Wagg'uq apqaraluku, question-arluku. Aptaqani qanrutaqani taum taūgaam tua-i kangirciaqluku. Wangkuta avatiini kegginquilngurni kangircisuunaku. Waten camek aptaqani qanrutaqluku. Tua apqaranek tamakut pilallruit maaken qasgim acianek nep'ngaqata. Taūgaam taum kegginaqulgem kangirciaqluku, wangkuta kangircisuunaku. Atam niillemni tavani tuarpiaq naken patuluni camek qang'a-llu qat'gami iluanek qanerlalria. Caperrsullruunga. Ansugsaaqeng'erma-ll' anevkarpek'nii tegulua tegumiaqlua, neplirpek'nii uitasqellua. Uitangnaqellrianga. Amik-llu umegturngatgu. Yugsaggarluni qasgim ilua. Tuani taūgaam alingsukallruunga.

Alma Keyes, May 1993

Once I saw a shaman performing a ritual. I have never forgotten how frightened I was. Because I was curious, my mother gave me permission to go with my late aunt to the *qasgiq* to see the shaman's performance. The late father of Aqaran, who was quite resourceful, did not perform out of necessity but perhaps to glorify himself.

The doorway was closed off, and the firepit was covered with planks. It was right after the men had had a firebath, and it was still warm inside the *qasgiq*. Since he wasn't a great hunter, he lacked his own *imarnin* [seal-gut raincoat] and borrowed somebody else's. While I watched him, he put on a mask. I watched although I became very frightened. I think there were four holes up on top of the great big *avangcaq* [mask]. When he straightened up, he pushed on it, but it could not come off. They called those masks *nepcetat*. They said they became fused to the face.

Great big *avangcat* were put away on a shelf of someone's home and were called *nepcetat*. They were masks with holes right here [gesturing]. The face of the *nepcetaq* was like a regular mask. Part of the mask was painted with *uiteraq* [red ocher]. And I don't know what they used to make the green color.

I didn't know or understand the purpose of the performance because I was young and at that time very frightened. They said he was giving a *nepcetaq* performance. Although he tried to remove it by pushing on it, he had difficulty prying it off. When he somehow removed the mask, he was covered with sweat. He started to make noises. When he did that, something seemed to enter from under the house. They say it was asking him questions, but we couldn't understand it. That was why I got so frightened. When it asked a question, he would answer. And whenever it asked him a question, he was the only one who understood it. Those of us that weren't wearing masks could not understand it. When it asked a question he would answer back. They called the ones under the *qasgiq* making the noises *apqarat* ["brief utterances," from *aper-*, "to say," plus *-qar*, "briefly"]. The person wearing the mask was the only one who understood while we, the audience, were unable to understand it. Although I heard the voice, it was muffled as if its mouth were covered with something or as if the noises were coming from its chest. It was hard to believe. Although I wanted to leave, they physically held me

Kegginaqut Inglukellriit

Justina Mike, March 1994

Ellaita kangilirluki waten kegginaqirluteng piaqameng yuraucirluteng amlleresqelluki tamakut cat ungungssit. Akusrarpiiqnateng-ll' pivkenateng wagg'uq agayuniluteng tuaten piaqameng caunguarturluteng pinaurtut. Tauna-llu angun kegginaqurluni caunguarturluni nepaitnek-llu neplirtureluteng. Taum imarpigmiutaam pikekaku nepaitnek neplirturluteng. Kaviarunguarqameng-llu tua uarpaaluteng pinaurtut. Tamakut tuaten piureluteng. Ataam umegngan taukuk kegginaqurlutek anlutek. Ataam cevv'arluteng allat tua-am kegginaquit cimirluteng , tavaten cimirtaarturluteng. Caunguarluteng

back, telling me to stay still and not make any noise. I was totally overwhelmed by the events. I restrained myself from fleeing. They had closed off the doorway. There were quite a few people in the *qasgiq*. That time I experienced the most fear in my whole life.

Pairs of Masks

Justina Mike, March 1994

They performed using masks with their songs so they would ensure that the animals be plentiful. They said that they were performing an *Agayu* and considered it a solemn occasion. The men wore masks that were made like a variety of animals, and they made their sounds. If he had on a sea mammal mask, he made sounds like one. And he cried out like a fox if he had on a fox mask. They presented a variety of animal masks. They had a curtain, and when it opened two masked men came forward. Each time the curtain opened, there were different performers with masks. The masks depicted sea mammals, land animals, plants,

George Bunyan-aam Naparyaarmium ukuk paluqtaruak kegginaquk pilialqak 1946-aami tangercetaalillratni Disney-nkut Alaska Eskimo-mek. Nertukmegnek naparuanek tegumiarlutek. Ukuk kegginaquk cali-ll' pingayuak alla Sam Hunter-aam piliara ilakluku tamarmeng ayuqluteng kangingqellruut. Alaska State Museum, Juneau

George Bunyan carved this pair of beaver masks at Hooper Bay in 1946 for a masked dance performed during the filming of the Disney movie *Alaskan Eskimo*. The feathered "trees" the beavers hold in their hands represent their food. These two masks, along with a third beaver mask (II-A-5393) made by Sam Hunter, told the same story. Alaska State Museum, Juneau, II-A-5395 (63.5 cm) and II-A-5396 (61 cm)

cat kegginaqut imarpigmiutaunguarluteng, nunamiutaat-llu ungungssit kegginait, naunraruanek-llu nausqelluki naunraat makut-llu muriit amllerresqelluki, imangat-llu. Tamakut nepaitnek qayuw' neplingnaqluteng taukuk pinaurtuk.

Malruulutek kegginaquk akiqlirraqlutek, cimirtaarturluteng. Patuqaqluni taũgaam kiugna. Kangcirarrlugaq capkutaqluku. Tuaten piureluteng, taungunguarturluteng aperluku kaigaluteng. Arnait-ll' tamakut kenugarrluteng. Canguat tamakut apalluqureluki tua-i kiaku amlleresqelluki. Tua-i nangniigaqameng taũgaam tuaten qanerturluteng pilkialartut.

Mary Mike, February 1994

Tuaten agayuliaqata unani wangkuta natermi aqumgavkayuunata maavet taũgaam inglernun aqumtaqluta. Kumgatakluta-w'. Kankuk arulalriik, ukuk-wa cali arnak arulalriik allamek taprunateng makunek taũgaam cauyalrianek. Malruuqerrlainarluteng arulalriit, angutek malruk arnak-llu malruk. Ayagniqataarrlainarluteng-llu pinaurtut, meng'ura'arqata arulalaagpek'nateng, ayagninqegcaarluteng taũgaam. Apalliraqatgu nutaan yaggluteng. Ilait tua-i arulamavkarnaurait.

Kegginaqurlutek-wa tua-i all'uki anlartuk tayima ellamun. Pakmavet taũgken egalrem ceñiinun mayurluteng—mayurluteng pilallinilriit, qalriuciriluteng. Tua-i-w' qalriaciitnek qalrialluki kegginaqut. Egalermun-llu waten pull'uteng pilalliameng erinvauvakarlalriik. Tamakunek-ll' keglunruanek piaqameng marurpagaluteng tuaten qakma pinaurtut. Canek qalriuciitnek ungungssit qalriagaqluteng.

Kay Hendrickson, January 1994

Takumni kegginaqirluteng yuralrianeg tangtullruunga. Ellimeq'ngag malruutullruug kwaten kegginaqurluteg yura'arkag. Tawa-llu taukug yuug malrug taum angalkum pisqestemeg kegginaqugkeneg all'uteg yurarluteg. Yurauteqainarluki taũgg'am makut allanret. Taw' ukug pisteg

wood, and blackfish to ensure that they would be plentiful. The performers made the sounds of the animals depicted.

They took turns presenting masks in pairs side by side. They used a canvas for a curtain and closed it each time between performances. They continued to perform, honoring each animal, plant, and fish. And their women dressed up for the presentation. They used animals depicted on the masks as *apallut* in hopes that they would be plentiful in the summer. They presented their last performances so that it was intelligible to the audience.

Mary Mike, February 1994

They had us sit on the *ingleret* [benches] during the *Agayu*. They wouldn't allow us to sit on the floor *?kumgatakluta*. Two men were dancing down there, and on the side two women danced to the drummers' beat. They always danced in pairs. Two men and two women. The dancers gradually start their movements to the beat of the soft drumming and singing [*meng'ura'arqata*, "as they begin to reverberate, resonate"; from *meng'e-* "to reverberate, resonate"], according to custom and protocol. When the singers start singing the *apalluq*, the dancers would start the motions that tell the story of the song. For some dances the audience requested many encores.

The two would go outside after putting on the masks they were presenting. They went on the roof of the *qasgiq* and made the calls of the masks depicted. Perhaps their cries were so loud because they were right next to the skylight.

Kay Hendrickson, January 1994

I used to observe people dancing with masks. Two dancers appointed by the *angalkuq* performed with the masks. The two appointees put on the masks and performed for the guests. Following the step-by-step instructions of the *angalkuq*, the two performers knelt on the floor, and

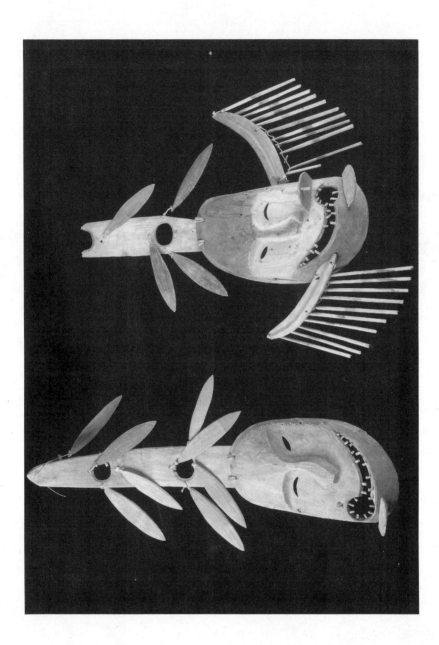

Sheldon Jackson-aam ukuk inglukellriik kegginaquk pilqak Andreafski-mek 1893-aami. Tamarmek cangungqanguarlutek iqgegkenka-llu aipagkek ukimalutek, kegguterualipiarlutek-llu. Johan Adrian Jacobsen-aaq-llu-gguq tamatum ciungani waten muragayagarnek agaluteng pilegmek kegginaqumek tamaaken pillruuq. Sheldon Jackson Museum, Sitka

Sheldon Jackson collected this asymmetrical pair of masks at Andreafski in 1893. Both have distorted faces. The round mouth corner, toothy grin, and wooden appendages are all reminiscent of the pair of *tuunraq* masks Johan Adrian Jacobsen collected from the same area ten years earlier. Sheldon Jackson Museum, Sitka, IIB45 (52.8 cm.) and IIB46 (61.3 cm)

Ayuqenrilnguugnek kegginaqurlutek angutek matarmek yuralriik can'get tupigat ciuqerratni. Milotte Collection, Alaska State Museum, Juneau

Bare-chested dancers performing in front of a grass screen using a pair of unmatched masks. Milotte Collection, Alaska State Museum, Juneau

ciisqumiggluteg ac'aqnegteki, qanertur tauna kegginaquni pitekluku, taum tayima angalkum alerquataciatun pilliur, ellii uitaniluni erenret qauratni. Erenret qauratni uitaniluni tauna tawa aapaa qaneryaaqur, kegginaquni tauna aperluku, ellii pinrilengremi. Aapaa-llu cali tauna qanerluni tawa taringevkarlua, imam atlirnerani uitaniluni. Tawaten taw' qanertug taukug. Qanrraarluteg nutaan yurartug.

Allakuragtug taukug kegginaqug atullekeg cauciitagka nutaan tawaten tangerrngama. Tawa aturciqiartua ukug arulalriig ivarucetaagneg angalkum taum piliaraneg. Kegginaqug tawa taukug ivarutkakegneg, kwaten aturtekegneka ivaruciagkeneg aturciqiartua. Tawa-qaa?

Uya-angu-ama
U-lla-ga-ta-rran
Uya-angu-ama
U-lla-ga-ta-rran
Cu-lu-nga-ma yu-ra-ra-tan
[Agenra/Its Chorus]
Yi-ya-ra-anga yi-ya-ara-nga yu-raa
Aya-yu-raa-nga-yii i-ya-ranga-aa yaa-aa-rraa
Yaa-aa-aa

Yug-ya-ma
Ma-lleg-yar-tu-ram-ke-rren
Aku-lu-rram ut-yar-ai-kun
Yi-ya-ra-anga yi-ya-ara-nga yu-raa
Aya-yu-raa-nga-yii i-ya-ranga-aa yaa-aa-rraa
Yaa-aa-aa

Ca-pu-ka-raat
Ta-lin-rat-neg
Uiv-tar-pag ui-vu-ma-yaa-qur
Yi-ya-ra-anga yi-ya-ara-nga yu-raa
Aya-yu-raa-nga-yii i-ya-ranga-aa yaa-aa-rraa
Yaa-aa-aa

then one of them said that he was at the crest of the daylight [*erenret qauratni*], as depicted by the mask. The other person said that he was at the ocean floor. That was what they said, and after that they danced.

I couldn't determine what the masks were depicting because that was the first time I had seen masks like that. I will sing a song for you that the two dancers performed which the *angalkuq* composed for the masks.

My ?
You're coming to it
My ?
You're coming to it
As I began to sing
you are dancing
Yi-ya-ra-anga yi-ya-ara-nga yu-raa
Aya-yu-raa-nga-yii iya-ranga-a yaa-aa-rraa
Ya-a-a-aa

My spirit
I come to be near
Through Akuluraq's ?
Yi-ya-ra-anga yi-ya-ara-nga yu-raa
Aya-yu-raa-nga-yii i-ya-ranga-aa yaa-aa-rraa
Yaa-aa-aa

?
From their shadow
? circled
Yi-ya-ra-anga yi-ya-ara-nga yu-raa
Aya-yu-raa-nga-yii i-ya-ranga-aa yaa-aa-rraa
Yaa-aa-aa

Yug-ya-ma
Ma-lleg-yar-tu-ram-ke-rren
Nu-na-lug-piam
U-lev-ya-raa-kun
Yi-ya-ra-anga yi-ya-ara-nga yu-raa
Aya-yu-raa-nga-yii i-ya-ranga-aa
Yaa-aa-rra-aa-yaa

Tun-tur-yuum
Ta-lin-ra-neg
Uya-vviar-lug e-llu-ra-ya-qur
Yi-ya-ra-anga yi-ya-ara-nga yu-raa
Aya-yu-raa-nga-yii i-ya-ranga-aa yaa-aa-rraa
Yaa-aa-aa

Yug-ya-ma
Ag-ya-yar-tu-ram-ke-rren
Ata-na-rram ing-ril-qit-ai-neg
Yi-ya-ra-anga yi-ya-ara-nga yu-raa
Aya-yu-raa-nga-yii i-ya-ranga-aa
Yaa-aa-rra-aa-yaa

Aru-la-tan
Ka-liv-ciur-luav-gu
Kalli-rraag-neg nav-rit-naum-ken
Yi-ya-ra-anga yi-ya-ara-nga yu-raa
Aya-yu-raa-nga-yii i-ya-ranga-aa yaa-aa-rraa
Yaa-aa-aa-ai

Yuungcautet Kegginaqut

Jasper Louise, February 1994

Waten-llu una apqucirrangqerqan waten ayuqellriamek, canek cikitullruat kegginaqunek anirtuutekaqeciqngalkaitnek taumun apquciatnun. Tua-i taum kangia tauna nallunritaqa tuaten taktalria. Picirrlumegcetun aruquteksuitait tamakut nakmiklermeggnun taũgaam.

My spirit
I come near you
Through the place
Where ? churns
Yi-ya-ra-anga yi-ya-ara-nga yu-raa
Aya-yu-raa-nga-yii i-ya-ranga-aa
Yaa-aa-rra-aa-yaa

Big Dipper's
From its shadow
? swooped down
Yi-ya-ra-anga yi-ya-ara-nga yu-raa
Aya-yu-raa-nga-yii i-ya-ranga-aa yaa-aa-rraa
Yaa-aa-aa

My spirit
I've come to ?
From ? ?
Yi-ya-ra-anga yi-ya-ara-nga yu-raa
Aya-yu-raa-nga-yii i-ya-ranga-aa
Yaa-aa-rra-aa-yaa

You're moving for it
Because you can't reach it
I'll lend you ?
Yi-ya-ra-anga yi-ya-ara-nga yu-raa
Aya-yu-raa-nga-yii i-ya-ranga-aa yaa-aa-rraa
Yaa-aa-aa-ai

Healing Masks

Jasper Louise, February 1994

There were different kinds of masks. When someone had a chronic illness, an *angalkuq* might give that person a mask with healing properties. That's how much I know about that. They didn't give them to just anyone, only to those they diagnosed.

Yuungcaristetun ayuqluteng. Cavtaqluki unatmeggnek akngirnarqekan, tua-i-ll' cavtesqelluku, cavvluku-ll' tua-i. Kem'ga tungairluk' cavingaluku. Tua-i-ll' assiriluni taun cavingallra. Tuaten tua-i tamakut ciuliaput ayuqellrulliniut yullret auġkut.

Arnat Kegginaqruit

Johnny Thompson, Negeqliq, February 1994

Tua-i arnat tua nasqurruterluteng canek nellevluteng tua pilalriit, uyamigluteng-llu. Tauġaam kegginaqulriamek arnamek tangerqerpailegma—cali kina qanemciksaituq arnamek kegginaqulriamek. Tauġaam waten inglukluteng nunat piaqameng tangerrlartua arnanek angutngunguarluteng pilriit tua kegginaqurmiluteng pilallrumiut, angutngunguarluteng pilriit.

Waten nunat inglukluteng arnat angutmeggnun waten kelelriacetun piluteng. Tua-i picingssaarlallruut kiani. Waten cacirkairutaqameng makunun avaqlirmeggnun ellmegteggun kiagmi-llu tua anglaningnaqu'uratullruut arnat angutet-llu inglukluteng. Arnat angutngunguaqluteng. Tua-i arnirluki-llu yurarmiaqluteng angutngunguarluteng tua-i angucetarnek-llu aturluteng. Tua-i tuaten anglaningnaqu'urlallruut. Tua-i iluriurulluteng tua-i. Anglanarqaqluteng tua-i kiingan tua-i anglanarqengnaquciqlaamegteggu tamaani tua-i.

Shamans were like medical doctors, they placed their hands directly on the flesh where there was pain. The pain would leave the place where they put their hand. That was the way our ancestors dealt with their illnesses.

Women's Masks

Johnny Thompson, St. Marys, February 1994

The women were all dressed up in headdresses and necklaces. I have not seen women presenting masks. But women dressed up as men and performed with masks within the village when the opposite sexes challenged each other.

The males of a village challenged their women in the same way a village challenged another. They amused the audience as comedians would. Men and women entertained each other in the village with humorous performances when they weren't hosting other villages. The women dressed as men and danced. Both sides danced accompanied by women dressed like men. That's how they entertained themselves. They had fun with their teasing cousins. They were enjoyable to watch because that was their way of amusing themselves.

Arnat kegginaqurluteng Akulurak Mission-aami tamaani 1900-aam nuniini. Angenkacagaq kegginaquq qukami aipaa-llu caniani ayuqsarpiaqii, tamarmek *nepcetauguk.* Malruk-wa cali tegumiarlutek uivenqellriignek cagnek tuarpiaq imkut Kusquqvagmek pillrita arnanun kegginaquqtuniluki ayuqegket. Jesuit Archives, Gonzaga University, Spokane, Washington

Women posing with masks at Akulurak Mission, early 1900s. The woman in the center wears a large *nepcetaq* while two girls hold concentric hoops similar to the women's masks collected along the Kuskokwim. Jesuit Archives, Gonzaga University, Spokane, Washington

Kegginaqut Auluksaraat

Jasper Louise, February 1994

Kegginaqut kenekluki agarrluki-llu. Agartaqamegteki qasgiq yuicecuirutaqluku. Yuitaqameng-gguq ilait anuralartut-llu kegginaqut kalgguurulluteng-llu waten agalriit. Tua-i yuitenritengnatuutiin qasgim kangia. Atuumariaqata taūgaam tua-i peggluki, qalriucimariaqamegteki.

Arnanun-llu agturavkayuitellruit. Arnaq-gguq man'a—maa-i-wa cali piyaaqellria nallukvut—cangerlauguq; arnaq arcaqerluni agleryuaq. Uuggun-llu-gguq camek maq'uq iiragmikun, pitarkaulriani anyurnarqellriamek. Naqugucirturluteng-llu tamaani arnat pitullruut kanvellerkarteng-gguq pitekluku piyuakuneng. Naqugucirturluki pisqellarait camek ik'imek sagcinayukluki anyurnamek natermun. Umyuartequrallemni tamaa-i, agnguaryaurcata-llu arnanek ingluteng, umyuartequrarqama tua-i neqe'urluput imkut pitarkat tamariinartut. Elpet-llu nallunritaten.

Care of the Masks

Jasper Louise, February 1994

They cared for masks with reverence and hung them up. Once they hung them, they made sure someone was always in the *qasgiq*. They said that if they were left alone, some of the masks would go out, knocking the other masks that were hanging. For that reason they kept the *qasgiq* occupied. After the masks were sounded out in performance, they could be released.

Women were not allowed to touch the masks. They say a woman—it is still true today, but we aren't aware of it—is *cangerlak* [can cause bad experiences], especially a pubescent girl. They say something emanates from her thyroid area that repels animals. Also, women always wore belts around their waists to block female emanations that might offend the animals. When I think about that, I'm reminded of the gradual decline of animals we depend on for food since men started to dance with women in their arms.

Chuna McIntyre-aaq yaquleguam qamiqurranek ciuqalegmek nacarluni kinguqlirmi John-am piliaranek, Marie Meade-aq-llu ellanguamek kegginaqurluni Chuna-m piliaranek. New York-ami Symphnoy Space-ami yurarraarlutek tarenraircetellrulliniut April 1995-aami. Chuna McIntyre

Chuna McIntyre, wearing a forehead bird mask made by his brother, John, and Marie Meade, wearing a *ellanguaq* mask, at Symphony Space in New York City, April 1995, on tour with the National Council on the Traditional Arts. Chuna McIntyre

Natmun Pegtellrat Kegginaqut

Kay Hendrickson, January 1994

Tawa taq'aqamegteki tamakut kegginaqut nutaan egtevkenaki anulluki ataucimun ellitulliniit cuilquunrilengraan nunat ukut yaakariitnun. Tamakuneg tangertallruunga amllerturluteng kegginaquneg ayuqenrilngurneg. Taum tawa-i imam atlirnerani uitaniluku qanellrem, erenret-llu qauratni uitaniluku qanellrem, taukug kegginaquutegni maqikevkallruag.

Willie Kamkoff, Qerrullik, Johnny Thompson-aaq-llu, February 1994

Willie Kamkoff: Egglarait cikirtuutekluki-llu mikelnguarnun pilarait. Tuani-wa takumni tuatnalriit qavcirqunek.

Johnny Thompson: Egterpallurlarait kiani-ll' [Tuutalgaq] atu'urqamegteki.

Willie Kamkoff: Naanguarkillarait tua-i makut caperrsuklanritliamegteki, Nunapiggluugarmi Caniliami tuaten. Cat taūgaam qel'kait. Kaviaruat tua cat qunukenritait.

Jasper Louise, February 1994

Aturlarait atunermek-llu taqngamegteki cikirtuutekluki mikelngurnun. Wii-ll' cikitullruatnga. Anglanitekluki taūgken enem iluani.

Mary Mike, February 1994

Taukuk egciyuitellruuk kegginaqutullrek Amigtulimi. Egcukluki cali pilallruyaaqekput, taūgaam egingalanritliniut, quyurrluki ellilalliniakek. Tekitellruapuk wangkuk anglicarteka-llu—wiinga-w' ciumek tekilluki. Egteqapigcimavkenateng taūgaam quyungqaluteng. Nanvam cenii ururrluum qaningani mat'um nunapiim—nanvaq taun'

"Putting Away" the Masks

Kay Hendrickson, January 1994

The masks were not thrown away when the performances were over. They were placed together not far from the village. I used to see a pile of different masks deposited that way. That shaman who presented two masks depicting creatures that reside at the crest of daybreak and the ocean floor burned his masks in the firebath.

Willie Kamkoff, Kotlik, and Johnny Thompson, February 1994

Willie Kamkoff: They put the masks away on the tundra, but some were given to children. That was what they did several times in my youth.

Johnny Thompson: When they used masks up there [at Pilot Station], they took most of them out to the wilderness after they presented them.

Willie Kamkoff: In Hamilton and Caniliaq some children received masks that *angalkut* weren't worried about discarding. The phemonenal and significant masks were not distributed in that way. But ones like fox masks and such were given away.

Jasper Louise, February 1994

They used the masks, and after they finished they gave them to children. They gave me some, too. We had fun with them in the house.

Mary Mike, February 1994

Those two who had masks in Amigtuli never discarded them. We thought they had thrown them away, but evidently they were carefully placed on the tundra away from the village. My stepmother and I happened upon such a stash—I actually found them first. They weren't casually thrown away but neatly arranged on the ground near a lake

cenengqelliniluni maraqcamek, meq-wa kan' ketvaarni. Maraqcam ngeliini, nunapiim ngeliini kegginaqut yaaqliqluteng. Quyurmeng uitaluteng canguat alingnarqellriit tamakut. Mikelngurnun naanguaqevkarlanricugnarqakek taukuk. Tamakut taūgaam pinguarraat, kegginaqucuaraat-llu tamakut yaquleguat mikelngurnun tunlarait.

Taumek taūgaam nepcetallranek-gguq Teggalqum Amigtulimi tangtullruunga. Qasgim elatiini uitaaqluni naparuciumaluni equyaarmek, qertuvkenani taūgaam. Yaassiigenqeggluni qukaani-w' kegginaquq. Tuantauratulun' tauna. Tauna-llu angalkuq Teggalquq nalallran kingurpiikun wii tua-i tangellruaqa. Arullerminun tuanlluni.

ringed by a wide marsh. The masks sat side by side on the marsh below the tundra edge. Different masks were all together, including powerful ones. I don't think those two shamans let children play with them. Generally, children received masks of ordinary beings, little masks, and bird masks.

In Amigtuli I saw a *nepcetaq* that belonged to Teggalquq nailed to a short post outside the *qasgiq*. It was a square mask with a face in the middle. It was always there in that place. I saw it there long after the *angalkuq* Teggalquq died. It remained there until it rotted.

4. Kegginaqut Kangiit-llu

William Tyson, Anchorage, February 1993

Kegginaquteng nalqigtaqamegteki camun atullerkaat nalqigtetullruat. Taumun ataucimun aturpek'naku, tau͡gaam kegginaqum kangia camun atullerkaa nalqigtelallruat.

Dick Andrew-m qanellra yuarun-llu atullra aniparuam kegginaqum tarenraa yuvrillerminiu, January 1994

Qulirat-wa ilakellikiit tauna anipaq. Anipaq irnillinilria tua-i. Tua-i-llu atulliniuq,

> *Aa-ya-guu-ma-rraa-ya-guu-ma*
> *Aa-ya-guu-ma-rraa-ya-guu-ma*
> *Ya-qiur-ci, ya-qiur-ci-i-i*
> *Ya-qiur-ci, ya-qiur-ci-i-i*
> *A-ta-si ima-qaa te-kis-kan*
> *Aa, ner-niar-tu-ci-i-i*
> *U-gen-vag-nek ta-lli-ma-neg*
> *Aa-ya-guu-maa*
> *Aa-ya-guu-ma-rraa-yag-uu-mai*
> *Ya-qiur-ci, ya-qiur-ci-i-i*

Tua-i-ggur-imkut irniari yaqiungarrnaurtut waten neqkameggnek qanrutaqateng taum anipam. Tua-i tuaten ayuquq taun' quliraq, taktanganani-ll' waten. Anipat iciw' uugnarnek avelngarnek nertulriit. Tua-i ner'aqluteng tamakunek. Tua-i ava-i quliraa. Ava-i taktacia. Qulirat piciatun wii nallunritanka takengraata-llu nanilengraata-llu. Tua-i au͡gna

Masks and the Stories They Tell

William Tyson, Anchorage, February 1993

They clarified the masks' significance [during performances]. They had many uses, and the origin and use of each mask was explained.

Dick Andrew's snowy owl song and story told when he was shown a snowy owl mask, January 1994

That owl [mask] is probably associated with a *quliraq* [story from the ancient times]. A snowy owl's eggs hatched, and she started to sing.

> *Aa-ya-guu-ma-rraa-ya-guu-ma*
> *Aa-ya-guu-ma-rraa-ya-guu-ma*
> *Flap your wings*
> *Flap your wings*
> *When your father comes*
> *Aa, you will eat*
> *Five big voles*
> *Aa-ya-guu-maa*
> *Aa-ya-guu-ma-rraa-yag-uu-mai*
> *Flap your wings, flap your wings*

The baby owls started flapping their wings when their mother told them about their food. That's how long the story is, being no longer than that. The snowy owls usually eat voles. They would eat that kind. That's the extent of the story. I know many *qulirat*, some long and some short. The song I just sang is a song I sing when I tell that story. There are

Inglukellriik aniparuak kegginaquk Sheldon Jackson-aam pillrek Kuigpagmek 1890s-aani. Pingayunek yungam teqsuqrinek melqurrarnek kanglegnek cikmiumalriignek iilek kangmikun kapusvikumaluni. Sheldon Jackson Museum, Sitka

An asymmetrical pair of owl masks collected by Sheldon Jackson on the lower Yukon in the 1890s. Three stripped jaeger feathers with downy tufts are atop the owl with closed eyes. Similar masks were collected by Edward Nelson (1899:197) from Sabotnisky. Sheldon Jackson Museum, Sitka, IIH11 (15.8 cm) and IIH14 (16.5 cm)

ava-i yuarutekluku atutuunga. Pingayurqunek yurautnguuq, quliraq taun' nanipakaami. Pingayurqunek allarrauluku aturarkauluku. Tuaten ayuqluni.

Aa-ya-guu-ma-ar
A-yai-yai-aa
Aa-rraa

Aa-ya-guu-maar
A-yai-yaa-nga
A-yai-yaa-aa-a-nga
A-ya-yii-i-yaa a-ya-rraa-ra-nga
Ya-qiur-ci-i-i-ii-ii-rrii-i-i

Yuraqelallruaput piani [Mamterilleq] ak'a imumi yuraryugangellemteni maani. Neq'angcaarlua tamakut yuarutait—augna apellra, "Atasi ima-qaa . . . ." Cukarikanirluku aturluku. Malruurrlainatuut yuarutet apalluit. Ayuqluteng tua-i yuarutait apalluit atauciuluteng allauyuunateng.

three parts to the song we dance to since the story is so short. It is sung three times, each time a little bit different. That's the way it is.

Aa-ya-guu-ma-ar
A-yai-yai-aa
Aa-rraa

Aa-ya-guu-maar
A-yai-yaa-nga
A-yai-yaa-aa-a-nga
A-ya-yii-i-yaa a-ya-rraa-ra-nga
Flap your wiiiiiii-nnnn-ggs

We danced it here [Bethel] when we began dancing long ago. I would think about the stories and their songs—for instance, one line in the song goes, "When your father . . . ." That part would be sung faster. Traditionally, a song always had two verses. The verses to the songs never changed.

5. Qasgim Iluani

Mary Mike, February 1994

Tua-i tauǥken tekicameng makut angutait qasgimun tua-i iterluteng arnait-ll' enenun tukurkameggnun piluteng. Ak'a-ll' tua-i ikna qasgi puyunglun'. Tua-i-w' piqainaurrluki, maqikait-llu, piqainaurrluki pilaamegteki kenillerkun imumi qasgikun maqitullermeggni. Qasgirpaulaameng-llu ilait imkut, quyurrvigmeggnek-wa qasgirpagmek pililalliniameng. Ak'aki-w' kan' kenillerpall'er. Maqirraarcelluki-llu qantatgun, qantarrarteggun payuggluki makut neviarcaraat taqnerurtenga'artellriit.

Aren tuani tekiyutiitni maqivailgata payugartellarait. Payugartemek-am aperluku. Itrumariqercata allanret tamalkuita qantarrarteggun canek neqpiggarnek imiqerluki, kinertarrarnek, payugarrluki tua-i tamakunek. Nunal'ircelluki-gguq.

Tuatnarraartelluki-am nutaan, utaqaluki tamakut qantat imairucata-ll' payugcestaita anulluki. Nutaan anngata qasgi ingna puyungluni. Kumarrluteng maqiluteng. Maqinermek-am taq'ercata nutaan payuggluki. Taukut tukunka, uitavipuk-w', angairutma-w' taukut Atsaruankut, Qetupan Leggleq-llu nulirrit uuqnarlinek egaluteng qantat imirluki. Kuigata taum akiani qasgi uitaluni. Kuigat cali taman' avayarrangqerrluni qasgim ketiikun kelutmun kuigmek Amelkilngurmek piaqluku. Nunat, net akiqliqu'urluteng, tauna-w' ik'um cingiim qaingani qasgiat. Tayima tua-i nutaan payugqaqnaurtut uuqnarlinek. Qagkut-llu-w' pilallilriit tuaten.

Nutaan nerluteng. Maqirraarluteng tua-i nererraarluteng-llu callerkairtaqameng ataam allanret arnartuumaita qasgilluki. Waten aklunek ciumek itrucuitut wii taukut tangvallrenka. Tua-i allanret

In the *Qasgiq*

Mary Mike, February 1994

When the invited guests arrived in the village their men would go to the *qasgiq* and their women would go to the homes of their hosts. Not long after the arrival, the smoke would start coming out the skylight of the *qasgiq*. At the time they still had firebaths, the hosts always got the wood ready before their guests arrived. Some settlements made huge *qasgit* for gatherings. A huge firepit would be down in the middle of the structure. After the men bathed, girls who were just becoming adults would bring them dishes of food.

Aren [expression], I meant to say that when they first arrived, they brought the male guests a little snack before they bathed. They would call it *payugarciyaraq* [presenting food to a friend or relative]. Once they were settled in the *qasgiq,* all the male guests received a little snack of dried fish and meat. It was their way of welcoming guests, *nunal'ircelluki.*

The food servers would wait until the guests had eaten, and when the bowls were empty they would leave. After they left, smoke would inevitably begin to rise from the skylight of the *qasgiq* as the men fired up for their firebath. As soon as the guests finished bathing, the servers returned with a full meal. The wives of our hosts, my late uncles Atsaruaq, Qetupan, and Leggleq, would cook fresh blackfish and dish them up into bowls when the bathers had finished. The *qasgiq* was on the opposite bank of their river. Just below the *qasgiq* was a little branch off the main river, a slough called Amelkilnguq [a narrow one]. The houses were on both sides of it, and the *qasgiq* was on the point across there. The servers would bring the men bowls of hot blackfish. The other families out there probably did the same thing.

Then they would finally eat. After they bathed and ate they would invite all the guests, including the women, to the *qasgiq*. The ones I observed didn't bring in the gifts at the beginning of the event. After all

quyurtelluki akma qasgimariata nutaan ukut nunalget arvirluteng qasgimun. Tua-i aturluteng. Yurarlaameng uksuaqvani, waten taũgken erenret takliriaqata agayuliluteng-gguq. Agayulimek un' apraqluku arulallerteng.

Tua-i taukut curukat taigaqata agayuliameggnek arulaluteng. Inglernek pilaraat aqumkallitaq pagaani qaillun waten qerratataluni, yuk-w' aciani aqumgaarkauluni. Pagna tua-i yungqerrnaurtuq kassuggluni, man'a-llu cali kassuggluni yungqerrluni inglerem acia. Kankut-w' qaũgkut-llu muragarmek cali aqumllitarluteng. Akiqliqluteng atulriit cauyarluteng. Una-w' tuskarraq waten ak'aki tak'urluni kaantelaanek yaaqliuqurluk' pingqerrluni. Ukuk-wa cali kenurrak ayagayarak ingleret qaingatnun ellilukek. Tua-i tanqigpagnaurtuq wangkutni.

Akiqliqluteng taukut cauyalriit nunalget curirluteng equgmek esrimaluni qaill' tayim qertutaluni. Tua-i taũgg' imna arulaluteng kanani malruuqaqluteng, angutek arnak-llu cali malruugaqlutek. Tuaten tua-i piurluteng. Nutaan taqngata nutaan makut pilluarqarkat-wa itrulluteng neqkanek ayuqenrilngurnek.

the guests assembled in the *qasgiq,* the village members would finally go across and join them. They would begin singing. During the fall season people would dance, and toward spring they composed *agayu* songs. The latter performance was called *Agayuliyaraq* [making requests or praying].

When the guests came, they would dance to the *agayu* songs they had composed. A long wooden plank called an *ingleq* was secured to the wall of the *qasgiq* high enough so a person could sit beneath it. People sat up on the *ingleq* all the way around, and the space beneath was also occupied. The singers and drummers would sit on two wooden benches on both sides of the middle stage area. And lighted candles were arranged across a rather long board right here, and two Coleman lanterns were sitting on the *ingleq* up there. It seemed to be very bright in the *qasgiq* to us at that time.

The host drummers and singers sat across from each other on a raised wooden plank. The dancers would dance on the stage in pairs, two men dancers and two women dancers. They would always do that. Then when they finished the dance performances, the host families would start bringing in a variety of foods they had harvested and prepared for distribution.

Qasgim ilua Tununermi, Qaluyaani, 1973

Inside the *qasgiq* in Tununak, Nelson Island, 1973

Ellanguaq

Martha Mann, Kangirnaq, July 1994

Iciw' angalkut taũgaam tuaten pitullrulriit. Angalkut iciw' ellanguatullrulriit, yuralriit-llu angalkunun ellanguaraqluteng.

Qilaamruyaanek apraqluki; waten yura'arqameng pagaavet agarrluki muriit piliat kenurranek imirluki. Waten yura'arqameng pagaavet agarrluki muriit piliat kenurranek imirluki, qilaamruyaanek apraqluteng. Tua-i tuaten pitullruut. Kenurranek imirluki kumarluki-ll' tamakut kenurrat, kenurraqluki tua-i tanqigcetaqluteng. Angalkut-am ilait, waten-llu imkunek agayunek piliaqameng pekceciinaurtut pikani—yuk pikna—tuar tang yuk. Tua-i taũgken apratni aqvaqurluni pagaaggun agqerrlun'. Pekcetaaq, imumek taprarmek cayugyarirluku, apraqatni taũgken aqvaqurluni iquvaarlun'. Tuar tang yuut. Tuaten pinaurtut pekceciluteng pagaaggun qasgim quliikun. Neviamek aci'irluku tauna tua pekcetaaq piaqluku. "Neviaraam-qaa paqtaaqai-qaa?"

Model of the Universe

Martha Mann, Kongiganak, July 1994

The *angalkut* were the ones that did that. The *angalkut* presented the *ellanguaq* and the dancers would perform for the *angalkut* during the *ellanguaq* presentation.

There were things they called *qilaamruyaat*, wooden pieces with lights inside which hung from the *qasgiq* ceiling as the people danced. They would dance with those *qilaamruyaat* lamps hanging from above. That's what they used to do. The lights inside those pieces would brighten up the *qasgiq*. When making presentations, some of the *angalkut* would make a figure of a person move up there—it looked just like a person. It would run across the ceiling when they called it. It was a puppetlike figure tied to a skin line that would run all the way across the area whenever it was called. Those figures looked just like people. The *angalkut* would make the hanging figures run across the ceiling of the *qasgiq*. The puppetlike figure would be called a *neviaq* [young girl]. "Is the *neviaq* coming to check on them?" [perhaps this is a line from a song].

Yuguaq agalria qukaani ellanguam yurellratni Mamterillerni 1981-aami. Iliit-wa uyungssuaralria eniraranterluni. Angucetaak-wa taruyamaarutek qacarnermi agalriik. James H. Barker

Yuguaq hanging in the center of a rope *ellanguaq* created for the 1981 masked dances in Bethel. A young man moves a dance wand to the drum's rhythm in the foreground. Six-feathered men's dance fans hang on the back wall. James H. Barker

Agayuaqameng—imna-am agayulilria, Qikertaugaam atii, imum-llu Arnaaqum Arnaan alqaan yurarluku. Qasgim-w' ilua tua-i qivyuaralirluni tangniqluni. Makut yurayaalriit yurarnaurtut kegginaquqtarluteng tan'gaurluut-llu. Tan'gaurluut kegginaqurluteng-llu yurarnaurtut yurauciaqaceteng. Cauyat-llu avatait waten allgiaraat teqsuqritnek kapusvikluki qivyurrarnek nuulirluki. Tangniqpiarluteng. Imkut-llu niirarautet cali tuaten qivyurrarnek nuulirluki.

Negeqlirmi Ciulirneret Quyurtellratni, February 1993

Ellanguamek, angalalluku, kegginaqut imkut aturlaqait. Taum ciungani tuaten pivailegmeng ircenrrarnun keleglartut, kevgirlartut. Niitnaqlartut kiugaqameng. Qasgimiut tem'irtaqluteng imkut nacitet piluki, tuaten pirraarluteng taq'eqaqluteng acimun aqumluteng. Nutaan taugken piuraqerluni naken unaken tem'illagluni. Tua-i-gguq angerluteng. Nutaan angrumariiceteng nutaan kassiyurluteng, tauna-ll' ellanguaq aturluku.

Mary Mike, February 1994

Wiinga-w' ellanguamek maani taugaam tangellrulrianga, kiani Tuutalgarmi aqvallratkut. Taum imum angukaraam tuqu'urlurpailegmi tauna tua alailliniluku ellanguaq. Qasgimi tua pikani agaluni, makut-w' pelaciniit aqesgiruanek maqaruaruanek-llu aqevlauqutarluteng. Una-w' yaqulpak, arnaruaq-wa cali, tauna-w' yaqulpak angelria.

Tauna-gguq arnaq mertallrani atakumi taum wani yaqulpiim tengutelliniluku natmun qavavet ingrimun qertulriamun Kuigpiim ceñiini, tuavet tua-i mis'ulluku. Tamariluku taukut kingunrin. Tuaken taugaam elakam ceñiinek qaltaa nalaqluku. Tua cayaaqluk' yuaryaaqluk' nalkevkenaku.

When they gathered for *Agayu* the father of Qikertaugaq presented a mask, and the sister of Arnaaqum Arnaan danced to the song composed for it. The interior of the *qasgiq* was beautifully decorated with white bird down feathers during the performance. The boys for whom songs were specifically composed were charming when they danced wearing masks. The drums also were decorated with old-squaw duck tail feathers with white down feathers on the tips. Their *enirarautet* [dance sticks, "pointers"] also had long bird quills with soft down feather at the tips. They were splendid to look at.

St. Marys Elders' Meeting, February 1993

A *ellanguaq,* which they moved about on stage, was used during performances when the masks were presented to the audience. Before people assembled in the *qasgiq* for the mask presentations, they invited the *ircenrrat* [extraordinary persons that appear in either animal or human form]. People could hear them when they responded. The residents of the *qasgiq* stamped their feet on the plank flooring and made thunderous sounds at intervals. After they did that they sat on the floor and listened. Then after a moment a thundering sound would suddenly erupt from down below. They say that's what the *ircenrrat* did when accepting the invitation. After that response the people would gather for the mask presentations and performances with the *ellanguaq.*

Mary Mike, February 1994

I saw a *ellanguaq* up at Tuutalgaq [Pilot Station] when they invited us for a dance festival. Before his death, a poor old man in the village presented the *ellanguaq.* The *ellanguaq* was spread across the ceiling in the community hall with ptarmigan and rabbit figures hanging from it. And [in the middle] was an eagle, the figure of a woman, and that huge bird.

When a woman fetched some water one evening, that eagle carried her away. It landed with her on a tall mountain somewhere up along the Yukon River. She had disappeared from the village. But they found her bucket by a hole in the ice. They searched for her but never found her.

Tamakunek taũgaam ungungssirrarnek, aqesginek maqaruanek-llu aqevlaunqutarluni ellanguaq, taum-gguq yaqulpiim pitaqlallri. Tauna-gguq tua ellanguaq, qanemcikluku tua-i Kumkallrem, angukaraam taum Uicimallermek piaqluku, taum-gguq alairesqengaku tauna alairluku. Taumek taũgaam tangellruunga ellanguamek [Tuutalgarmi].

Tuutalgarmiu Ciulirneq, February 1994

Tamakucimek wangkuta pingqertukut qama-i, cellanguamek. Qavcirqunek atullruuq kian' nunamteñi. Taũgaam nanluciitaqa tayima. Iliitni tayima uitauq. Tuutalgarmi cellanguaq malrurqugnek atullruarput qamani. Yungqenricaaquq taũgaam tengmiaruamek pingqerrluni. Taum tua-i ilai amllertut. Amllellruut taũgaam watua wangkuta nanluciitaput, nalluaput. Tangtullruyaaqaput. Ilaita-llu kangirtaqluku caucia. Wii tua-i nalluyagutenritellrenka qanruteksugngaanka.

Aũgna cellanguaq tauna kiugkumiutaunricaaquq nutem [Tuutalgaq]. Ak'a tamaani imumi waten kevgirluteng pitullermeggni kiani Iqugmi— Iqugmiutaullrulliniuq taun' cellanguaq. Teglegaqat ukut Tuutalgarmiut. Iqugmiutaullruuq-gguq.

Dick Andrew, January 1994

Yurallruukut-ll'-am pian' ellanguamek elitnaurluk' piani high school-ami [Bethel high school]. Ellanguarluta-gguq kuvyamek aũg'umek. Atraqtaarlun' yuguaq pikna. Ellanguam-w' aciani taun' yuguaq atraqtaarluni, atraraqluni mayuraqluni. Tua-i tangnirqutekluki pitullruut imkut ellanguat, qasgi tangniringnaqluku cakneq, qasgim ilua. Tuaten pingatetullruat.

Justina Mike, March 1994

Allakarrauluteng tua pagna-ll' tangnirpak qayuw' pilaqiit, qilii pagna tangnircarluk'. Camek-kiq tayim kangingqerrlarta? Wall'u-qaa cella assisqelluku pilaraat. Cellanguarnaurtut-gguq. Cella-gguq quinatullruuq kaingluteng-llu. Agniluku pinaurtut palungluteng-llu. Maa-i pilarsallilriakut laavkaat makut ikasuumakaitkut.

Little animal models such as ptarmigans and rabbits hung from it, the animals the eagle caught and ate. The late Kumkaq [Noel Polty] told the assembled audience that the old man named Uicimalleq had given the village permission to present the *ellanguaq*.

Pilot Station Elder, February 1994

We have a *cellanguaq* like that up there [in Pilot Station]. We used it several times up at our place. But I don't know where it is now. Someone must have it now. We presented a *cellanguaq* twice up at Pilot Station. It didn't have a human figure on it, but it had a bird. There were other pieces that came with the *cellanguaq,* but we don't know where they are now. We used to see them. Some people would explain the meaning behind it. I can talk about what I have not forgotten.

The *cellanguaq* didn't actually originate from up there [Pilot Station]. Long ago when they gathered for dances and ceremonies up in Iquk— that particular *cellanguaq* belonged to people of Iquk [Russian Mission]. The people of Pilot Station stole it from them. They said it belonged to the Iugmiut.

Dick Andrew, January 1994

We danced with a *ellanguaq* up at the [Bethel high school] for the students. The *ellanguaq* was made out of fish net. The human figure hanging up there would come down and go up. The human figure hanging below the *ellanguaq* would go up and down, up and down. The *ellanguat* made the *qasgiq* interior look grand. I think that's what they used to do.

Justina Mike, March 1994

The presentation [of the *cellanguaq*] was different, being a spectacular ceiling decoration. I wonder what it originally meant? Perhaps they used it to make sure *Cella* remained good to them. They called it *cellanguaryaraq* [the way of doing *cellanguaq*]. They say when *Cella* turned against people, they would begin to starve. The adage was *"Cella agniluku"* [lit.,

Andy Kinzy, Negeqliq, February 1993

Una cella maliggluku pingnatulleq wii taringumallemni, tua-i elluarrluku taũgaam atuqeryuumirluku pilriim tauna cella maliggluku eglertarkauguq. Taũgken asgurluku pikuniu, caunrilkiciquq taũgaam qaneryaramek. Tuaten wii kangingumaaqa tauna. Tua-i elluarrluku ikayuutekani caunrilkeciqaa asgurluku pikuniu. Maliggluku taũgken pikuniu elluamun atalria iliini tekiqurainaraa. Assinruuq tuani wangni tua-i taun' taringumallemni.

Mary Mike, February 1994

Tamakunek alingnarqellrianek piaqameng anluteng pilarait. Makut tam' kegginaqungssaarnek canguangsaarnek piaqameng tamaani nem'i anevkenateng qalriuciaqluki. Pikna-wa aniparuaq pelacinagnek nuqsuguterluni. Tengaurturcelluk'. Aciani-w' yaqulkussak—aqesgiq-w' pilallilria. Cetuni taum aniparuam waten, cetui nengingaluteng. Tauna aqesgiruaq teguqataruarluku. Yaqiurturcelluku tua-i pelaciniik tamakuk nuqtarturlukek akiqliqlutek. Tua-i imutun yaqiurturalriatun pinaurtuq taun' anipaq yurainanratni.

"*Cella* is going over," having a negative implication, such as uncooperative weather]. We probably would still do that, but the modern stores are helping us now.

Andy Kinzy, St. Marys, February 1993

This is the way I understand that adage, *Cella maliggluku*. A person should follow the way of *Cella* [the universe] and live in accordance with nature's laws if he wants to lead a good life. However, if he goes against *Cella,* he will forsake the traditional teachings. That's how I understand that phrase. If he goes against *Cella,* he will reject the very thing that will help him attain a humane and noble life. But if his life is in harmony with Nature, he will continuously arrive at the true or correct way. As far as I understand, that's a better way to live.

Mary Mike, February 1994

When they presented the powerful animals, they would go outside the *qasgiq*. However, when they presented the little animals, they stayed inside and called out their cries. A model of a snowy owl would be suspended on a string from above. They made it fly continuously. Below the owl hung a smaller bird—perhaps a ptarmigan. The talons of the snowy owl were drawn as if it was about to seize the ptarmigan. There would be two people on either side pulling the strings, making the owl look like it was flying. While they were dancing, the snowy owl's wings were flapping and appeared to be actually flying.

6. Taqraarluteng Ataam Kegginaqirluteng Yuralangellrat

Justina Mike, March 1994

Taũgaam kingunemteñi tamatumek piurelartut yurarluteng kegginaquunateng. Fr. Lunum taum pivkaraqluki. Ellmegteggun waten, mat'um-ll' Eyagem nalliini, Paaskaam nalliini pivkenateng, taũgaam yaani iquklitesmiaqan tua-i yurangluteng tuaten piaqluteng. Pivkaraqluki taum. Kevgirluteng taũgaam pinrirluteng, caluteng tuaten-llu kegginaqunek atevkenateng. Assikluku taun' elliin, elliin-llu taum ilagarluta pimiaqluni, yuraturimiluni.

Mary Mike, February 1994

Taukut tua-i nangneqlilirillruut Anagcirmiut tuani. Qakuani-llu qayutun allrakut piqerluki cali, wall'u-q' pingayun, ataam Uksuqallermi elriluteng. Cunaw' tua-i nangnermek cali elrimillinilriit taukucicetun. Cali tua-i piyuirulluteng.

Taum-w' agayulirtem nengakluki. Agayulirtet-gguq nengakluki tuaten pillrat assiilnguuniluku. Tua-i piyungermeng nagingaaqluteng. Cikirturisqevkenaki-llu aklunek makunek yugnun. Ellaitnun pikestaitnun pikesqelluki. Tamana tang niiteqaqsailkeka waten pikesqelluki ellaitnun qanelriamek.

Paul John, April 1994

Tamana tua-i pegcunaicaaqellruciqlun' wangtuktaulriani aviukaqsaraq, tarvaryaraq-llu. Tamaa-i tamakut kayulriit ciuliamta

Suppression and Revival of Masked Dancing

Justina Mike, March 1994

In our home village they danced without masks. Fr. Lonneux allowed them to dance. The village people would dance without inviting people from another village. They would stop during Lent and Easter, but when that period ended they resumed dancing. He allowed them to do that. But people stopped doing *Kevgiryaraq* and mask performances. He enjoyed the dancing and even joined us, actually learning how to dance *yuraq*-style, too.

Mary Mike, February 1994

Anagcirmiut people celebrated *Elriq* [ceremony for clothing the namesake of the deceased] for the last time. Then several years later, perhaps it was three years after that, *Elriq* was celebrated in Uksuqalleq. Evidently, just like the other village, it was their last time, too. They also stopped doing it.

The priests disapproved. The priests frowned upon the ceremonial festivals, saying they were evil. Thus, though they wanted to continue, they were held back by the priests. The priests also told them not to give away goods or clothes to other people. They told the people to keep the things for themselves. Before that I had never heard people saying that they should keep the goods themselves.

Paul John, April 1994

Aviukaqsaraq [offering food to spirits of the dead] and *tarvaryaraq* [purification with smoke] were customs that we should not have aban-

asrurtuutellrit ellmeggnun, aviukaqsarat, tarvaryarat, neqlicarat-llu. Tang imkut-ll' angllurcecitullrulriit apeqmeggnek merqelluki. Tua-i wangkutnek unguvavut man' aulukellrulliaput ayagmek, ciuliamta. Pegcanricaaqellrulliniaput cali tamakut eyagyarat. Taũgaam tua-i wangkuta Catholic-aani aũgkut agayulirtet caumastekqerraallemta tuunrangayagtaunilug-yuurcirput qanraqluteng. Pegteluuqertellrulliniit.

Tang imkut piicalallrullinilriit tua-i cikluteng tuarpiaq Agayutmun ellangellemni; pissuqatalriit arcaqerluteng. Yug-una picuumirtacini niilluku, melqulegcuqatalria, anluni tua-i nut'ni teguluku aturani-ll' qaternitni aturluku, pitarkami tangellrani caarrluunani tua-i ullagyugnaqsuumirluni, aũgkut-ll' ikiituaraat qang'a-llu ayurrluaraat kuma'arrluk' puy'illakata avelruarrluki iluminun itertelluk', 'gguun puyuq anevkarluku. Amllirluku-ll' tua-i taun' taqkuni ayagluni evcuglun' tuaten. Tua-i piicalallrulliniut pitarkamek unangyugluteng, caarrluiryuumirluteng. Nunanek ayakuneng caarrluunateng ayagyugluteng.

Tuamta-llu qamigaqatalria tangvalriani ayautarkani cailkamun quyurqurarraarluki, qayani-llu mengleminun elliluku, keneq kuma'arrluku, ayautarkani imkut kenrem tuavet puyuanun piqa'aqluku evcugarraarluk' qayaminun ek'aqluki. Tua-i-gguq tarvarluki taukut ayautarkani ellii-ll' tapqullun'. Tuaten-am cali tua-i puyumek pilun' 'gguun anevkarluk; amllirluk' puyuq, qayani-ll' ciunga un' cayukanirluku tumekluku qayaminun, tumkevkarluku ayagluteng. Tarvaq tua-i un' kayulria tamayunaicaaqellrulliuq.

Tua-i-lli ilumun ataucimek taqestengqellinivagceta wangkuta. Cali-llu taum taqestemta ilumun allakamta piciryararkirluta caggluta ellillrullinivaa tamarngaicaaqelrianek nutem pikarkauyaaqellemnek ellam piunrirvianun.

Mary Mike, February 1994

Maa-i taũgken nutaan allrakuaqan tua kassiyurturangelriit maa-i. Agayulirtem-ll' uum [Fr. Astruc] ilagaarluki tua piaqluni. Arulangucia-ll' akaurrluni. Tua-i-am ak'a aturlallrit atungevkaqait. Aciritullruut-ll'

doned. *Aviukaqsaraq, tarvaryaraq* and *neqlicaraq* [offering food to the living namesake of a deceased one] were powerful ways that our old ones blessed each other. They actually did a kind of baptismal rite for children by offering libations of water, *merqelluki*. Our ancestors truly led their lives according to design. We also should not have abandoned *eyagyarat* [abstaining from certain foods or activities during pregnancy, death, illness, puberty, etc.]. However, the first Catholic priests that came to us said that our ways were evil. So we suddenly abandoned them.

The old ones, especially the hunters, actually prayed by bowing to God. When one wished to catch an animal, in preparation for the hunt he would put his white canvas *qaspeq* [cloth parka cover] over his parka, then take his gun and go out, and with the goal in mind to be pure in the eyes of his prey, he would burn a few wild celery plants or tundra tea, wafting the smoke in under his parka and allowing it to escape out the neck opening. He would step over the plants while brushing off his body with his hands. For them this was a form of prayer in hopes of catching game, a rite of self-purification. They wanted to be clean and pure when they left the village for the hunt.

And when a hunter was getting ready to go seal hunting on the ocean, he gathered his hunting gear on the ground and placed the kayak beside him. He would light a fire and lift each item over the smoke, then shake it and load it into his kayak. He would purify everything he was bringing out to the ocean, including himself, with the wild celery and parsnip smoke. Smoke would enter his parka and come out through the neck opening. He would step over the lit plants, pull his kayak in front of the smoke, and leave the village. This powerful *tarvaryaraq* definitely should not have been abandoned by our people.

We truly are made by one Creator. Our Maker designed all of us and placed us in different places all over the world, granting us our own customs and traditions that we should never have abandoned and should maintain until the end of the world.

Mary Mike, February 1994

During this time we are beginning to have dance festivals every year. One particular priest [Fr. Astruc] is always at the dance gatherings. He started dancing a long time ago. They are beginning to revive some of

tamaani, yug-una alairqan yuurtaqan. Tua-i piyullermeggnek acirturnaurait mermek kuciqaqluki. Ilait-llu kakgaitgun piluki acirluki-gguq. Taqevkallruyaaqaat cali taman'. Aviukarqesqevkenaki-llu cali merquuresqevkenaki-llu. Tua-i im' allragnirpak maani tamana ellimertuutekaa, aviukarqelluki merquuresqelluki-llu angllurteqatarqamegteki. Angllurtaqamegteki maurluitnun merquurcet'larait agayulirtem. Merquurluku tua-i pimeg-uumek acirniluki.

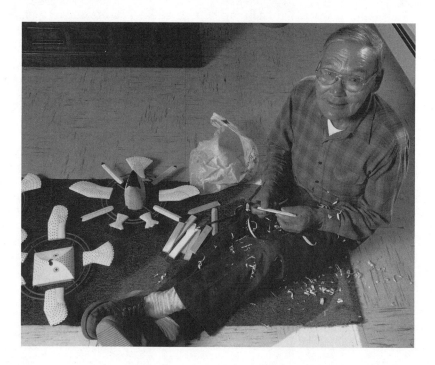

the old customs. When children were born they used to have naming rituals. They sprinkled water on them and gave them names of the deceased. They also sprinkled water on the crowns of their heads and named them. The early priests made people stop practicing that custom. They also told people not to give food offerings and water offerings to the deceased. Since last year the aforementioned priest has been telling us to renew some of our traditions. He told us to give food and water offerings when children are baptized. Now, before baptisms, they let the childrens' grandmothers give water offerings. They sprinkle water and give the child the name of a certain deceased individual.

Nick Charles, Sr.-am, atra canalria kegginaqum qirussirkaanek mellgarmek aturluni, Mamterillerni 1985-ami. Barry McWayne

The late Nick Charles, Sr., using a traditional *mellgar* (curved knife) to shape a mask's appendages, Bethel, 1985. Barry McWayne

7. Kegginaqulineq

Kay Hendrickson, January 1994

Tamakut agayulilriit murilkervarluki nalluyugnaunaki. Ciumeg keputerraarluki piyunarikata-llu mellgarameg, teguyaralegmeg cavigluki elagluku man'a uum enkaa. Nutaan-llu cali elaggaarluku man'a kegginar qukaakun qengirluku una elagluku. Taw' makut ayuqeliluki. Qengangqerrarkaukan-llu qengirluku qengag ukug ukillukeg, iilirluku-llu.

Piyaurtellrunritua tamaani tawa. Yaqvanun-llu ayallerkaqa alikellruaqa nunat taluggluki, nunat taluggluki ayakuma tunramun nernayuklua. [*Ngelartuq*]

Kass'at maa-i makuneg kegginaquneg piyungellrata nalliini piliyaurtellruunga tamakuneg akikiurlua. Ayuqenrilngurneg piliyaurtellruunga makuneg kwangkutneg ayuqeliluta tuullegneg, qilanganeg, naruyaneg, tamakuneg piliyaurtellruunga. Makuneg-llu ircinguaneg makuneg piaqlua.

Imna napam mat'um acia kan'a mimeryangqetuyukur, qamiqungqetuyukur nunamun kapusngallra camavet. Napam pagg'um acianeg un'umeg ukatmun talliruaruaneg tauna kepluku pitulqait. Piciatun-am pisuitellruut. Teplerraarneg pitullruut, tepelriit equut mimernaitneg. Qamiqunaneg pituit maani (Kusquqvak). Mimernaneg pituit. Tamakut-llu camani nunam aciani cali talliruaritneg piaqluki. Una-llu kangiat mimernameg piluku.

Maaken atertellerneg nunameg mat'umeg (mainland), kuigneg maaken, imarpigmun unavet anutaqateng Nuniwaamun napat illait atertelartut. Maaken napam temiineg agayuliaqameng piyuunateng.

Making a Mask

Kay Hendrickson, January 1994

I observed the old ones carefully when they made masks. First they began cutting the wood with an adze, and when the piece began to take shape, the *mellgar* [man's carving knife with a bent blade] was used to hollow out the back for fitting it on a face. Next they worked on carving the front, shaping the nose and other parts of the face. Once the nose was shaped, they made holes for the nostrils and for the eyes as well.

I didn't learn to carve when I was a young. I was very timid and afraid to wander away from the village by myself, thinking that if I did wander off *tunrar* [spirit, bad one implied] would eat me. [*Laughter*]

When white people became interested in buying masks, I started to make them to earn money. I began making different kinds like common loon masks, puffin masks, and seagull masks. I started making *ircir* masks, too.

The base of a tree has a section above the roots which we call *mimernar* [tree stump], and the bottom part of a tree just below the ground is referred to as the *qamiquq* [head]. The roots of the tree, called *talliruat* [imitation arms], are used for making masks. They never used just any kind of wood for masks. They used the *mimernar* and the root section of trees that had drifted onto the shores [of Nunivak Island]. People around here [Kuskokwim area] call that piece *qamiqurnaq*. We call it *mimernar*. And the roots are called *talliruat*. And the base of the tree from which the roots grow is called *mimernar*.

When trees drift out into the ocean from the rivers on the mainland, some land on the shores of Nunivak Island. When they made masks they didn't use the main body of the tree [and this is still true today]. The

Temait makut taw' cali qupurrluki cakluki, taluyaqluki, caskunun epukluki, anguarutekluki, qalussuuciluki-llu tawaten pitulqait. Tawa teguyaraqetulqait tamakut equut.

Mingugaqamegteki cali Nuniwaar kan'a piilan Qaluyaaneg yaaken, yaaken Nelson Island uiterner imkuneg kawinqeggilrianeg pikartetuut, imkuneg-llu qatelrianeg kegginaqut mingugkaitneg. Tamakuneg pikartequtullruut, kwiinga-llu pikartequtallruunga calliama pikaitneg. Akulurakun anguarlua ayaglua Nelson Island-aamek pikarcuraqluanga. Una-llu [nuliani-llu] maliklunug angyaryaurcata angyarlunug taglunug pikartaqlunug. Yaaqsinritur. Piuraqernaqsaqur. Anguarluni kessianeg qelalernarqur, nerininarqur. Kenimarraarluni qang'a-ll' ulumarraarluni kenteqataaraallra angu-llu ulqataaraallra maliggluku tagelriani man'a taq'ertevkarluku carvaner tutnarqetuluni.

Kiarrluteng pinarqut. White-at imkut cenameg unaken pituluki, kavirutet-llu teggalqut akulaitneg cenameg. Teggalqut akluliitneg elagluteng tamakuneg kawirutneg piaqluteng nallunrilnguut. Kwiinga elalleraarneg nallungamki pit'allruunga. Tamakut elalleraaraat tekitaqamki pinauranka kawirutet makut. Tamakuneg piuratullruunga.

Tungulriameg piqeqsaatua. Makut cali cuputngulliniut. Una elavuralria siimar teggalqur piluku mermeg imirluku, tungulrianeg piyugaqameng, tauna taw' tungulria asngeruqurluku cali atutullruat. Auḡ'umeg ilaluku nutaan nassiim auganeg tauna tungulria nutaan aturluku. Cuputnguur. School-arviit tamakuneg murangqetullruut. Angyarpiit tekiutequtulqait. Tamakuneg tamaa aturluteng pitullrulliniut. Uiter cali tawaten mermeg cali imirluku upluku urrluku, urqurluku, cali tangellra assiriaqan aturluku. Urasqer cali mermeg aturluku.

Kinraqata kinerciaramaaqerluki asngerrluki keneggluki cakneq. Keneggluki cakneq asngerrluki tawa ur'arkaunrirluteng taqluteng. Canun atungraiceteng urarkauvkenateng. Mermun-llu atungraiteng urarkaunrirluteng.

Tamakuneg tamaa-i cuputneg augneg awuluki pirraarluk', equar cawigturluku nuulirluku qanganaam pamyuan melqurraneg. Una tungulria augmeg ilaluku equgmun mat'umun, tauna aturluku qanganaam pamyua muragmun mat'umun minguucimaaqerluku kenermun mac'arcarcuaraumaaqani ecqerciqur—ceq'erciqur. Tawa tamta-llu piurerraarluku minguucimaaqaqerluku mac'artuqani

main body of the tree was used to make fishtraps, weapon handles, paddles, and ladles. Driftwood was used for many things.

Since Nunivak didn't have any pigment sources, carvers went to Nelson Island to get *uiter* [red ocher] for their masks, getting white pigment [perhaps *urasqer* or white clay] as well. Like them, I also secured those colors for my work. I used to travel across Akulurar [Etolin Strait] to Nelson Island in a kayak to gather the paints. When people began using boats, I used to take my wife with me. It's not far, but it takes a while to get there. It's a longer trip by kayak. When you are going with the current, or when you go with the tide in either direction, you reach the other side more quickly.

You have to scan the area for them. The white clay is found on the beach. Red ocher is found between the rocks on the shore. Those who knew where to find the ocher would dig between rocks to find it. I got some from holes that people had dug previously since I didn't know where they were. When I looked into a hole where someone had already dug, I would find red ocher. That's how I got pigments for my work.

I never looked for black pigment since coal worked for that. If you wanted black you would fill an indentation in a flat stone with water, mix it with coal, and after adding hair-seal blood to the mixture use it as black paint. It works just like charcoal. They used to burn that [coal] to heat the school. Big boats brought it in bags for the school. That's what they used for black paint. They carefully mixed red ocher with water, and they used it as paint when it was ready. White clay was also mixed with water.

After the paint dried, you would rub it, pressing very hard. You rubbed it until you were sure the paint was set. And even when the piece was used in water, the paint would not dissolve.

After they mixed the charcoal with blood, they carved a piece of wood and attached a squirrel's tail to its tip. After dipping the squirrel's tail into the mixture they would paint the wood, and the painted wood would suddenly "sweat" when they put it near the fire. Then after they brushed more paint on it and put it near the fire, it would look very good. Then they would stop applying paint. It would be ready to use,

assirtacia. Tawaten taqluku, taqluni. Nutaan-llu aturluku atungraani erevyugnaarulluni. Minguucugnairulluni-llu. Nutaan taqqunegtegu tauna maqiluteng kiiwet ingelret qaangatnun qantat akiwiggluk' elliluki maqiluteng. Tamakut alngalteng pisqelluki, tawa ervigyuirutesqelluki qantam illuani. Nutaan taqkunegteki asngerqurluki erevyugnaunaki taqluki. Illait taūgg'am tawa taqnerrlugguarumalriit aturaqateng erevqertutuut. Illait erevyugnaunateng.

Qantam pikestiin cameg taqukanguarmeg-llu nayiruameg qaralirluku angu-llu cukcunguaremeng qamiqurluku temii-llu man'a qaqilluk' elliluku. Tawa-i-am piciryaramegcetun. Pikngamegteki tamakut ellaita nalluyugnaunaki. Tamakut-llu qaralit ellaita pikngamegteki cali piciryaraqngamegteki cali aturluki.

Jasper Louise, May 1993

Kiingan kela'askaqluku tungulria kangipluk, cameg-avuluku. Tua-i kela'askatun ayuquq kiiyuunani. Kavircetellria-ll' tamana cuukvaguam qeltii egevkarluku. Kavirilartuq. Tua-i kegginaqut mingugkautiit-llu tamana.

Tamaani wangkuta qugtarqamta-llu alerquutarluta, kiima-ll' alerqualanrilkiitnga, qugtarqamta qakineruarnek uqviarnek ekqutkamteñek, "Asmarqaarluku ata un' qakineq yurrmiguarlarru asemtellerpeggun tuaggun." Iquakun ayimnerrarkun tanqia yuurrmilriatun ayuqluku. Qakinret-gguq makut equut tanqingqertut. Alerquuteksaaqaput wangkuta yuulriani. Watua maa-i superstition-aunilarait.

Mary Mike, February 1994

Waten ilait kegginaqut qirussingqerrlallruut, cat imarpigmiutaat tengmilqut—murag-man'a, waten taūgaam akagenqeggaqluni canek melqunek pingqerraqlun'. Unatnek-llu agaluteng, unaksuarnek, qirussit iliitnun pimaluteng. Nalqigteqatarqamegteki angalkut pikestaita nepaitnek neplirluteng pituut. Kavcagpak tauna agalria muragmun—qirussiinun kalguurulluteng tamakut agalriit, qalrialluku qalriacianek

and the paint would not rub off. But when the bowl was done they would put it on the *ingleq* and would leave it there while the men took their firebath. Men would take a firebath with many bowls sitting on the *ingleq*, in this way allowing the paint on the bowls to set well. When that was done they would rub them some more for the final touch. Paint would come off some of the bowls that were not processed correctly. But others were perfect.

The bowl's owner would paint a seal, hair seal, or a human figure with a head and body as a design. They would make the figure with a head and body and all the parts to the form. It was their custom. They knew their own bowls by the design. They knew by tradition exactly what kinds of designs to put on their own bowls.

Jasper Louise, May 1993

Black charcoal, mixed with something, was the only black color they had. It didn't come off and worked exactly like paint. Red color was processed from alder bark. Alder bark was also used to paint masks.

When we went out to collect dried willow sticks for kindling, the elders would say to us, "When you pick up a dried willow stick, snap it and put the cut end in your mouth and *yurrmiguarlarru* [inhale it]." What you are inhaling is its light. They say dried willow sticks have light in them. We Yupiit had always been told to do that. At the present time people think it's a superstition.

Mary Mike, February 1994

Some of the masks had *qirussit* [appendages]. Certain ocean bird masks were ringed with wooden strips with feathers on them. Little human hand carvings would hang from the *qirussit*. When the shamans, the owners of the masks, explained the stories behind the masks they would first cry out the call of the animal depicted. When a shaman put the mask on, turned his head from side to side, and mimicked the call of

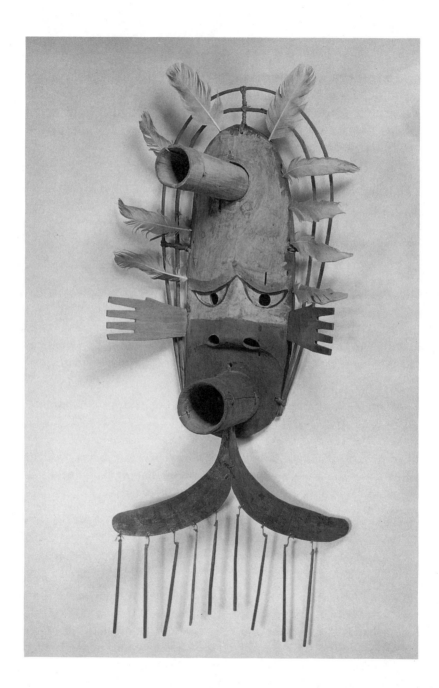

Napaskiarmiutaq kegginaquq "Tomanik" wall'u-gguq anuqessuun. Qatellria-gguq cupluq uksum anuqekluku tungulria-llu-gguq kiagem anuqekluku. National Museum of the American Indian, New York

Mask from Napaskiak representing "Tomanik" or Wind-maker. The white tube is for winter and the black for summer. National Museum of the American Indian, New York, 9/3427 (105.4 cm)

tuaten all'uku pilaraat. Aren, ilait tua-i yugcetun kegginaqruluteng kegginaqucuaraugaqluteng, taũgaam qirussingqerraqluteng.

Mary Mike, October 1994

Qantaliamek mingulriamek tangellruunga. Qancungamun ek'arrluku kavirlirraq kan'a, urkili kana-i kaviriluku meq. Kavirpak. Tuluvkuyuggaq taũgaam meciqerluku qantar-im' mingugluku. Qaqiucamiu qaituumaan minguggaarluk' uqupiarrarmek ataam mingugluku aug'aryailkucirluku, kinercinqegcaararraarluki nutaan.

Qatellriamek-gguq Ingrill'er-llu-ggur-ing' pitangqellruuq. Tamaani Qip'ngayiim kangrani uitalria tauna Ingrill'er. Aciani-wa Kassiglurmiut Ulukarqurvigmiut-llu uitaluteng. Tua-i-lli-wa-gguq irr'inarqellrianek-gguq iliini pitullruut Ingrill'ermi. Kela'askaq qatellria waten, tua-i-gguq ingrim qacarneranek caarvamek pinganani qatellria tauna. Ellaita-am taukut kela'askauniluku piaqluku. Kela'askamun ayuqekulluku yaaqvanun tangenrrilamegteggu. Amta-llu-gguq paqcaaqekiit ercan cataunani.

the animal, the objects hanging from the appendages would jingle and rattle loudly. *Aren* [expression], some of the little masks would resemble human faces, but they would have the *qirrusit.*

Mary Mike, October 1994

I saw a person painting a wooden bowl he made. He dropped *uiter* in a small bowl with a little bit of water in it. When the pigment dissolved, the whole mixture turned red. It was scarlet red. Then he took a *tuluvkuyuggaq* [feather] and dipped it into the mixture and painted the bowl. When he finished painting the entire surface of the bowl, he rubbed it with seal oil to keep the paint from coming off and carefully dried it.

They say Ingrill'er [lit., bad mountain, Kusilvak Mountain] had white pigment paint. Ingrill'er is located at the head of Qip'ngayak river. At the base of the mountain was Kassigluq and Ulukarqurvik. They say people had awesome experiences in Ingrill'er. One time they saw a white color that seemed to flow from the mountain side. They said it was paint. They observed it up close, and it looked like paint. When they looked for it the next day it was gone.

8. Alairiyaraq Kegginaqunek: Yuarutetaa Arulatii-llu

Paul John, April 1994

Tuamta-ll'-am aũg'um angayuqriutemta, tutgariurturyuani ukut aaniit, itellrani pia, "Aling Apacuu, tang yuaruciqaa piyugngakuvet." Aren, elliini-gguq yuarutet nurnaitut. Atam'aaraa, "Atam-am qagaa-i imumek ellami anuqem can'get uggaaraurcet'laqai. Wii tang waniw' aturturalriaruluki niiskengaqetukenka, waniwa-ll' yuarutait qemangqaluki." Tuaten-am tua-i kiullrukii imum Billy Lincoln-am. Can'get-gguq imumek ugg'agqurluteng arulaqu'urqateng aturturalartut, elliin-llu-gguq waniw' yuarutait elisngaluki.

Jasper Louise, May 1993

Angelriaruluku wangkuta yurar-alerquutekarput. Tamaani-llu cellangeqarraallemni yuramek piyuitaat ellugturturmek taũgaam, ugaani anerteqeq'allerkarteng pitekluku. Tamaani yuraasqaitkut yuralria una ayuqeliurluku yagiraurallra. Ciin yuraasqatkut? Yuralriani-gguq germsaq ellugturlartuq. Ellugturturluki yuraasqetullruit. Apqucirkaa yaaqvaqaningnaqesqelluku yuraasqaat. Ellugturturmek wangkuta taringumaarput ayanirilriani.

Mary Mike, May 1993

Tua-i-wa evcugturaasqelluku-am alerquutngumiyaaquq. Alerquutnguyaaqelliniuq-am tua-i caarrluni-gguq yuum katagciqaa [yuraquni]. Cali waten alerquutnguluni arca qerringavkenaku qasgimi, tua-i waten yuralriit nuniitni qerringavkenaku ilai maligtaqungnaqluki yurarlaasqelluku. Makut-gguq ayagcetellrit ilulliqaqellriit una

108

Presenting a Mask: Its Song and Dance

Paul John, April 1994

Our late parent always came to our house to see his grandchildren, and when he came in my wife said, "*Aling Apacuu* [Oh my, Little Grandfather], please compose a song if you can." He responded immediately saying, "*Atam* [expression], you see the grasses outside, the wind constantly makes them sing. I can hear their songs myself, and I have their songs with me." That was what Billy Lincoln said to her. He said that when wind moves the grasses they sing and that he knew their songs very well.

Jasper Louise, May 1993

Dancing was very important to our people. Back in those days when I first became aware, they didn't call it *yuraq*, they called it *ellugturyaraq* [way of brushing away, brushing off]. They told us to dance following the dancer's motions. Why did they tell us to dance? They said when you danced you were brushing off germs from your body. They told us to use those brushing off motions when we danced. They told us to dance to push away illness and disease. We older folks call that *ellugturyaraq*.

Mary Mike, May 1993

A person was directed to always brush themselves off. Evidently, it was a tradition we were asked to follow to brush away dirt or offensive things from oneself. When people were dancing in the *qasgiq* we were advised to join in, not to try to hold back and hide away. They say the ones we let go, our departed ones, would be sad because they were aware

kingunerteng anglaninritellra nalluvkenaku. Amutequteklarait-gguq tamakut ayagcetaita ciin ilagaucuunaku anglanilrianun qerringauratullra piluku. Tama'antellaameng-gguq anglanilriit nuniitni makut ayagcetelput—yuum-w' ayagcetellri. Tamana-ll'-am tua-i pitekluku waten yuraqangnaqesqelluku yug-alerquutekaat. Yuraqtalalrianga—yuramek-ll' iliini umyuarteq'lanricaaqellrianga, taūgaam qaneryaraq taman' ukvekluku--ukvekellrunricaaqaqa young-allemni. Catkevkenaku tua-i. Waniwa tang arnasagaama qaneryarat-ll' ilait elitaqsaurcamki ukveryaguskeka-ll'-am tamana tua-i.

Yurayuitellruyaaqua tua-i tuarpiaq kasnguyuglalrianga yuramek. Cami-am Cakitellrem nulirran pikilia, "Usuuq iqlutmuartuten." Yura'arqata yuramek tengrunrilngerma nangertaqlua pisqellua. Camalriarita-gguq ilulluklaqait. Tamakut-gguq kingunerteng un' anglaninritaqan maliggluku qiaguratuut. Atrarlua yura'aqlua pisqellua. Tua-i im' yurangnaqsaurrlua. Kiituan tua-i cangalkenringaqa.

of one who was not enjoying the event. They did not like to see a person hiding or holding back. They say the departed ones actually joined the crowd in the *qasgiq* unseen. So, with everyone being aware of that, each person should always stand up and dance. I've always stood up and danced, believing what I had been told, even though at times I did not feel like dancing. I didn't think that what they said was true when I was young. However, now that I'm getting to be an old woman and have begun to understand the old sayings, I believe in that tradition.

I never used to dance as if I were ashamed to dance. Then one day Cakitelleq's wife said, "*Usuuq* [Listen you], you're going in the wrong direction." She told me to stand up and dance even though I wasn't enthusiastic about it. She said when the departed ones see you unhappy, they in turn begin to cry with you. She told me to get up and dance. I began forcing myself to dance. Soon I began to feel comfortable about it.

Joe Chief, Jr.-aq yurarlria Ississaayuguamek kegginaqurluni. Ak'a-gguq tamaani Angalkullrem Ississaayuum Kass'at iluvararkaullrat qanrutkellrua. Kegginaqum kangra sun'aruartarluni tauna-qquq-wa angalkuq qanellruan Kass'at tekiciiqniluki sun'atgun. Qanellran-gguq kinguani sun'aq tekitelllruuq, yuut-llu-gguq sun'armiunun canek naverrniaraluteng. Tuani-llu-gguq sun'aq ayiin cat tun'ellrit tamakunun yugnun tevirluteng. James H. Barker

Joe Chief, Jr., performing with a mask that tells the story of the *angalkuq* Ississaayuq, who foretold the coming of the first white people. He predicted that they would come in ships, represented on the mask by the carving atop the *angalkuq*'s head. The ship did come, and the men traded with the people, but when it left, all the goods the strangers had brought disappeared. James H. Barker

Dick Andrew, January 1994

Imkut yurapianek ak'a tamaani tallimegteggun qanemciluteng yurapiarluteng arnat. Imkunek tamakunek anguyiim nalliini tua-i caqallerteng-llu tauna yurautekluku. Atauciq arnaq yuraucingqerraqluni wall' malruk, ataucimek. Qanemciluni talligmikun qavaruarluni. Iciw' uyungssuarluteng pilalriit. Qavaruarluteng piciatun yagiraluteng akiciuruaraqluteng, qamigaruaraqluteng-llu ayarurluteng. Tua-i piciatun yagiratengqerrluteng tamakut yuut piciryarait.

Uksullranek ayagluteng tua-i yaavet anglaniuralartut caqtaarturluteng nunalget man'a-llu Christmas-aaq tekilluku. Anglaningelartut, tua-i-wa ellait nunaniryugluteng, umyuartequa wii tuar Christmas-aarluteng angnirturluteng tua-i yaavet. Tayima-ll' mat'umi December-aami nutaan taqluteng caqtaarturanermek, nutaan kevgirluteng nunanun yurarluteng aklunek yuraulluteng.

Imkut-llu irniateng pitqerraarqata kalukarluteng. Tuamtellu ineqsuyugluteng-gguq kalukarluteng, nunanek kevgirluteng kelgiluteng. Tua-i-llu nunat imkut canek tua-i neqkarugarnek amllernek aruqluteng. Caperrnarqut tamaani yullret aūgkut, yuk'egtaaraat assilriit tangvallrenka.

Ingulalriit-llu cali allakarmeng ingularluteng. Tua-i canguarturluteng. Waten-ll' iqvaruarturluteng piaqluteng. Imarniterluteng arnat ingularaqluteng. Tamakucinek-llu tangerqallrulua tuaten ingulalrianek.

Jasper Louise, February 1994

Ingulautet qaill' ayuqat? Ingulautet allay'uggaugut. Nutaraunritut makut ingulautet. Ingularlallruut yurapiam aipaqluku. Ingulalriit pikangqerraqameng-llu qantamek itrutlartut qasgimi neqkautekesqelluku. Ellirraarluku-ll' nutaan ingularluni. Kenaatguiluni arulalartut

Dick Andrew, January 1994

Long ago women did *yurapiat* [genuine dances], telling stories with their arm movements. They would story-dance about something that was done during warfare. Sometimes a story-dance would be shared by two women. A woman would begin her story-dance by doing the *qavaruaq* [pretend sleep] motion with her arms. As you know, women always bend their knees slightly in a rhythmic up-and-down motion as they dance. So doing the arm movements pretending to be sleeping, they would then push away their bedding and begin their story, pretending to be those going ocean-hunting using walking sticks. With those different dance motions, the women would present daily village activities to the audience.

Starting in the fall when it froze, the village people began having fun, participating in different events all the way to Christmas time. In my mind it was as if people were celebrating Christmas continuously from the fall all the way into December. When the village people finally finished with these different events, *Kevgiryaraq* was celebrated, and they exchanged goods with another village.

When their children caught their first animals, the families celebrated the occasion by food and gift distribution to invited guests, *kalukarluteng*. And when a child did a task or action that pleased the parents, they celebrated *ineqsuyugluteng* [lit., "they are joyfully moved"] by food and gift giving. The people in the village would distribute many different foods to the invited guests. People in the past were amazing. They were wonderful and kind people of superb quality.

The *ingula* dances were different, too. A dancer told a story of a certain activity with hand movements. Some presented berry-picking stories. Women did *ingula* dances wearing seal-gut raincoats. I saw a little bit of *ingula* dancing in my youth.

Jasper Louise, February 1994

What were the *ingulautet* like? *Ingulautet* [*ingula* songs] were different from regular songs. *Ingulautet* were old songs. *Ingula* dances were similiar to *yurapiaq* dances. Women performing *ingula* dances brought food to the residents of the *qasgiq* as part of the presentation. Upon entering,

cukaunateng. Cukavkenani arulaurluni. Tua-i-gguq inglaluni. Cauyallrit-llu yuarutaita cukaunani waten kaugtuarluteng. Uyungssuarluteng-llu cukaunateng kaugtuallra maligtaquluku.

Nickolai Berlin, Nunapicuar, January 1994

Tutgara'urluq Nukalpiartam atkugkarcuryugluku nulirruciutekainek tunturaagnek pirraarluku, allamun-llu ciunirluni tekicami. Maurluan-llu tua-i yuarutkaanek elitnaurluku tua-i qiagura'urluan taun' uikeqataryaaqellni allamun ciunian. Maurluan yuarutkiurluku inglautesqelluku Nukalpiartaq qasgimi. Tua-i-llu-gguq elicamiu payuggluku nukalpiaq tauna, ketiini ellminek atuulluni ingularluni yurarluni. Tuqulliniluni-llu-gguq tauna nukalpiaq, taun' quliraq. Quliraq tauna, nukalpiaq taun' qetqaci'irtellermini tua-i qetqaciraucimitun tuqulliniluni. Waten tua-i ayagnengqerrngat'lalria yuarutii.

> *Nu-na-qa-am*
> *Ke-lua-ni*
> *Pa-ma-ni*
> *Kia-rri-yaa*
> *Nu-raag' mal-ruuk*
> *A-lii-rri-yal-riik*
> *Ak-qu-teg-ken*
> *Uu-uu-u i-yaa-aa*
> *Aa-gi-ii-i-yaa-rra-ngaa*
> *Aa-a-ngaa ggi-yaa*
> *Aa-gii-rri-yaa*

Ingulautet tamakut allayuugut. Angalkurtauvkenateng-wa, ak'a taũgaam tamaaken ayagluteng piuluteng ciuliamteñek, ciuliapiamteñek.

Aũgna-ll' cali issaluuq imna—ingulautngungatuq—issaluuq at'reskii kuimarciiganani, tunturyuaryuk-ll' ingluklermegni. Tunturyuaryuum pairrsaagyungraani qessaqtarluni ellminek piarkauniluni. Tua-i-ll' aterrluk' imaanun-ll' anulluku. Tua-i atercani qiagura'urlurluni ayagluni camani imarpigmun anucani mer'em. Tua-i-ll' arrluuyugluni, "Tuaten-llu-qaa-rraa, qaillun ayaullia mer'em arrluut ilagaraqnianka."

one first placed the food on the floor and then danced. The dance was slow. The dancers would move slowly, rhythmically bending their knees slightly as they danced, following the beat of the drum.

Nickolai Berlin, Nunapitchuk, January 1994

A *nukalpiartaq* [a very accomplished hunter] promised *tutgara'urluq* [an orphan child] he would marry her after hunting two young caribou for her parka, but when he returned from hunting he went to the home of another girl. As she sat heartbroken and crying, her grandmother composed an *ingulaun* for her. She taught her the song she was to sing in the *qasgiq*. When she learned it, she brought a bowl of food for the *nukalpiartaq*. She stood in front of him, sang the song, and danced. Then the *nukalpiartaq*, the *quliraq* [persona in ancient story], died. As soon as he fell on his back, he died. I think this is the way the song begins.

> *The land*
> *Behind it*
> *Back there*
> *Look around and see*
> *Two fawn caribou*
> *?Aliirriyalriik*
> *Two you promised me*
> *Uu-uu-u i-yaa-aa*
> *Aa-gi-ii-i-yaa-rra-ngaa*
> *Aa-a-ngaa ggi-yaa*
> *Aa-gii-rri-yaa*

The *ingulautet* were different. They weren't shaman songs, but they were ones passed down from generation to generation since time immemorial. They came from our real ancestors.

There is another story about a porcupine—I think it's an *ingulaun*, too—the porcupine couldn't swim and was floating in the water. It was when Issaluuq [porcupine] and *tunturyuaryuk* [a legendary cariboulike creature] were rivals. Although *tunturyuaryuk* wanted to meet him, he refused and said he could make it to land by himself. He floated and soon drifted out on the ocean. While drifting on the ocean he began to cry. Wanting to become a killer whale he sang, "Let the water move me,

Tua-i-llu-gguq tuaten pirraarlun' qaklun' angllurluni. Pug'uq-gguq arrluuluni.

Justina Mike, March 1994

Puallalrianek niillartuten. Tuaten puallanaurtut atakurpak. Pinginanratni taũgken yug-una iternaurtuq qalcirluni. Qaltarrarmek equggarmek tegumiarluni, imarnitegnek all'uni. Mecarpak taukug-imarnitek ua-i iternaurtuq taumek qaltarrarmek tegumiarluni. Tua-llu kanavet ellinauraa, imkut-ll' puallalriit taqluteng. Yuum-am ullagluku kan'a qanerturnaurtuq, avga-ggur-man' cikuuguq avga-llu-ggur-man'a nunauluni. Caneg-kiq tayim kangilirlartaitki. Qanertura'arnaurtuq. Tauna taũgaam elpektaaraqa. Avga-gguq man' cikuulliniuq avga-llu-gguq man'a nunauluni. Cameg-kiq tayim kangilirlartaiteki.

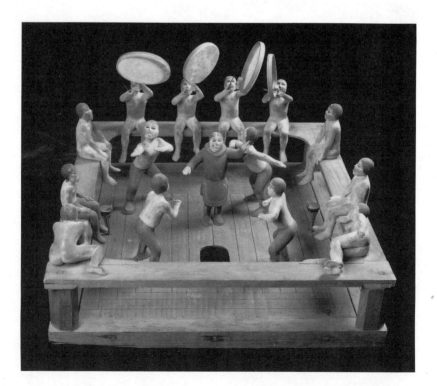

so I can be one among the killer whales." Then after he sang he rose straight up from the water and dove in. When he came back up he was a killer whale.

Justina Mike, March 1994

You have heard of people doing *pualla* [fast-paced, northern-style standing dance performed by men]. People did *pualla* dancing all evening. While they were dancing a person would enter the *qasgiq* wearing an *imarnin* [seal-gut rain garment] and holding a little wooden bucket. He would enter with his *imarnin* crackling. As he placed the bucket in the middle of the performance area, the people doing the *pualla* would stop. Then a person from the side would come down to the man with the bucket and begin talking, saying half of his bucket contained ice and the other half was earth. I wonder what that meant? I remember the person talking to the man, saying that one side of his bucket was ice and the other half was earth. I wonder what it was about?

Kuigpagmiut iliita piliara qasgiruaq yuguarluni. Angutet cetaman nangermeng puallalriit arnaq-wa qukaatni putulria. Arnam-wa ciuqerrani kalvagyaraq kenurrarviik-wa akiqliqlutek caniqaagkeni qasgim. Sheldon Jackson Musuem, Sitka

Wooden dance house model from the lower Yukon showing four men performing a northern-style *pualla* dance while a single woman *putuluni* in their midst. The underground entryway is visible in front of the woman, and she is flanked by two lamp stands. Sheldon Jackson Museum, Sitka, IIH46 (42 cm by 37.5 cm)

Angutet puallaaqluteng arnirluteng. Waten tua puallanaurtut angutet, arnaq-wa kanani qukaatni yuralria. Yaani [St. Marys community hall] akwaugaq atucuaqalriit cukaluteng. Wangkug-am arnagni atracuaqerlunuk. Taũgaam tamaani makut angutet puallalriit qayuw' pilartat? Kayullerteng-ll' man'a piluku pilliat. Arnaq-wa atraucirrauluni kanan' qukaatni putulria. Putumek acirnauraat. Tuani pinginanratni taun' iterlartuq.

Puallassuutet tamakut cukaluteng. Nangermeng yuraraqluteng. Naken-llu allaneq tekitaqan taukut nunat tauna allaneq puallaqautnauraat. Puallaureluteng tuaten allaneq tauna tangkevkarluku. Maani uksumi piciatun allaneq tekitaqan, atraucirraungraan-llu pitullruut tavaten taukut nunat.

Johnny Thompson, February 1994

Tua-i waten tukerceciluteng-gguq piaqameng—tua-wa waten waniw'-am akwaugaq pilriakut. Tua-i tuaten piaqameng tukercecinilartut. Tua-i piciryararraqmiluku. Puallalriamek tua-i ayagniqaurcirluteng pilartut tukerceciqata'arqameng tua puallaqerlalriit. Angutet puallaluteng arnat-llu putuluteng.

Qagkurmiutaugut tamakut; qagkurmiutarpalluuguq. Tua maani kiani [Tuutalgaq] cellangellemni qagkumiunek-llu ilangqerrlaameng. Atakuaqan tua-i tamakunek elicugallermeggni atakurpak tuaten puallassuuterrlainarnek-llu piurnaurtut. Pinrilmiameng tua talircuutnek. Iciw' imkut qagkurmiut aqumqerluteng iqukliqa'arrluteng, tua-i-gguq talirluteng. Tua-i talirlartut tuatnaci'irqameng. Aqumluteng sagg'arrluteng ataucikun tua-i piurluteng. Tua-i tuaten nallunricet'aci'irramtun pingnaqu'uraramken.

The men *pualla* with women. The men would dance on the sides and a woman would be dancing in the middle. As you remember, yesterday over at the gathering [at St. Marys community hall] they sang a short *pualla* song which was fast. Then another woman and I went down and danced briefly. Back in those days when men did *pualla,* what did they do? Perhaps they were demonstrating their strength while one woman danced in the middle, *putuluni.* When the woman danced in the middle they called it *putu.* As I watched them dancing like that, the man [with the bucket] entered the *qasgiq.*

Pualla songs were fast. Everyone would stand and dance. And when someone from another place arrived, they would do a short *pualla* dance for the visitor. They regularly did *pualla* dances for visitors. Anytime during the winter when people arrived from another village, even if it was only one visitor, they would do *pualla* dances. They always did this in my village.

Johnny Thompson, February 1994

When they gathered to present children, *tukerceciluteng* [a debut, formal presentation in public, coming-out ceremony; lit., "letting one hatch"]—as you remember there were some children presented at our gathering last night [at St. Marys community hall]. In the past the same kind of presentation was called *tukerceciyaraq.* When they presented children they would begin with a short *pualla* dance. Men would *pualla* and women would *putu.*

Pualla-style dancing came mainly from the north. When I became aware [in Pilot Station], some of the village members were from the north. When people first learned to *pualla* dance, they would sing *pualla* songs and dance all evening. And if they weren't doing *pualla* songs, they would sing *talircuutet* [line-dance songs]. You know when people up north sat in a line and danced, they called that style *talirluteng* [line dancing]. The dancers would sit in a line and move in unison. I'm telling you things the best way I can according to what I know.

Yuranrarat

Mary Mike, February 1994

Ak'a tamaani ellangua tua-i yuranrarcecinaurtut-llu tua-i.
Nutemllaugut avaken tamana piciryaraq. Mikelnguut tuaten, tua-i-w'
iliit taqnerurrluni yuralalria, yurayuicimalleq pillilria. Wiinga tua-i maaten
ellangua yuratulua [temciyukartuq]. Yuraryunqeggnaurtua tua-i.
Mikelnguut tua-i yuraqerraarqata nangercetniluki piaqluteng.
Kassiyurluteng tua-i kassiyuutekluki yuranrarat. Wii'urluq tua-i maaten
ellangua yuratulua. Taumek yurarcetlinikiignga taukuk angayuqaagma
irniangyuilamek caitqapiar. Aklirluki nangertaqata yurarcetaqluki
cakegciqercelluki yurarcuucirluki.

Cauyarvigmi-gguq cauyanglartut yurarluteng. Yurapiggluteng piluteng
Cauyarvigmi cauyarluteng. Imutun tua-i practice-aangluteng pilallilriit
nunalget taukut.

Mary Mike, October 1994

Tua-i-w' kevgirluteng taukut piyugvikqatalteng, kevgag-ayagcellukek
tuavet qanrucarturcelluki. Piyugvikluki taūgaam ingluteng.
Nallunritevkarluki makunek-llu piyugvikqatallermeggnek. Canek tua-i
qasgim aklukainek ciumek piyugviku'urluki. Alkungyugvikluki,
egaleryugvikluki, nacitengyugvikluki-llu. Qanirtuusqelluku-llu iliin qasgi
qanikciurutmek. Aperluku una taitnauraa pim, taitesqelluku pimek—
piciatun-w' tua. Wiinga-w' pingenratgun pillruama, iliit-llu tulvaarrarmek
itrutlalria alkungyugvikaqatni. Kingullugqaqluki-llu ilurateng.

First-time Dancers

Mary Mike, February 1994

Long ago, when I became aware, they presented their children and let them perform their first dance before the audience. They did that with young children and even grown children. When I became aware, I knew how to dance already [*chuckle*]. I loved to dance. When children had their first public dance, they called it *nangerceciyaraq* [way to make one stand up]. When a child did his first dance, people would assemble in the *qasgiq* to celebrate. When I became fully aware, I was already dancing [having learned before I knew it]. Having had no children of their own, my step-parents had me honored at my first dance quite early. Children would wear new garments and dance with appropriate dance paraphernalia.

In the fall, at the time they called *Cauyarvik* [Place or Time for Drumming], they began drumming and dancing. During that time they did the *yurapiat* [story dances performed by women]. The village people got together and danced, just like we get together and practice our dances today.

Mary Mike, October 1994

One village would send two delegates to the other village to tell them what they wanted from them. They would inform the people in their counter-village about their wishes. Items for the *qasgiq* were the first things asked for. They would ask for a new inside wall covering, a window, and flooring for it. One of them would request a shovel for the *qasgiq*, too. They would mention the name of a child in the invited village and ask that the child's parents fulfill a particular request. At the time I observed these events, cloth goods had already been introduced, so people would often bring some kind of material for inside wall covering for the *qasgiq* in response to a request. Some of the men who had requested certain items to be brought by their teasing cousins or *ilurait* [men's male cross-cousins] would sing certain teasing or ridicule songs, *kingullugqaqluki*, after the gift was presented.

Iraluq taũgaam kenurraqlalliamegteggu iralviim nalliini pitullruut. Iralvagqan taigaqluteng curukat. Tanqigcetetullrungalami-ll' tamaani iralirqami. Tua-i tanqigpagluni ella tarenriirluteng-llu makut cat tamarmeng.

Kegginaqirluteng-llu arulaluteng, taitnaurluteng kevgillrata-ll' kinguani. Usguklukek tua-i ak'aniqerpek'nateng amkut-llu inglumeng akimariaqaceteng pilartut ingluku'urulluteng pituameng. Amkut taimariata-ll' nutaan arulanek atuangluteng. Imkut ukut ciumek pillret ataam arulakameggnek atuangluteng elicarluteng. Tuaten atam piurlartut. Tua-i imarpik ciumek apernauraat. Pulengcamegteggu-ll' nuna cali aperluku. Tuaten tua-i piurngat'lartut. Allat-llu nunat tuaten cali pituyugnarqut.

Arulamek piyaurtait Agayutmun ukvengameng. Agayun nall'arrluku una agayulitullruut. Maa-i agayulimek qanernanrirluteng, arulamek taũgaam.

Tuani nangniillratni murilketariqerrnemkun piyaaqut. Arenqiatua alingyugtua qalriuciriaqata waten alingnaqluteng qalrialaameng. Wani-llu qasgim iluani qalriuciriyuilameng ellamun taũgaam anluteng. Egalrem ceñiini pakma qalriuciriluteng. Neplirluteng taũgken iteryarturluteng cakma qasgim amiigakun. Nepliinanermeggni-ll' qasgimun iterluteng nepairrluteng. Qayuturqunek arulaliyaaqut ciungani wii murilkessuitanka qavarlaama-ll' tayim atungartaqata.

Alingnarqellriamek kegginaqumek, nangniillratni cunaw'— yuirulluteng, yuut nalaurluteng imkut ellangellemni· ilaklallrit qasgimtellallret tamaani. Amllerpek'nateng taukut kegginaqullermeggni alairilriit. Imkut-wa aturlalteng minggugluki uiterinqiggluki nutarrluki aturngalkait tuani allanek pilivkenateng. Tuani taũgaam ciungani allanek pilillrulriit. Payugtellria-ll' taun' ilungallraqa, angama taum pania payugtaqan maligtelallrukeka qasgimun. Iternaurtukuk qaũgna capumaluni cingyaamek. Iciw' cingyaangqetullrulriit tamaan' tulvaanek qatellrianek, tiignek-llu imkunek pilallritnek patumalalliuq qaũgna. Ak'a tua-i inglerem qaũg'um acia patumaluni. Cunaw' tua-i kegginaqunek imalek. Allanret tekipailgata patumaurluki.

Using the full moon as a natural light, people gathered at that time for events. The *curukat* [guests from the counter-village; from *curug-*, "to challenge, attack"] came when the moon was full. Back in those days when the moon was full it seemed very bright. It would be brilliant outside, and there were shadows all around.

Then they did the *arula* dancing with masks after they did the *Kevgiryaraq* singing *taitnauq* [gift request] songs. They did the mask dancing after the two counter-villages were done with *Kevgiryaraq*. The village would begin doing the *arula* dances after their guests returned to their village. The first village to host would start practicing the new *arula* songs. That's what the villages used to do. In their songs they would sing about the ocean first, then the land. That's what they always did, it seems. I think that's what the other villages did, too.

The *arula*-style dancing is not referred to as *agayu* anymore since people started believing in God. They used to compose *agayu* songs precisely about God. Nowadays, people use the term *arula* for traditional dancing and not *agayu*.

I was quite aware [ten years old, in 1922] when they danced with masks the last time. I used to get frightened when they mimicked the sounds of the animals depicted on the mask. They didn't call out the cries in the *qasgiq* but went outside to make their sounds. They climbed up on the *qasgiq* and stood by the skylight when they called out. Then they would come in through the underground entrance making noises, and when they emerged through the entrance hole they suddenly became quiet. Several times they presented masks, but I didn't pay much attention to them because as soon as they began singing I fell asleep.

There was a very frightening mask I saw—evidently it was the last masked dancing in that area. Many elders I used to see participating in *qasgiq* events had already died. At that time a few shamans presented their masks. It appeared that they repainted masks that they had presented before instead of making new ones. Before that time they presented new masks each time. I used to go with my cousin, my uncle's daughter, when she brought food to the *qasgiq*. At the back wall of the *qasgiq* I saw a canvas curtain. White canvas and another kind they called *tiik* [mattress ticking] was available back then. The space under the *ingleq* was covered with cloth. Evidently, behind it were many masks. They kept them covered before the guests arrived from another village.

Allanret-wa tekicimariaqata nererraarluteng-wa piyararteng tekitaqan atakumi pilalriit. Itruarrluteng-wa canek pilaryaaqellilriit wiinga tang murilkenrilkenka. Maaten itertukuk tuani ak'a makut aqumengllinilriit. Equgpallraak akiqliqlukek, iquklilluk' angutet aqumluteng. Arnat taũgken pagaani inglermi. Makut-llu cali allanret inglerni aqumgaluteng.

Kegginaqruit patumaluteng. Uum pikestiin pini allakaita pilarngatai. Uum cali pini taukut allakarrluki. At'eqatarqatki taũgaam tua-i teguluki all'uki yurarlutek Pikestiignek qanaatekaqlukek.

[Leggleq] alairiyaaqellria amllernek ayuqenrilngurnek, amikugmek-llu, yungamek-llu. Tauna taũgaam neq'aklarqa. Tauna tua-i yungaq pikavet agarrluku pilacinagmek piluku. Cag-imkuk akiqliqlutek nuqtaarturluku pikna-w' tengaurturalria yungaruaq piliaq. Taukuk tua-i amikuunkuk yungaq-llu ataucikun tegumiaqlukek qanaatekellruak. Apalluqlukek yuarutminun.

Arnak-llu taukuk nangerrlutek alairillrani taukugnek. Angutekakek-llu-w' kana-i ciisqumingqalutek. Apalliaku-am, arnaq taun' maaten murilkaqa atkumi qaingakun tuulvaarrallermek allguumalriamek atkuni qasgperrluku atullia. Tua-llu cam nalliini tayim piagu, apallillerminiu, wall'u-qaa apallua nangellrani, arnaq tauna taum imum, kegginaqum pikestiin nangerrluni pugyaraanek ayagluku qaspeq taun' alkii aũg'arluku-llu. Maaten tang piaput atkukegciyaaqellinilria. Tua-i kanani nangerngallrani allegluku aũg'arluku taun' qaspell'er. Apallinanrani pillrua wall'u-q' apallua iqukliartellrani. Tauna tua-i akiqlia-llu.

Tuani tua-i anirtualukek-llu calriik taukuk pingatak, apqucirralgek. Wall'u-qaa aaqluk' irnikan—iciw' augem kingukurlaqai ilait. Wiinga-am umyuarteqngellruunga tauna yuarucetaa apallillermeggni pillruan: "Aunralriamun aturaniaran. Iluqsingraan-qaa melugarniaran." Ciuqliullrungatuq una amikuk. Nunamiutaq yungaq kinguani pillrungataat. Neq'aklaryaaqaqa-am. Neq'akellrin-ll' nunat allat aturlaryaaqekiit Imangami-llu allaurrluki taũgaam ilaita pilaraat. Imangami-llu-w' aturlaryaaqellikii taum' Legellrem Imangamtellermini. Yaani tang nunamni atullrunrilkii. Aturyugngangataqa.

After the guests arrived and ate, they began dancing in the evening. I suppose people brought a little bit of something, but I don't remember. When my step-mother and I came into the *qasgiq*, many people were already waiting there. Men were sitting on two huge split logs across the stage from each other. Women and children sat on the *ingleq* up there. The guests were sitting on the *ingleq*, too.

Their masks would be covered. Each group of masks belonging to a given person was covered separately. When the masks were ready to be presented, two men dancers put them on and danced. The owners explained the story behind each mask.

[Leggleq] presented many kinds of masks, including an *amikuk* mask and a jaeger mask. The figure of a jaeger was hanging up there attached with a string. Two people on either side kept pulling the strings to flap its wings, giving the appearance of flight. [Leggleq] held the jaeger and *amikuk* together while he told the story about them. The two animals depicted provided the two *apalluk* of the song he composed for the masks.

Two women stood up on the stage when the masks were presented. Two men dancers were kneeling down in the middle. When the *apalluq* was sung, I noticed a woman wearing an old ragged and torn *qaspeq*. Then, either at the time the *apalluq* was being sung or after it had finished, the owner of the mask approached the woman, and beginning from the neck hole he tore at the *qaspeq*, removing it. Underneath she wore a beautiful parka. He just tore off and removed the old *qaspeq*. He did the same thing to the other woman.

I think he was doctoring the two women, who had some kind of ailment. Or maybe people were worried about them delivering children. You know, some women hemorrhage and die in delivery. I figure he was trying to help them, as the lyrics of one of the *apalluk* were: "Use it on one who is bleeding. Suck it even though it is deep." I think the first *apalluq* was about *amikuk*. I think the second *apalluq* was about the jaeger, a species that resides on land. I do remember the song. Some villages that remember it still sing it, including the singers from Imangaq [Emmonak], but some groups change it slightly when they sing it. When Leggleq lived in Imangaq he probably sang it, too. He never sang it over in my village [St. Marys]. I think I can sing it.

A-ru-la-lua ka-na-ni-aa
A-ru-la-lua ka-na-ni-aa-nga-aa
Aa-rraa-rraa a-nga-li-yaa
Ii-rrii-rrii i-nga-li-yaa
Yaa-a-nga-rraa-aa-aa

A-ru-la-lua ka-na-ni-aa
A-ru-la-lua ka-na-ni-aa-nga-aa
Aa-rra-rraa a-nga-li-yaa
Ii-rrii-rrii i-nga-li-yaa
Yaa-a-nga-rraa-aa-aa

Tua-ll' apalliqatarluku.

Nak-leng u-na-qaa
U-ru-ma-vi-ka wii
A-mu-lu-ni i-nar-ngal-ria una
Aa-rraa-raa a-nga-li-yaa
Ii-rrii-rrii i-nga-li-yaa
Yaa-a-nga-rraa-aa-aa

Yu-ngar-pam-nek uu-mek
a-mi-lir-lua-nga wii
Aa-rraa-rraa a-nga-li-yaa
Ii-rrii-rrii i-nga-li-yaa
Yaa-a-nga-rraa-aa-aa

Ak-ngil-ria-mun
A-tu-ra-nia-ran
I-luq-sing-raan-qaa
Me-lu-gar-nia-ran u-na
Aa-rraa-rraa a-nga-li-yaa
Ii-rrii-rrii i-nga-li-yaa
Yaa-a-nga-rraa-aa-aa

Aipaa-llu, kinguqlia—naliak-wa [*temciyukartuq*]. Ciuqliunricaaqngatuq
aũgna.

I'm dancing down there
I'm moving down there
Aa-rraa-rraa a-nga-li-yaa
Ii-rrii-rrii i-nga-li-yaa
Yaa-a-nga-rraa-aa-aa

I'm dancing down there
I'm moving down there
Aa-rra-rraa a-nga-li-yaa
Ii-rrii-rrii i-nga-li-yaa
Yaa-a-nga-rraa-aa-aa

Now I'm going to sing the *apalluq*.

This poor one here
One who keeps me warm
She lies here ill
Aa-rraa-raa a-nga-li-yaa
Ii-rrii-rrii i-nga-li-yaa
Yaa-a-nga-rraa-aa-aa

My big jaeger here
Using it as my skin
Aa-rraa-rraa a-nga-li-yaa
Ii-rrii-rrii i-nga-li-yaa
Yaa-a-nga-rraa-aa-aa

Where there's pain
You can use it
Though it's deep
You can suck it out
Aa-rraa-rraa a-nga-li-yaa
Ii-rrii-rrii i-nga-li-yaa
Yaa-a-nga-rraa-aa-aa

And the second verse—one of them, I'm not sure which one though [*chuckle*]. The *apalluq* I just sang, I don't think it's the first verse.

Nak-leng u-na-qaa
U-ru-ma-vi-ka wii
A-mu-lu-ni i-nar-ngal-ria u-na
Aa-rraa-rraa a-nga-li-yaa
Ii-rrii-rrii i-nga-li-yaa
Yaa-a-nga-rraa-aa-aa

U-ru-ma-vii a-mun-ri-lu-qaa
A-mi-kug-mek uu-mek
A-mi-lir-lua-nga wii
Aa-rraa-rraa a-nga-li-yaa
Ii-rrii-rrii i-nga-li-yaa
Yaa-a-nga-rraa-aa-aa

Aun-ral-ria-mun
A-tu-ra-nia-ran
I-luq-sing-raan-qaa
Me-lu-gar-nia-ran u-na
Aa-rraa-rraa a-nga-li-yaa
Ii-rrii-rrii i-nga-li-yaa
Yaa-a-nga-rraa-aa-aa

Tua-i-w' waniw' apalluk iquklitellriik. Tuaten ayuqluni, taum Legglerem yuarutii. Atullra elliin elicautekluk' yugnun makunun elicelluku. Legllermek atengqerrlun' taun' Tommy-m atallra. Taukuk kegginaquk yuarutiik, yuarutetaak arulatii-ll' nalluyagucuunaku. Tauna ciuqliq, "Akngilriamun melugarniaran." Iluqsingraan-llu tua-i yungamun meluusqelluku.

Tuaten atam piurlartut. Tua-i imarpik ciumek apernauraat. Pulengcamegteggu-ll' nuna cali aperluku. Allat-llu nunat tuaten cali pituyugnarqut.

This poor one here
One who keeps me warm
She lies here ill
Aa-rraa-rraa a-nga-li-yaa
Ii-rrii-rrii i-nga-li-yaa
Yaa-a-nga-rraa-aa-aa

Don't remain ill here
Using this amikuk
As my skin
Aa-rraa-rraa a-nga-li-yaa
Ii-rrii-rrii i-nga-li-yaa
Yaa-a-nga-rraa-aa-aa

Place where it bleeds
You can use it
Though it is deep
You can suck it out
Aa-rraa-rraa a-nga-li-yaa
Ii-rrii-rrii i-nga-li-yaa
Yaa-a-nga-rraa-aa-aa

That is the end of the two *apalluk*. The song Leggleq composed is like that. He taught the people how to sing it. Leggleq was his name, Tommy's late father. It was the song for the two masks. I haven't forgotten the song and the dance motions that go with it. The verse goes, "Suck at the place where it hurts." Though it was in deep, the jaeger was to suck it out.

That's what they always did. [When they composed songs for masks] they mentioned the ocean [animals] first. And the second *apalluq* would talk about an animal from the land. Other villages did the same, I think.

9. Kuigpagmiut Qanemciit Qulirait-llu, Kuigpagmiutaat-llu Kegginaqut

Kegginuqut Nulirruaruaq, Tuulleguak,
Keglunruak, Amikuguankuk-llu
Mary Mike, May 1993

Murilkellukek malrurqugnek kegginaqurluteng pillrat. Avaken tua-i ayagluteng piuratullrullinilriit. Taukugnek taũgaam malrurqugnek allrakugni murilkeqapiggluki tua-i tangvallruanka. Kegginaqunek-ll' nalqigciaqluteng. Tamakut-wa tua-i allanret tekirqellratni yuut, yuarun tamana iquklitaqan, kegginaqut taq'aqata, yuugaqateki, pikestiin taum ullagluki nalqigtaqluki-gguq tamakut kegginaqut. Qaillun tua-i nalqiggluki callrat. Murilkeqapigcuitanka-am tamakut. Alingnarqut ilait keglunruat, amikuguat—cat-ll' imkut amikugnek pilartatki—cat tua-i tuntut-llu. Unguvalriit-w' tua-i unkumiutaat-ll' mermiutaat alingnarqaqluteng ilait.

Tauna-ll'-am tua-i Quscuarmek piaqluku kegginaquq arnaruaq nalqigeskiliu-am qerruyarpiallermegni taumun anirtullrunilutek, kinguqliirutni-ll' tauna-ll' Atakirraller. Qip'ngayagmi-gguq amani Black River-ami uksumi March-ami pilarngatut—wii March-amun maa-i ellilarqa—atrarlartut neqkamek nurutellriit qimugcitkamek-ll' nurutellriit, tuavet Qip'ngayagmun. Quarruulillruuq tauna. Quarruugcurluteng. Quarruulillrani qimugciteklartut. Naken-lli-qaa nunanek tekiqluteng tuavet tua-i tamakunek neqcuarnek pissurluteng.

Tuani-gguq-am tua-i atrarqurrluteng Qip'ngayagmun. Taũgaam merrliquq-gguq tua-i-wa cuuriluni. Taũgaam cikumek qang'a-ll' qanikcaq urugqurluku merlalliniut. Mertarvingqerrluteng-llu nanvamek nunapigmi. Cikutaqluteng-llu. Natqugpagmi-gguq-am mertaqilit arnat tayima nunapigmek paũgken. Nunapik-ll' taman' Qip'ngayagmek

Yukon Stories,
Yukon Masks

Nulirruaq Masks, Two Common Loon Masks,
Wolf Mask Pair, and Amikuk Masks
Mary Mike, May 1993

I paid attention twice when they danced with masks. Evidently, it was a custom that was practiced from generation to generation. I seriously paid attention only during those two years. They would explain the stories behind the masks. When the song and mask performance ended and the dancers had taken the masks off, the owners of the masks would come forward and tell the stories about them to the many guests present for the event. Previous to the two years I mentioned, I didn't pay close attention when they explained the stories about them. Some masks depicting wolves and *amikuk* were quite frightening. I'm not sure what an *amikuk* is exactly. There were also caribou masks. Some of the masks depicting sea mammals and other creatures were very frightening.

There was a man we called Quscuar who explained the mask depicting a woman he said had saved him and his brother Atakirraller when they almost died of hypothermia. They say it was at Qip'ngayak, on the Black River, perhaps in March. I say it was March. The people who ran out of food for themselves and their dogs would go down to Qip'ngayak. The river had a lot of needlefish, so they would go there to harvest them. When there were a lot of needlefish, some were given to the dogs. People from different places would come to that river and gather the little fish.

At that time they moved down to Qip'ngayak. However, he said the water there was not good to drink, having gotten dark and murky. But they would melt ice and snow for drinking water. There was also a lake on the tundra where they would get some. They would get ice from there, too. One day during a blizzard some women went to get water

yaaqsiggartuq. Catun tayim yaaqsigtaa? Ak'aki-w' ingigun taman' yaaqsiggalria. Ikamratgun-gguq ayakatarluteng. Alqangqertuk-gguq taukuk Quscuaraankuk Atakirraller-llu kat'um-w' kanani Mike, Maigem-w' angaagiin aaniinek. Imangarmiungurtellria. Tauna alqaak kinkunek tayim ilaluni mertalliniluni. Naciglutek-am taukuk kinguqliik tan'gaurluuk. Natqugpaglun' negerrlugluni-gguq pircirrlugluni, taũgken-gguq avairyaaqluni. Kingunratgun qialutek tua-i ayalliuk tua atakuarmi.

Angli-gguq tua ayagaaraqerlutek natetmuruciiruskilik. Aũgkut-ll' tangvanrilamegenki natqugpiim tayim pulalluk' natmun. Natetmuruciirucamek tua-i uqumigglutek ayalliuk. Cunawa-gguq kiatmun ayalliuk. Ing'umek tekicartulliuk tunguluni ca ingna. Maaten-gguq tang ullagluku tekitaak muragpag-man'a nasqunarpagtuumaluni. Tua-i qaill' picirkailamek, natetmuruciilamek, anngaa taun' usvitunruami, tuavet nasqunam uqranun qungceq'allinilutek taun' kinguqlini manuminun elliluku manuqliuvkarluku. Uitalutek tua-i tan'gerian tayim qavaq'alliuk. Tuani-gguq qavarpailegmek nenglliunglutek tua-i nengllian. Tua-i-llu-gguq piinanermegni tayim qavaq'allinilutek. Maaten-gguq tang ellanguq tauna, wall'u-q' tupagluni piuq, Quscuar tauna, nenglliullra im' tayima. Naken-gguq taũgaam puqlam, tunua-ll' pamna agtuumaluku. Epsalnguluni-am tupalliuq. Yuilqumtellni-ll' umyuaqertevkenaku qavallruami.

Maaten-gguq murilkenaurluni piuq yuum tegumiaqellinikek waten akiqliqlukek. Maaten-gguq tang pia yuum uum mugtellinikek. Evsaigminek tamarkenka cikiumalukek. Maaten-gguq tangengnaqluku piuq arnar una. Tua-i-llu-gguq pikilikek tua-i nanikuangagnek qerruarkaungagnek waniw' elliin pinilukek qelleklukek.

Tua-i uitalutek. Tanqigian tauna-ll' arnaq tayim tangenrrirluku; tangerqengaqenriqerrluku. Yuarastekenka tua-i nalkellinilukek. Ut'rullukek.

from that tundra back there. The tundra was quite a distance from Qip'ngayak. I don't know how far it was. The *ingigun* [topographical indication of a natural feature] was pretty far out. They were going to go with sleds. Quscuar and Atakirraller had an older sister who was Mike's uncle's mother. Mike lives down in Emmonak now. Their sister had gone to fetch some water with some other women. Her two younger brothers fussed and cried wanting to go with them. With the wind blowing from the north causing a blizzard, the weather had been bad, but it had begun to ease up. Crying, the younger brothers followed them in the early evening.

As they were going, the two became confused about their direction. They couldn't see the others up ahead anymore, for the drifting snow had obscured their view. When they became disoriented, they began to go with the wind. To their chagrin, they found they had headed upstream. On their way they approached a black object. When they got to it they saw it was a huge uprooted tree with massive roots. Being unsure of what to do or where to go, the older brother, being wiser, had his younger brother nestle in front of him as they crouched down and huddled together on the lee side of those huge roots. There they remained and fell asleep when it got dark. Before they had fallen asleep they had gotten very cold, for it was quite cold outside. So both of them had fallen asleep. Soon Quscuar became aware, perhaps awakening to the realization that he wasn't cold anymore! But he could feel heat emanating from somewhere, feeling it on his back, too. He awoke feeling suffocated. And because he had been sleeping he didn't even remember that he was outside in the cold!

Then, trying to focus his mind, Quscuar realized that a person was holding them in her arms, one on each side. Then he realized the person was breastfeeding them. She had presented a breast to each of them. Making an effort to identify the person, he looked and saw a woman there. She began to speak to him and said that since they were experiencing a life-and-death situation, she was protecting them from freezing to death.

They remained there. When daylight came, they could no longer see that woman; she had vanished. Their search party found them there. They took them home.

Cunaw' tua-i alairtullia tauna ikayuasteklertek arnaruaq mugtesteklertek kegginaquuluku. Nalqiggluku tua-i taumun tua-i anirtuallrunilutek. Nulirruaruuq-gguq tauna. Nulirruam-gguq kegginaqaa.

Nulirruamek acirluku. Iciw' maa-i ak'a tamaani waten arnamek pivailegmi, arnamun-gguq agtuupailegmeng, nulirturpailegmeng nurciluteng caqeryukaarallermeggni angutet, yun'erraat, nulirruatulriit usvillugqaqluteng. Arniqluteng. Taum-gguq tua-i taun' kangikaa.

Taum tua-i ullaglukek anirtullinilukek qavaagni ullaglukek. Ellii-am tua-i yuk'apiunritliami tuunrarralgulliami tuunraqsagulluku tauna arnaq anirturcetlertek. Tauna tua-i alairturlaraa. Canek-w' alairturiyaaqelria, iciw' kangiit-wa tua-i qanruteksaaqlaqai, wiinga tang avaurlaranka.

Cali-ll' alairikili yaqulecungarmek imarpigtarmek. Evunernun-gguq mill'uni qalriaguratuuq taun' imarpigmi. Cameg-am aciryaaqaa cali. Avaurlaranka tang iquitnek ayagniryungramki-llu. Unuakumi-gguq qavallermini imarpigmi tuani qamigaumallermini, tupagtuq-gguq yaqulecungaq pakemna qanerturalria anuqengqatarniluku tamaancunaitniluku tagesqelluku. Maaten-gguq tang paqluku caullra uyangtuq, evunret natiitni tamaan' qavallermeggni, yaqulecungaq taun' qanerturallinilria. Tua-llu-gguq waten piani, "Kitek anuqekaan tungiinun tengi," ungalatmun-gguq tayim tengkili. Tua-i asgurakevkenaku anuqengqatarngatuq-gguq qakemna.

Tauna-ll' angairutka, qangvaq-wa tua-i, Tommy-m kat'um atallra, nalqigciaqluni cali taun' piminek tamakunek pillilria. Qanrutkaqluki-w' tamakut keglunruat, amikuguat, tuulleguak-llu. Tauna-am tauğaam atauciq taringluku tua-i avauqsaunaku-ll' maa-i pikeka. Imarpigtellermegni-gguur-am, maligutlermini, anuqaunani-gguq camani tamaani imarpigmi. Anuqlirpek'nani. Cunawa-ggur-am qeculliuq pamaggun tunuatgun. Murilkengamegteggu-gguq tua-i up'arrluteng kelutmun tua ayagarrluteng. Maaten-gguq tang qecuneq tamana piat, ak'aki tua-i pirlaak ikavet nuryagutellinilriik akianun. Iqua-gguq paqluku paqtaa ayuqluni tua-i qecullinilria. Amta-llu-gguq anuqaunani!

Quscuar presented a mask of the woman who had come to their aid and given them breast milk. He explained that she was the one who saved them. He said it was Nulirruaq. He said it was the face of Nulirruaq, "Wife-Woman."

He called her Nulirruaq. You know, a long time ago, young men at a vulnerable age, before they were properly married, could become possessed by Nulirruaq and become obsessed with sexual fantasies. They would actually believe and begin to act as if they were with a woman. Nulirruaq [from *nulirruar-*, "to have delusions about wife-possession, to act as if one has a wife"] was the source of such obsessions.

She came to them and saved them, coming to them while they were sleeping. Since he probably wasn't an ordinary human but an *angalkuq*, she became his *tuunraq*. He would regularly reveal her in a mask. He presented other masks as well, explaining the background for each, but I have forgotten those explanations.

He also presented a little ocean-bird mask, representing a bird they say liked to land on ice pile-ups on the ocean and sing. I can't remember the name of the bird. I would like to be able to tell some of these stories from the beginning, but I have forgotten them. Anyway Quscuar said that when he was out seal-hunting he woke up one morning and heard a bird singing outside, telling him to go up on land because it was going to get stormy on the ocean. Being curious about what kind of bird it was, he looked out from among the ice pile-ups where they were sleeping, and he saw that it was a cute little bird that had been talking. Then when he said, "Please fly into the direction from which the wind will be blowing," it flew away toward the south. He believed what the little bird had said and told the others that a storm was likely to come.

And also some time back my late uncle, Tommy's late father [Leggleq], would tell people stories about his own masks. He would tell stories about the wolf masks, *amikuk* masks, and common loon masks. One particular story he told about masks I have not forgotten to this day. One day when he accompanied his brother seal-hunting out on the ocean, it was very calm. There wasn't any wind at all. It turned out that the ice they were on had broken away from the area behind them. Once they realized that, they quickly got ready and rushed toward the shore. But lo and behold, the crack in the ice was already too wide for the sled runners. They ran to check the other end and discovered they were actually on an ice floe drifting away. But it wasn't even windy outside!

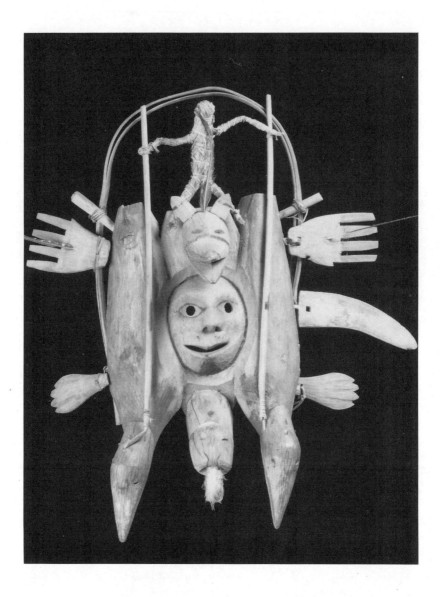

Kegginaquq avategmikun yaquleguarluni, tuar Mary Mike-am angiin tuulleguak kegginaquk alairtellerminikek kangiagnek qanemcillracetun ayuqellria. Canguaq can'guluni nangengqaluni tunuagni. Mamterarmiunek Ellis Allen-aam pillra 1912-aami. Burke Museum, Seattle

A large, powerful mask showing two birds moving side by side, reminiscent of Mary Mike's uncle's encounter with loons. A grass figure rides on their backs. Collected by Ellis Allen at Goodnews Bay in 1912. Thomas Burke Memorial Museum, Seattle, 4530 (57 cm)

Qairvaarluni-gguq. Qairvaamek-am taun' acillrua. Qairvaallinilria-gguq cunawa.

Tua-llu-gguq qaill' tua-i picirkailameng qayangqerrameng qayamun eklutek anngani-llu, wall'u-q' kinguqlini-llu. Pulavkarluku aipani. Una-ll' ket'garluku anuqailengraan painga imarnitegnek all'uni. Murilkellemni pitullruut neqet qeltaitnek, teggmaarrluut qeltaitnek waten ituqurluki tua-i. Canek imna-tanem atengqerrsaaqellriit. Atunem-ll' makuk nungirucirlukek, cillarrluni tauna waten ciqay'agcetun ayuqluni. Neqet qeltait imkut kangitneret amiit ituqurluki tua-i piurrluki tuaten avatiinun qayam elliarkaurrluku. Atunem-llu nungirucirluku qayam painganun una qillertarkauluku, maavet qukamegteggun imarnicetuumarmeng ellikunegteggu man'a cali qillerrluku cagnilluk' mer-iterngairulluku. Caulria-ll' ima-tanem tauna. Atra-am nallunricaaqaqa kit'ur-am tayima.

Tua-i-gguq pulavkarluku tauna, wall'u-q' ellii piuq, ellii-ll' Leggleq pingatuq. Anngarminek anguarcirluni. Tagluteng kelutmun anguarturluteng tua-i. Man'a tua-i aterqurluku uitallrat, tauna ugingallrat. Ak'aki-w' pamna. Yaaqsigillinilriit. Tua-i-am encuum tamana cukarivkalliniluku; aren carvaneq-wa tua-i tunerturivkallia. Qavangelliniluni-am ellii. Tauna-llu anguartii anguarutni qillrulluku pitsaqa'artevkenani qavarangareskuni pegtuqernayukluku. Anguarutni qillrulluku maavet qayaminun anguallinilria. Mernungami-llu-w' tayim pillilria, qavaq'alliuq-gguq anguartii tauna. Ellii-ll' qavarluni. Maaten-gguq tupagyarturtuq ellerrar-man'a. Ellerrarrluni man'a, amta-llu-gguq qayaak-llu uvaavkenani. Tua-i arenqianani eglerrluni man'a amta-llu-gguq pakemna-ll' angualriartailnganani. Pillia qaill' pillranek taum, qavaqeryukluku-llu.

Maaten-gguq tauna pug'llerkani piluku pilliuq tuullgek akiqliqlutek kuimutlinikiik kelutmun. Elpeka'arrlukek-llu taukuk kuimucilriik camani qayam avategkeni. Kuimutlinikiik kelutmun. Tauna-gguq tua-i tupak'aan anguartii imkuk tayimqerrlutek. Maa-i-gguq tua-i tekitellinilutek

The ocean moved in huge rolls even though the wind wasn't blowing. It was a condition called *qairvaaq*.

Then, since everybody had their own kayaks with them and they had no alternative but to use them, he and his brother doubled up in their one kayak. One let the other crawl inside the kayak. And even though it wasn't windy, he put on his *imarnin* [seal-gut raincoat] and secured the spray-cover to the coaming of the kayak hole. I remember they made that cover by sewing spawned chum salmon skins together. But I can't remember what they called that piece. It looked like a short flared skirt with drawstrings on the top and bottom. They would sew the spawned chum salmon skins together, finishing them so that they would fit securely around the kayak-hole coaming. They made drawstrings for both the top and bottom of the piece, tying this part around the coaming and fitting the top part over the *imarnin*, tying the strings tightly around the waist to keep the water from coming in. What was it called now? I know the name of that piece, but it has slipped my mind.

So, he had the other crawl inside the kayak, or perhaps it was Leggleq himself who had crawled in. The brother was paddling. They began paddling up toward the shore. The ice floe they had been on was drifting alongside them. Way up in the distance they could see land. Goodness, they had drifted way out! The tide going out had caused them to drift out faster than they realized. The ocean current had gotten stronger with the tide. The one inside the kayak, Leggleq, had begun to doze off. And the other person who was paddling had tied the paddle to the kayak in case he dropped it into the water if he dozed off. He tied a line from the paddle to the side of the kayak and continued to paddle. Perhaps it was because the paddler got weary that he fell asleep. Inside the kayak Leggleq was also asleep. Then he slowly awoke from his sleep to a loud, swishing, gurgling sound. He heard the loud swishing sound, and yet their kayak wasn't making a rocking motion. He could feel the kayak moving along swiftly, and yet his brother was sitting still and it didn't sound as if he were paddling out there. He asked his brother what was going on and asked him if he had fallen asleep, too.

And when he found a way to move his head up and look around outside, he saw two common loons swimming, one on each side of the kayak, propelling it to the shore. Then he suddenly felt their presence at the sides of the kayak. They were bringing it up toward the land. And when his brother woke up, the two loons suddenly vanished. He looked

ceñamun, qecullrem tamatum iliinun. Tuanllutek tua-i. Yuulutek-wa tua-i. Ilakek-llu tua-i tamaa-i tekismilliniluteng.

Tauna cali tuaten nalqigtellrua. Taukuk tua-i alairlarak tuulleguak kegginaquk. Ukugnun tua-i tuani atertauyaaqellermeggni anirtullrunilutek. Ikayullrunilutek. Pitsaqlukek-wa qavaq'ercetlikegket elkenka eglerutnalukek. Qavamek cikirlukek elkenka kuimullukek tuani tagullukek. Tekiullukek-llu, waniw' tekiteqatallinilutek tupak'arluni. Tauna cali nalqigtellrukii.

Tamakut tang nalqigtengraitki keglunruat-llu, cat-wa tua-i kegginaqut alingnarqellriit avaurluki. Alingnarqellruut tuani. Ukuk-llu keglunruankuk, aturtek-w' all'ukek, akiqliqlutek angutek askekek, tauna tua-i aipaa Atakirralleraam all'uku. Tuqullrulria-w' taun' aipaa kituuciiruskeka.

Anlutek tua-i qakma tuar tang qasgim qainganun pilutek, egalrem tuar yaaqsinrilkiinun pilutek, marurpagalriik tua-i qakma. Tua-i tuar imkuk qimugteqapiik marurpagalriik. Iterlutek-llu waten unat'megnek ayaperturlutek, aurrlutek. Itramek-llu tuavet tua-i arulavigkamegnun pilutek maruallagaqlutek. Tua-i nepaitevkenatek maruallagaqlutek. Tua-i-ll' arulackarlutek kankuk, apallirtum kinguani piyugnarqellriik, apallirraartelluku, ellmegnun tang uirruskilik. Uirrullutek tuarpiaq-ll' augtangelria qaingak. Matarmeng-llu waten arulatulliniameng, kemek taũgaam man'a.

Kana-i tua-i uirruskilik, arenqianatek tua-i uirrutqapiarlutek. Wii-am ilii tangvanritaqa augtanga'arcan-w' natiin imna aipaagnek qainga. Tua-i aukapik kana-i. Ilii tangvagpek'naku. Taum tua-i pikestiignek, angutngurpailegmi-ll' tamaani yun'erraqsigluni taun' Leggleq, pikilikek uirrutenrircellukek. Natiik im' aunrangluni. Tua-i kiliucuksaaqlukek. Tua-i kiima-ll' pivkenaku yuut-ll' makut tua-i kiliryuklukek aipaak piluku, uirrucagnek palartevkenakek. Cunawa-gguq kiliutenricaaqliuk. Amta-ll' augurruteklutek. Arulairrlukek ullaglukek. Qaill' tayim pilukek piakek. Tua-i-w' qanruteksaaqekek avauqeka qaill' qanellra. Amlleruluta alingamta uirrut'ngellragni.

around, and they found themselves already at the shore where the ice had broken away. So there they were. They came out of the kayak. The other hunters had also arrived.

So that was the explanation for the mask. He would bring out those two common loon masks for presentation to the people. He told them that when he and his brother had drifted out on the ice floe, those two had saved them. He said that they helped them. They, the common loons, probably intentionally cast a spell on them so they could move them to shore. They gave them sleep, during which they could propel them to shore. The loons brought them to the shore, and he woke up right before they reached their destination. That was his explanation for the mask.

Although they told stories behind the masks, including the wolf masks, I have forgotten the stories behind those that looked frightening. At that time they were frightening. And I do remember the two wolf masks being put on by two men who were across from each other, Atakirraller being one of them. The other person died, and I don't remember his name.

They went outside on top of the *qasgiq* and began howling. It sounded as if the two of them were next to the smokehole on top of the *qasgiq*. They sounded exactly like dogs howling. Hands flat on the floor, they entered crawling. They would suddenly howl as they continued to crawl to their place. Howling intermittently, they were not quiet at all. They danced for a while, and probably after the *apallut* were sung, they fought like wolves. They danced bare-chested when they did this. As they were fighting like wolves, their bodies appeared to get all bloody.

They were fighting down there, fighting each other viciously. I didn't watch anymore after I saw blood on one of them. It was real blood. I didn't watch the rest of their fight. Then the owner of the masks, Leggleq, who was quite young at the time, did something to stop them from fighting. They had begun to bleed. I thought they had actually wounded each other. The other people there also thought that one of them had been wounded. They had really fought each other ferociously. Unexpectedly, neither had received cuts from the fight. Yet we had seen blood on them while they were fighting. Leggleq went up to them and stopped the fight. I don't know what he did to them. Actually he talked about it, but I don't remember what he said. Many of us were scared when they were fighting so ferociously.

Tauna-am cali, taum cali aipaan, Quscuarallrem amikuk taun' pikngataa. Arnak tua-i, panini kiavet nangerteskiliu aaniinek akiqlilirluku. Aanakellriik-wa taukuk. Una qaspell'er allgurluni, atkutek melqulget elatmun caumalriik, allgulriamek tulvaarrall'ermek, ciqay'allermek ac'imalutek. Tua-i im' ciin tuaten atkukegtaaratek qallilirluki pillragnek wii tuaten umyuaqa pikili. Ciin-kiq atkukegtaaratek elatmun caumalriit, qallilirtanki aūg'umek allgulriamek tulvaarrall'ermek. Cunaw' tua-i allguriciqliniicetek pillinilriik.

And also I think his companion, the late Quscuar, owned an *amikuk* mask. He had his daughter stand at the back of the *qasgiq,* and had her mother stand on the opposite side. The two women were [biologically] mother and daughter. They both wore long, tattered full-length *qasperek* [*ciqay'allraak*] over their fancy fur parkas. I asked myself why they had done that to their beautiful parkas. I wondered why they had covered their gorgeous parkas with tattered cloth garments. Apparently, they had done that because someone was going to tear up the outer cover during the presentation.

A. H. Twithchell-aaq pingayunek waten ayuqellrianek kegginaqunek amikuguanek pillrulliniuq 1900-aam nuniini. Una waniw' iliit taukut pingayun pillrin. Twitchell-aaq igamini waten piuq, "Kegginaqrua amikuum [Amekak] uitatulim nunam akuliini. Iliini pugtuluni nunamek tumliavkenani. Iliini-llu yuk assikenrilkeni temiikun nuv'arkauluku tauna-llu yuk cailkamun iquluni anernerirluni qainga taugken cacurlaumavkenani ayuqucirmitun ayuqluni."

Ukaqvaggun-llu kiagmi 1994-aami Joseph Evan-aq piuq: "Up'nerkami-gguq iliini yuk pektaqami yuilqumi niitelartuq amikuum nepiinek taugken-gguq naken piciinani. Nunamek-llu-gguq pingaleng'ermi nepem tungii cataunani camek-llu-gguq tangerrnaunani. Yuk-gguq niiskuni tamakucimek nepii qasturiinarciquq. Nepii-gguq taqeksaunani niiqurciqaa. Yuum-gguq avatiini tamakuciq kuimangkan nuna qalviryatun ellirciquq. Yuk-llu-gguq ayarungqerqan taum yuum ayuqucia allayuurciiquq unaqsertengluni-llu. Tuaten-gguq ellircuquq amikuum nuvkani kuimangluni temiini." National Museum of the American Indian, New York

One of three *amikuk* masks collected by A. H. Twitchell in the early 1900s. Twitchell wrote, "Mask representing Amekak [*amikuk*], a spirit that lives in the ground. He comes out at times but leaves no hole in the ground. He sometimes dislikes men and will jump through them, but leaves no mark. The man then lies down and dies."

More recently, Joseph Evan (July 12, 1994) recalled: "It is said that some people hear *amikuk* out in the wilderness as they move about in the spring. It's hard to tell where the sound is coming from. And though it sounds like it's coming from the land, there's nothing there. It isn't visible. When a person hears the sound it would get louder and louder. S/he would keep hearing the sound. They say when the creature swims around in the earth near the person, the ground s/he is walking on becomes like quicksand. And if a person is holding an *ayaruq* [walking stick] when an *amikuk* comes, he begins to feel very different. He becomes weak. They say this happens when the creature begins entering inside him and begins to swim in his body." National Museum of the American Indian, New York, 9/3421 (26.9 cm)

Tauna pania anerteqiiyuunani irniaminek. Cunawa-m' tamana pitekluku anerteqiiyuitellra tuatnallinilriit. Tauna-ll' cali aanii taumek tang paniggaminek, paniminek kiingan tua-i anerteqiillrulliniluni. Yurainanragni piut, kegginaqum-am taum ullagluku, taum-gguq amikuguam, apalliinanratni piyugnarquq, pikaken tua-i ayagluku qaspeq im' allgurluku kivgeskiliu kanavet acianun. Ataam-ll' aipaa. Ataam qaspell'er atrarrluku. Nutaan atkukek tamakuk tungairrlutek. Capairrlutek nutaan arulalutek.

Taukuk-wa angutek kegginaqurlutek tua-i-gguq amikuguamek. Aipaan-am tua-i nangerrluni allgurilukek taukuk tamakunek qaspell'ernek at'ellregkegnek. Kanavet tua-i aciagun atrartaqlukek. Tua-i-am caak tamakuk, callrak pillrak cangerliullrak atrarrluku pinikait, anerteqiiyuitellrak man'a pitekluku. Tauna-ll' tua-i pania uini tuqullrani, uilinqigcami qayutunek ukunek irniluni. Ataucirraq-w'-am taũgaam cama-i Nunam Iquani anerteqellria. Aqumgaũrlurmek piaqluku. Taum-gguq atiin apa'urluan tuunramikun Aqumgaũrlurmek acillrua tuunrartarmek. Ukug-am taũgaam yuunrillrulutek ilak.

Cauga-w' amikuk tauna? Ungungssiq. Unguvalria. Cauga-kiq amikuk? Irnilrianun-gguq atutua. Irnilrianun-gguq atauq tauna amikuk. Iciw' ilait-llu irniaqameng waten aunrarlalriit cakneq tuquyarpiaqluteng ilii-ll' tuquaqluni. Tamakunun-gguq cali ikayuuteklaraa taum' pikestiin. Yuarullungqertuq-ll' atam. Atúrlartuq apalluqluku tauna amikuk. Apallirnauraa: "Amikugmek uumek amilirluanga. Iluqsingraan-qaa melugarniaran una. Aunralriamun aturaniaran. Iluqsingraan-qaa melugarniaran." Tuaten-llu yuarucetangqertuq tauna amikuk.

Tua-i-w' amikugmek apallirlaqii,
Aunralriamun aturaniaran.
Iluqsingraan-qaa melugarniaran.
Waten tua-i apallitullrua. Apallinqigtaatullrua. Uumikuani allrakuani qakuani atu'urqamiu tuaten apalliqluku. Una taũgaam cimi'iqluku, "Iluqsingraan-qaa anuratniaran." Tuaten apallitullrua.

The babies the daughter bore had not been able to survive. That was why they were making the presentation. And her mother, having had the same problem, had successfully raised only that daughter standing with her. While they were dancing, perhaps during the *apalluq,* a dancer wearing an *amikuk* mask approached her. Starting from the hood of the *qaspeq,* the person with the mask began to tear the *qaspeq,* shredding it apart until it fell to the floor. He did this again to the other woman. He shredded the old *qaspeq* down to the floor. Their beautiful parkas were exposed for all to see. Freed at last from those old coverings, the two of them began to dance.

There were two men wearing *amikuk* masks. Then one of them stood up and tore up the *qasperek* the two women were wearing. He tore them all the way down to the floor. That ritual signified the removal from the women of the negative aura that caused them their great affliction. They were undergoing the ritual because their babies always died. When his daughter's husband died, she remarried and bore several children. Only one of her children is still alive, down at Sheldon's Point. His/her name is Aqumgaurluq. They say that his/her father's grandfather, an *angalkuq,* named her/him Aqumgaurluq, which is a *tuunraq* name. Her other two children are already dead.

What is an *amikuk,* anyway? It's an animal. It's a living creature. I wonder what an *amikuk* is. He used his *tuunraq,* the *amikuk,* on mothers-to-be during delivery. That *amikuk* is associated with childbirth. You know, some women hemorrhage when they deliver babies, to the point of near-death or even actual death. That person who owned the mask would use it to help these women. And indeed there is a ritual song that goes with it. I've heard him sing a song that mentions the *amikuk* in the lyrics. The verse would include mention of the *amikuk* in one line, and in another line he would be telling the *amikuk* to suck it [the placenta?] out even though it was deep inside the person who was hemorrhaging. So there's a song like that about the *amikuk.*

The *apalluq* of the song mentioned the *amikuk,*
> *Use it on the one who is bleeding.*
> *Though it is deep, would you suck it out?*

These were the words in the *apalluq.* He always changed the words in the *apalluq.* When he sang it the next time, the following year or whenever, he would sing it the new way. The only line he ever changed in the *apalluq* of the song would be the one that goes, "Though it is deep, would you pull it out?" He would make a new *apalluq* for it that way.

Tauna-gguq tua-i irnilrianun atauq amikuk. Iciw' irnicurlagluteng ilait aunrarluteng nalalalriit irnirraarluteng. Taum-w' tua anirtuuteklikii tuatnalriim irniyulriim tauna amikuk. Tuaten ciin yuarutengqerta, "Iluqsingraan-qaa melugarniaran." qang'a-llu "anuratniaran." Mikelnguum kingunra, qamna kingunra—iciw' augmun ilait kingukurnilarait; tamatuuyugnarquq. Tamatuuciqsugnarquq. Tua-i-am tuaten atutullruuq. Atutullruat. Atulgullruat tamana. Taũgaam apallui ukut cimiqetaararluki. Yuarun taũgken taman' cimirpakanritliniuq.

Aren ilait, kingunermeggnun waten pistekameggnun, tungelqumeggnun-llu, eliteqaasqumaluki piyaaqlallinilriit. Kingumeggni eliteqaasqumaluki makunun pistekameggnun cameggnun tungayameggnun, tamakut elluam tungiinun ikayuutekengnaqkengateng.

Nepcetaq
Johnny Thompson, Negeqliq, February 1994

Tua-i avani tarenrani yuaralaakaryaaqaqa tauna nepcetaq pitsaqevkenaku-llu alaiteqernayukluku tarenraan kangia qanemciknaluku. Tua-i waniwa una qanemcikengssaarqata'arqa, tua-i-wa tauna nallunritevguaralqa, angalkum taum angalkuurcartulriim-wa, ayuqucillra. Nani qavani [Qissunami] taum wani nepcetam pikestii uksiyalliniuq. Tua-i-am tuaten uksillerminek utercan caqerluni tauna angutet iliit ayalliniuq tamaavet uksillran nuniinun. Tekicami-am tuavet arulairluni tayima callilria, nerllilria-llu nem'i tuani.

Tua-i tuanelnginanermini anaqsartulliniluni wavet elliviim canianun. Tuani tua-i anarnginanrani naken im' maaken qalrialriamek niitlalliniluni. Kangiiturluku pillia nepcetaq tauna elliviim qacarnerani agalria. Tua-i-am tua-wa picingssaungameng yuut, quyakenritliamiu-llu, taqngami anaminek taũgken tua-i agciuqaarluni tauna quka'arrluku tua-i mingulliniluku anaminek. Tua-i utertelliniluni tuaten.

They say the *amikuk* was used for women delivering babies. As mentioned before, some women die of complications during delivery. It was the one that would save women who were having such complications while giving birth. That was why the words to the song say, "Would you suck or pull it out even though it's deep?" *Mikelnguum kingunra* [the placenta, lit., "one behind the child"; also called *neqii*, "its food"]—you know, some women die after hemorrhaging. It's probably that. You know, they say sometimes a woman died from bleeding too much. That's probably what it was. That's probably what it would be. So he would sing that way. The song they sang was like that. They would sing that song all the time during those presentations. However, they would change the words in the *apalluq* of the song. But actually the song didn't change very much.

No doubt they wished intensely that the generation that followed them, including their own relatives, would learn some of the songs. After they had departed this world, they would want those songs that were used for healing and general well-being to be passed on so that they would be carried forward from generation to generation.

One That Sticks to the Face
Johnny Thompson, St. Marys, February 1994

Among these pictures here, I immediately looked for the picture of the *nepcetaq* mask I used to see so I could tell its story, but I didn't find it. I'll tell a little bit of what I know about what happened to a man destined to become an *angalkuq*. Somewhere up river [Qissunaq River] an *angalkuq*, owner of the *nepcetaq* mask, had a fall camp. One time when this *angalkuq* wasn't staying at his camp, a man was hunting around there. When he arrived at the camp he stopped, perhaps to eat or to do something.

Before he left the shaman's camp he defecated not far from the cache. While he was in the act, he began to hear a sound from nearby. When he finished he walked toward the sound and found a *nepcetaq* mask hanging on the wall of the cache. Then, since some people are strange in their ways, or perhaps because he didn't appreciate the *nepcetaq*'s sounds, he picked up his feces and smeared them across the middle of the mask. Then he went home.

Ikani tua-i wangkuta uksuilaamta, Qissunam-gguq ceñiini maani, Qanagpagmek piaqluku. Angli taūgken pamani, tamaani ten miles pitangatuq-llu tuaken, up'nerkillertangqertuq Akagcullermek piaqluku. Taukut ellait tuanlluteng. Ca-wa imainerpak pamani keluatni Petmiim-gguq maan' ceñiini. Una-llu Alirnaq kuik eq'uqerrluni tua-i nanvamun keluani up'nerkillrata. Tuani tua-i qallanermi angungnaqu'uratulliniluteng.

Caqerluni-am unuakumi tuaten takuilliniluni tauna imna anaminek mingugilleq nepcetamek. Tuavet tekiteqerluku ungungssik malruk tekitelliniluku. Tua-i arenqialluga'arrluni. Tua-i taūgken taukuk ungungssik tamarmek kegginakek una qatellriamek tua-i kep'arluni akitmun minguglluni. Aulukelnguagni taukuk, qiluminek-llu maqellruniyugnarqaat, yaaqsinrilan pingna nanvaq cilraaraungan-llu

My family also had a fall camp at Qanagpak along the Qissunaq River. About ten miles back from our camp, there was a spring camp called Akagculleq. This man and his family were staying at that camp. Behind their place was a huge dried-up lake along the Petmik River. The Alirnaq River flowed out to a lake behind their camp. People in that area always hunted there around the eddy.

One day that man who had smeared feces on the *nepcetaq* mask went out to check his traps. Just when he got to that area, two bears met him. His life was in jeopardy. The bears had white streaks across their faces, and by the time they had finished mauling him to their satisfaction, his guts were literally hanging out of his stomach. He slowly crawled away, pulling his small sled toward the newly frozen lake not far from where

Nepcataq Sheldon Jackson-aam pillra Andreafski-mek 1893-aami. Sheldon Jackson Museum, Sitka

Nepcetaq mask collected at Andreafski by Sheldon Jackson in 1893. Sheldon Jackson Museum, Sitka, IIB8 (32.7 high)

tua-i tagengnaqu'uralliniluni tuavet. Manigian-am qamigautegminun ekluni tuavet asaurturluni tua-i aka'aktara'aralliniluni.

Tauna-am aanii angalkuumilliniluni, tua-i pulayarat tekipailgaki wani kelumeggni taum wani aaniin alakelliniluku. Alakngamiu-am elpengcautelliniluku ukunun ilaminun pairtuusqelluku tua-i. Egmian-am tua-i tekican, taicatgu tua-i, imutun mikelngut pilauciatun tua-i evsaiminek mugtelliniluku. Akwaugarpak tuaten mugtaqluku pilliniluku. Tuaten-wa pinginarpek'naku tayima qayuwa anirtuangnaqluku-llu ·pilallrullikii. Assiriluni tua cangatenrirluni.

Tua-am caqerluteng tauna elicalliniluni. Waten tamakut agayunek pilarait, tamakut yuaruteteng—tamaani agayuliniluteng qanerlallruut. Wangkuta yurarcuutnek pilaqeput maa-i. Tua-i imum wani aũg'um ciuqlima qanruciatun picirrluatun tua-i piyuitellruameng tamaani. Una tua-i ilii waten elicarqan kangianek kangircilluku pitullruat.

Tua-i-am tamana yuarun atullni tamaa elicaqatallermini kangia qanrutkuralliniluku tua-i taum tamakunguaruniluku. Pitarkallruaruniluku. Tua-i taumek-gguq tuani tua-i unicagni pikliutellruak-gguq taukuk.

Tauna imna pikestepiarak, taum nepcetam kegginaqum pikestepiara allurrluku taukugnek tuan' pitarkallraruagnek caskugkenek. Tua-am cam iliini old man-ama—taum-llu tangvallrullinikii tan'gurrauluni tamaani. Tua-gguq yuarun tamana atuqerluku apallirluku, tamaani murullliniluku tamatum, pitarkallraruaran tamatum. Murungamiu-gguq tua-i angun-ggur' imna unani tua-i ellminek tua-i uirrluni tua-i. Nateq-gguq tauna, qasgim un'a natra, tua-i augurrluku tua-i. Ellminek tua-i kilirturluni. Taqngami-llu-gguq, tamatum unicani, imkut tua-i kilirtullri tayima cataunateng mamluteng ataam. Mamluteng tua-i.

Tua-llu tua-i qanrutliniluki taum' tamatumek tauna allurtellruniluku pissuutiinek tamatumek. Tua-gguq qunukellruat-gguq tauna angalkuqngamegteggu tua kiiran, waten anirturituluni-llu pian. Tua-i tamatumek tua-i qanemcicuaqertua elluarrluku pinrilengramku.

Tangvaglallruunga [kegginaqulrianek] tan'gurralleraullemni murilketarissiyaagpek'nii taũgaam. Tamakut-llu waten ilait kangirciqapiggluki kangirciyuitellruamki. Taũgaam tua old man-ama

he was. On the smooth ice he pulled himself into his small, flat sled. Riding on his belly, he moved along slowly, pushing himself along with his arms.

Evidently because his mother was a shaman, just as he got to a trail in the thicket right behind their place, she sensed him. When she felt his presence nearby she summoned others and told them to go out to meet him. As soon as they brought him home, she let him suckle her breasts like a baby. She continued to suckle him for two days. She probably did other things to save him. Soon his wounds healed, and he was well again.

Then one day he began to compose a song. They composed songs called *agayut* [prayers or supplications]. When they composed dance songs they said they were making *agayu*. We call them *yurarcuutet* today. Just as Willie Kamkoff said, people did not do things frivolously in those days. When a person learned a dance song, they always made sure the person understood the origin and purpose of the composition.

When that man was ready to practice the song he had composed, he told the people that it was about that kind of animal. He said it was about a bear. He said that after the two bears fought him and left, they became his *tuunraq*.

This man had snatched away from the *nepcetaq* owner the bears that he had used as *tuunraq*. One time when my old man was a boy, he saw that man perform. He said when the man began to sing the *apalluq*, his *tuunraq* entered him. When the spirit of the bear had overtaken him, the man began to growl like an animal and wrestled with himself down there [on stage]. There was blood all over the floor in the *qasgiq*. He was scratching and cutting himself. When he finished and his *tuunraq* had left him, his wounds disappeared. They all healed.

Then after the presentation he told the audience that he had stripped the other person [the shaman] of his power source. They say when the man died it was a great loss, for he was the only *angalkuq* in that village who could heal people. I'm telling you a little bit of the story even though I didn't narrate it perfectly.

I saw [mask presentations] when I was a boy, but I didn't pay close attention. I didn't quite understand what they were doing. But when my old man talked about them, he would say that masks were not made for

taum qanrutkaqaki tua tamakut pilinguarularlanritniluki tua-i tamatumun yuarutmun kangikluki pituniluki tua-i. Nepcetaq taũgaam tauna tua, nepcetait-gguq cimirtaayuitut. Tua-i nepcetani tauna tua pikluku avaliqluku-llu [angalkum] pitunilaqait.

Tauna-llu-am cali iillakluku qanemcikellrumikii, waten qamaken Takcanek curukallrat kiagmi. Tekiqata'arluteng-gguq kanani Tuutalgarmiut ketiitni, tamaaken eglertessuutmeggnek tagvailegmeng, arulamek waten tekiqata'arcuutmeggnek-wa pilliniluteng.

Tua-gguq tauna angalkuat qayamek tagceciuq tamaaken qayat iliitnek. Tagcetaa tua mengvailegmeng piqainaurrluku. Tua-am cali tuaten imum qanellratun cetamanek atkugnek ayuqenrilngurnek piteklilliniluni. Tua-gguq qayam painganun taukut elliluki qayamek nepcetamek pillruuq. Tua-gguq im' qayaq takuyartaarulluku. Taũgaam yuarun iquklilluku pivkenaku tua maniqernginarluku taũgaam tua piyugngallinillni tamana nasvagluku.

Nepcetaarqameng cukanrarturluni tua kaugtuarturluteng pilarait. Tua taũgken taun' maligtaquurluku arulaluteng tua-i nepcetalria. Amllernek arulastengqessuitut, taũgaam kiimi nepcetalria tua pituuq waten arnangqerrsaaqeng'ermi. Taũgaam angun kanani pilria. Tua wii tangllemni taũgaam tuaten pillrunrituq, pelacinagmek pilirluku agalirluku atullrua. Tamakucetun pivkenani. Tua-i taun' angalkuuvkenani-llu taun' pilria. Maniqatallermeggni cali tua-i taum tauna cali nepcetaq aturluku nangneq old man-ama tua atullrua. Cakatgu-kiq tayima tauna.

Qatellriamek mingungqellruuq, maaggun-llu avatmikun pitarkaruanek tua-i pingqerrluni tuaten-ll' qugyinrarnek avatii pikna. Tua-i tauna kiiran tua-i tauna tangerqallruaqa wii. Taumek qanemciqallruuq iillagyugluni nepcetalriamek qayamek.

Tutgara'urluq Iilek Ataucimek
Mary Mike, Negeqliq, February 1994

Quliramek taũgaam niitlartua ataucimek iilegmek. Tauna tutgara'urluq nunanun tekilluni. Iiqerlun'-am uitauralriim tauna nukangqurra'urluq cali anmiluni elliicetun pirpauvkenani. Tutgara'urluulliami-llu-w' pilria. Ataucimek waten iingqerrluni. Tua-i kiingan iikluku. Cauga? Inglupgayuuguq-qaa?

amusement but were the inspiration for the *yuraq* performances. They say the *nepcetat* masks were never discarded. A specific *nepcetaq* mask was always kept by its owner [the shaman].

He [Johnny's father] also told another story about the time some people from Takcat arrived in Pilot Station for a dance festival in the summer. They did the *tekiqata'arcuun* [proper arrival or entrance dance] down in front of the village before they disembarked from their boats.

Then their *angalkuq* asked that one of the kayaks be hauled up on land. He made them bring it up [to the *qasgiq*] before they started the preliminary singing. He then asked for four different kinds of parkas. When the parkas were placed on the kayak, he used his kayak as a *nepcetaq*. With the kayak stuck on his face he swung his head left and right. However, he didn't perform like this throughout the whole song. He [shaman] was just demonstrating his ability to the people.

When they gave *nepcetaq* mask presentations, the drummers would beat the drums rather rapidly. Other dancers joined the person presenting the *nepcetaq* mask, but not many. There were women dancers too, but the one who was presenting the *nepcetaq* mask would be the main attraction. When I watched a man performing with a *nepcetaq,* the mask was tied to his head with strings. He didn't perform with it like the ones my old man saw. The presenter wasn't a shaman. When that particular *nepcetaq* mask I used to see was used for the last time, my old man performed with it. I wonder what they did with it?

The mask was painted white, with carvings of various animal figures along either side and swan feathers around the top. That was the only one I saw briefly. He [my father] was totally fascinated by the man who used a kayak as a *nepcetaq.*

Orphan Child With One Eye
Mary Mike, St. Marys, February 1994

I've heard a *quliraq* [traditional tale] about a creature with one eye. In the story a *tutgara'urluq* [orphan child] arrived in a village. As he hid himself just beyond the village, he observed a poor young boy like himself coming out of a house. The boy probably was an orphan, too. He had one eye. It was his only eye. Who was it? Perhaps he was the person called Inglupgayuk [one-eyed person].

Inglupgayugmek atengqerrluni. Calnguamiu-wa tua-i cam iliini caullranek apluku. Inglupgayuuguq-gguq. Tua-i-gguq caqelngaurturluni pinaurtuq. Nunat iquatni ualirnermi-gguq uitallinilutek tauna-ll' anuurluni-llu. Inglupiarrarmek iingqerrluni. Una kegginaquq taungulliuq.

Equguaq Kegginaquq
Willie Kamkoff, Qerrullik, February 1994

Uumek tangllemni kegginaqumek taum piliaqestiin, nangnermek Imangami kegginaqurluteng pillratni, equguaruniluku qanrutkellrua. Tamaani-gguq tamakut angalkut waten apalliriluteng yuarutnek camek pinguarsugaqameng waten kegginaqirluki, tauna yuarutseng, apallua, cassuutseng, kaigatseng, waten yugnun tangkevkarluku pilaraat.

Taūgaam-gguq amlleq, tamaani tuunralegteggun pitullermeggni, amlleq-gguq nalkuqaqlartuq tamakut tuunralget pisuutiitnek. Uksumi waten pinguarqameng, waten yura'arqameng equgualriit-llu makut unakluaqarqamegteggu-gguq equk amlleq Kuigpagkun anlartuq. Tua-wa man' kiiran tamaani cassuutekngamegteggu man' equk, cakluku canun equgglainarmek atutullermeggni. Equgnek-llu calianek nerengnaqutengqerrluteng. Tuatnamek-gguq equguanricuitellruut tamaani tamakut kegginaqulriit ilangqerrlainatuut-wa equguamek. Tavaten niillarqa aūg'umek qanrutesteklallemnek.

Equguaruuq-gguq. Tamana pitekluku equguanricuitellruut-gguq equgmek calissuutengqerrngameng cakluku-gguq amalkuan. Qayaliluteng, enliluteng-llu equgmek, neqsurcuutekameggnek-llu equgnek caliarluteng. Equk kiingan aklukluk' piamegtegg'u. Tavaten taktalriamek una qanruteksuumaaqa.

Keglunruamek Kegginaqurluni Tuunrilria
Willie Kamkoff and Johnny Thompson, February 1994

Willie Kamkoff: Una-llu waniwa keglunruarulria. Kangingumaq'apiaranritaqa taūgaam keglunrem ayuqucia. Taūgaam-gguq tamaani tamakut tuunralget amllerem una kegluneq tuunraqaa. Tauna-llu Nakacuk tauna niitnaqlalria pilagturituniluku maani yuungcaristet alairpailgata. Pilagturqamiu-gguq yuk tauna nangtequtii

His name was Inglupgayuk. After being curious for some time, the one who arrived asked him who he was. The boy said his name was Inglupgayuk. [Inglupgayuk] always hopped around with one leg. He lived with his grandmother at the end of the village. He had one eye. Perhaps this mask is an image of him.

Driftwood Mask
Willie Kamkoff, Kotlik, February 1994

When I saw a mask like this one [see photo on next page] in Emmonak at the last mask presentation, the owner of the mask said it was an image of *Equk* [driftwood]. They say back in those days the *angalkut* composed songs with *apallut* for masks and presented them to people. The masks represented things they needed to survive.

When they relied on those who had *tuunrat,* people received many of the things the *angalkut* asked for. When people performed with masks during the winter, including the *Equk* masks, and their plea had been granted, an abundance of driftwood came down the Yukon River. They used driftwood for everything. Hunting equipment used for acquiring food was made mostly of driftwood. That was why the *Equk* masks were always presented. I heard this from my mentor.

They talked about *Equk* masks. They always presented an *Equk* mask since they used driftwood for everything. They made their kayaks out of it, they made their homes out of wood, and they used it for tools to acquire food. They used wood for everything. That's the extent of my story about these [masks].

Wolf Mask Used in Healing
Willie Kamkoff and Johnny Thompson, February 1994

Willie Kamkoff: This is a wolf image. However, I know very little about the wolf. They say back in those days many *tuunralget* [lit., "ones with *tuunraq*"; another term for *angalkuq* or shaman] had the wolf as their *tuunraq*. They also talked about a person named Nakacuk, who operated on people before medical doctors came. They say when he

Una kegginaquq ilakaat pingayun kegginaqut Henry Neumann-aam pillrin St. Micheal-aamek 1890-mi. H. M. W. Edmonds-aaq-llu cali pillruuq waten ayuqellriamek kegginaqumek St. Micheal-aamek ukut allrakut iliitni, 1890–1899 piluku-llu-gguq "equum yua." Sheldon Jackson Museum, Sitka

One of three masks collected at St. Michael by Henry Neumann in 1890. H. M. W. Edmonds collected a similar mask from St. Michael between 1890 and 1899, which he labeled "the spirit of the driftwood." Sheldon Jackson Museum, Sitka, IIG8 (26.6 cm)

egcuillaraa, nerluku-gguq taũgaam uum muruaqani tuunrami keglunrem. Nerluku-gguq tua augmek qurrlurluni qanra nerlaraa taun' aũg'allni.

Angalkuuluni taun' Nakacuk. Amlleret nallunritaat niiqlaraat. Ak'a avani tayima angama tangkellrullinikii. Tangerrlallruaqa-llu taun' arnaq qetunraa-llu. Anginrarmek taun' atengqellruuq arnaq tauna, qetunraa-ll' taun' Cakiceñamek. Nunapiggluugarmi-gguq cakmani nanikuatellrua atiin taun' Anginraq. Ellii-llu piusaaqmiluni taũgaam tamakut-gguq tuunralget nakmiin ilateng ellmeggnek aulukesciigallarait. Allamun taũgaam tuunralegmun aulukevkaqluki.

Itrutliniat alliranek curirluk kevegluku taun' pektesciiganan', kanavet-llu qasgim qukaanun piluku. Taum-llu angama Sinka-m tangkellrullinikii tuan' pillrani. Aũg'umek-gguq tengmiam yaqruanek takelriamek cavilirluni pillruuq. Alarcaqiqelliniluni-gguq. Pilagturluku-gguq taun' alarcaqrua aũg'allrua. Ancamiu-llu nerluku tauna uum wani keglunruami muruani. Tamatumek-gguq aturluni-gguq tamakut aũg'allri nertullrui egtevkenaki. Nutaan tua-i taqngamiu, tauna nerumariamiu, ataam imna pilagtullni anemluku. Taqngamiu-gguq pia nangerrluk' anesqelluku. Tua-gguq pisqengani nangerrlun', im' pekcuunan' itleq watava, nangerrluni tayim anellruuq taun' arnaq.

Johnny Thompson: Iquvanrilnguum tamana qanemcikellrua qamani Massercullermi agayulirtem takuani. Waten-llu qanerluni maa-i waniwa tauna arnaq anirtullra maa-i cali unguvaniluku. That was back in late 40s. Tua-i nutaan agayulirta pucigngauraqerluni qanertuq, angalkut-gguq tamakut assiitellriarrlainarmek caliyuitelliniut. Tua-i-w' kiingita tamaani waten yuungcaristekngamegteki. Assiiterrlainanritliniameng assilrianek tua caliangqerrlarmilliniut ilait. Uum-llu qanellra waten wani, tua waten nakmiin ilani pisciigatlarniluku. Maa-i cali mat'um nalliini yuungcaristet yuungcaristenguming'ermeng nakmiin ilateng ellmegtun pisciigatlarmiut. Aulukesciigatlarmiit. Tua-i tamakut ciuliaput tuaten ayuqut.

Willie Kamkoff: Tungulriit-am aũgkut qerrircautnek pilarait un'gani, tunguq'apiararluteng. Tamakucimek-gguq taum kinguakun qupurillrani tangkellrua taun' Nakacuk taum angama. Tangkuraamiu-gguq yaaqvanun pivkenaku imumek-gguq waten cavigtun pilalriacetun piaqani tupailgani-gguq qup'arrlartuq. Tau-wa tamatumek waten yugnginauluteng pilanrilameng cassuutmeggnek waten aturluteng pilaameng mumiggluk' ayuqucirteng. Man'a wangkucetun waten

removed the cause of the person's illness, he never threw it away. His *tuunraq,* the wolf, entered him and he would eat it. He ate what he had removed as blood dripped down his mouth.

Nakacuk was an *angalkuq.* Many people knew him. Once long ago my uncle watched him perform. I myself used to see the woman he cured and her son. Her name was Anginraq, and her son was Cakicenaq. Down in Nunapigglugaq, Anginraq became ill and her father grew concerned for her life. Her father was an *angalkuq,* too, but those with *tuunrat* never doctored their blood relatives back in those days. They let other shamans take care of them.

Since she couldn't move, they put her on a skin pad and carried her into the *qasgiq,* placing her in the center. My uncle Sinka watched Nakacuk that time. He said he used a wing-feather/quill as a surgical tool, using the longest wing-feather of a bird. Apparently, the woman had appendicitis. My uncle said Nakacuk opened her up and took out her appendix. When he took it out he ate it, since the wolf spirit [his *tuunraq*] had entered him. With his *tuunraq* taking over, he was able to eat the parts he had removed from people. Then after he ate it, he closed the incision. When he was finished he told her to get up and go outside. She stood up as she was told and walked out the door.

Johnny Thompson: Iquvanrilnguq told that story up in Masserculleq [Marshall] with a priest present. He said the shaman's patient was still alive. That was back in the late 1940s. After the priest looked down contemplating that for a while, he said he had begun to understand that the *angalkuq's* work wasn't all bad. They were the only healers around, so some of them obviously did help people. And like he [Willie Kamkoff] mentioned, they did not take care of their own relatives. Even at the present time, medical doctors are reluctant to care for their own families. Our ancestors were like that, too.

Willie Kamkoff: There are black stones found down on the coast called *qerrircautet.* My uncle saw Nakacuk cutting that kind of a stone. He observed him from close by. He said that whenever he lowered the feather, holding it like a knife, [the stone] would split before it was touched. They were able to do that because their human selves were transformed into something totally different. They didn't behave in their usual human ways. Since their *tuunraq* knew exactly who they

yuugsararteng aturpek'naku. Tuunrateng aturluki cimirluteng-gguq pilartut. Tuatelluni tauna pilagturiaqami-llu egcuitellinii nerngermi-llu mirsalnguarkauvkenani taumek tuunraminek aturluni pilaami.

Johnny Thompson: Tua-wa elliin tua tangvagyaaqluku taum wani atullran. Tua-w' tuunraan amiqluku. Elliin nerlanricaaqaa taũgaam taum wani caskuan keglunrem nerlaraa. Elliin tungaunani nerlanricaaqaa.

Willie Kamkoff: Ayuqenrilngurnek-gguq tamakut tuunralget tuunrangqertut. Uurrlainarmek pivkenateng ungungssinek canek tuunrangqerrlartut. Tuaten aulukikuneng yuuluku taũgaam yuut tangeksaaqaqluku taũgaam cimirsaaqengraan tangeksuunaku, yuuluku taũgaam tangkaqluku. Tuaten-gguq tamaani tamakut tuaten pituut.

were, they were able to transform them. That was why Nakacuk never threw away the parts he removed when he operated on people. And he did not even become nauseated after he ate them.

Johnny Thompson: Transformed into his *tuunraq,* the shaman actually saw what he was doing. He personally didn't eat the part, but his *tuunraq,* the wolf, would eat it. Nakacuk's true self did not actually eat the part.

Willie Kamkoff: Shamans had many kinds of *tuunrat.* They didn't have just one but different kinds of animals as *tuunrat.* Everyone observing would actually see the shaman as a person when he worked on someone, even though he had been transformed into that animal. They say that was what they did back in those days.

Keglunruaq kegginaquq pillra J. H. Turner-aam 1891-aami. National Museum of the American Indian, New York

Wolf mask collected by J. H. Turner, 1891. National Museum of the American Indian, New York, 2/446 (20 cm)

Tutgara'urluq Siimarmek Kegginalek
Justina Mike, Negeqliq, March 1994

Taukuk-llu-qaa niilaragken cali maurluqellriik nunani ukuni uitalriik? Tauna tutgara'urlua waten aquilriit-llu ullagaqateng alingqerrluteng-gguq uniarrnauraat. Kiituani-gguq iluteq'nguq maurluni-llu pinauraa, "Ciin makut wii, ellait aquiluteng, ullagaqamteng tayim qimagnaurtut." Tua-llu-gguq ilutequarlurlun' qialuni-ll'. Kiituan anglinguq arnararpaurrluni. Tava-ggur-am mertaullaamiu tauna maurluni, mertarluni. Kan'a cam iliitni-gguq uyangtaa ik'iki kan' yungnaaq ciimarnek cangqerrluni. Ciimarnek makut cai, qerralernaqlun' kan'a tangellra. Alingqerrluni-gguq uitasaaqluni qaltani taun' imiqsaitellian. Tau-ggur-am uyangtaa, uyangcamiu-gguq qayuwa-gguq piaqan ayuqelinauraa kat'um. Nakleng. Tua-gguq umsuartequq, "Wall'u-qaa wanguuq kan'a. Wang'ungatuq kan'a." Tangerrluku ellminek nallunrian ellminek piuq, "Anirta-wa makut yuulgutenka aquigaqata ullagaqamteng alingqerrluteng ayakaqulartut."

Mertani taun' tagulluku qialuni tuaten maurluni pia, "Anirta-wa makut ilama aliklaraatnga alingnarqelliniama, kegginaqa pakemna catangqerrniluku ciimarnek." Tua-llu-gguq pia nani uluani taiteqaasqelluku. Taicaku im' tamakut qayuw' piluki kiiqluki maurluan taum aūg'allii.

Tua-llu-gguq atakuan iralirluni, pillia pakmani ca imna qungasviggani aqvasqell'uku mamterami tayim aganiluku. Tua-llu-gguq tayim anluni. Antai-gguq ik'ik piluguqegtaaraat aturat-llu kenugcimaluteng. Atkukegtaaraat-llu-gguq cai makut kenugcimaluteng. Aturaqegtaaraat. Pilliniluk', "Kitek-wa all'uki tamakut pakmavet nerrlugamegnuk qainganun ugglluten atuqina yuarutmek." Yuarutii tang nalluqereskeka. Atuusqelluku tamatumek elicarluku yuarutmek. Yuarun tamana aturluni, ernernun—iciw' erenret alairtelalriit akerta pugqataraqan. Ernernek taukut aperlaqait. Tavani uitaciqniluku. Yugnun amllernun tangerrlarciqniluku.

Tua mayurluni pisqengani atulliniluni. Aturluni. Yuqertetuameng tamakut qasgim imai, tua-gguq nukalpiam qetunraa yuqercungami-gguq an'uq. Anluni yuqerrnginanermini niiskili atulriamek imumek. Kiartengluku tamana maaten-gguq piuq taum maurluum eniin

Stone-faced Girl

Justina Mike, St. Marys, March 1994

Have you heard the story about a grandmother and her grandchild who lived in a certain village? When the grandchild approached other children playing outside, they would run away frightened. Hurt and sad she asked her grandmother, "Why do the kids run away when I go join them as they play?" Then after she asked her she cried. Soon she grew to be a big girl. As she usually did, one day she went to fetch some water for her grandmother. Just as she was dipping, she looked down at the water and noticed something down there with pieces of stone on its face. She became frightened but stayed there because her bucket was still empty. Then when she looked again she noticed an image in the water that mirrored all her movements. Poor thing! Then she thought, "Perhaps that's my reflection down there. It must be my reflection." When she realized that, she said to herself, "So that's why my peers run away from me in fright whenever I approach them."

Crying, she carried the bucket of water up to their house. Sobbing loudly she said to her grandmother, "I now realize why the others are frightened of me and run away. It's because I look so hideous with stones on my face." Then the grandmother asked her to bring her *uluaq* over. She took the *uluaq* and began prying off the stones from her grandchild's face, removing each of them.

Then when the moon rose in the evening she asked her to get a bag that was hanging in the food cache. She went out to get it. When she came in her grandmother started pulling beautiful garments out of the bag. There was a pair of fancy boots and a beautifully decorated parka. She said to her, "Put these on and climb up on top of this old house and sing a song." I have forgotten the song, but she taught her the song to sing. There's a phrase in the song that says, "To the *erenret* [dawning light]"—as you know the *erenret* appears right before the sun comes up. The grandmother told her grandchild that she was going to be transformed into that dimension. She said that many people would then look at her without fright.

She went up as instructed and began singing. She sang her song. And since the residents of the *qasgiq* invariably had to relieve themselves, a *nukalpiaq* [a young man in the prime of life] came out at that moment to urinate. As he relieved himself he heard someone singing. He looked

qaingani arnaqegtaaraq pikna aturturalria. Kenegnaqapiggluni. Aturaqegciqapiggluni. Cameg-negciurcuutminek piluni ullagluku-gguq negcigsaaqluku tegungnaqluku, nurturluku-gguq. Arenqialluni-gguq nurluku. Arnaqegtaar kenegnaqapiggluni. Ava-gguq tangkurluku. Tavavet-gguq ernernun tayim pulakili. Maurluan-gguq piluku ernernun tavavet ayagciqniluku. Yugnun tangtuciqniluku-llu erenret taukut nugqataraqan im' akerta, pugqataraqan. Taumek-gguq aturluni-gguq taukunun tayima pulaluni. Neq'akucimtun ilii antaqa.

Tutgara'urluum Nat'rallran Quliraa
Cecilia Foxie, Qerrullik, May 1993

Tutgara'urluqellriik kuigem ceniini uitalriik.
Tauna-gguq tutgara'urlua tanektallrauluni
angevkenani tua-i.
Maurlurluni-gguq tua-i
waten negarcuraqan aqesgirrarnek
maligqurnauraa.
Atmacicaurtengluku-llu aqesgirrarnek makunek pitaqan.
Taugken-gguq tua utertaqamek qakinerrarnek makunek
tegumkussaarlutek uterrnaurtuk.

around and saw a beautiful girl singing on top of the grandmother's house. She was radiant. She wore exquisitely made new clothes. Quickly, he grabbed his gaff and, walking over to where she was, tried to hook her with it, but she was out of reach. To his great disappointment he couldn't reach her. She was immensely beautiful. He watched her ascend into the sky. As he gazed, she disappeared into the *erenret*. Her grandmother had told her that she would merge with the *erenret*. She told her that the people here would see her just before the sun comes up. She told her that she would go there, and she taught her a song. As she sang, she disappeared into the morning twilight. I'm telling part of the story as I remember it.

Story of the Grandchild's Old Boot Sole[1]
Cecilia Foxie, Kotlik, May 1993

A grandmother and grandson lived along a river.
Her grandson was just a young boy
not very big.
When his grandmother
went out to set snares for ptarmigans
he always went with her.
Soon he was able to pack for her when she caught ptarmigans.
When they returned home
they carried a few pieces of driftwood in their arms.

---

[1]This is an example of a different transcription style, which some Yup'ik readers find better reflects the rhythm and cadence of the oral account. At the most basic level, each line break indicates a brief pause in the speaker's delivery, whereas longer pauses are marked by a period. Each new stanza marks a complete stop in speech and the beginning of a new thought. Along with pause length, the line and verse format reflects changes in the speaker's intonation, points in the story-telling process when the listener responds with cues such as "mm-hmm," as well as other aspects of Yup'ik rhetoric. Anthony Woodbury (1984, 1987) originally applied this transcription method to Yup'ik, and his publications give a detailed explanation of the rhetorical structure of Yup'ik narrative.

Tua-i
egallilria-w' tua maurlurlua
tua-i neqkiuraqluni.
[Naken-ll' uqungqelartak.
Naken-llu makunek imanganek pilartak.
Camiutauga man'a Acukalugaam quliraa.]
Tan'gurraurluq taun' miksaaqluni anglinglliniluni tua-i.
Maurlurluni tauna ayagavkanringllinia
negarrai makut paqequrluki.
Takuiyaurrluni.
Waten-llu mertaraqluku.
Qakinernek-llu piaqluni.
Tua-i aulukluk' taun' maurluni.
[Tua-i nallunritacimtun
tua-i iqluqungatua-llu.]

Tua-ll' cat iliitni
unuakumi maurlurlua keluliulliuq
ancilliniluni urluveq tamana.
Ataam anciuq pitegcaun tamana.
"Tutgarrluk,
atam anqerluk."
Tua-ll' anllinilutek.
Pillia,
"Kitaki ikavet . . ."
Una equggaq tegungamiu pillia,
"Kitaki yuq'uli ikavet.
Ikavet kapuareskiu
Una-llu aipaa yaavet."
Tutgara'uluni wan' nangercetaa piluku-llu,
"Waten atam pitgaqina.
Ikna nall'artengnaqluku piniaran."
Anuurlua pitgartuq.
Tangvagaa tutgara'urluum.
Aqvangagu pia,
"Kitak elpet."
Wavet tua pingnaqsaaqaa,
igtaqluni.
Kiituani pingaa.
Pakiucamiu pia anuurluan,

His grandmother
would cook
and prepare food for them.
[I wonder where they got seal oil?
Where did they get the blackfish, too?
I don't know where Acukallugaq's story is from.]
After time passed the boy grew older.
Soon he would let his grandmother stay home
and checked the snares himself.
He was able to check them alone.
He fetched water for her
and gathered driftwood.
He began taking care of his grandmother.
[I'm telling the story the best way I know how.
Perhaps I'm fabricating parts of it.]

Then one day
in the morning, his grandmother reached behind her
and pulled out a bow.
She reached around again and pulled out an arrow.
"*Tutgarrluk* [Grandchild],
let's go outside."
They both went out.
She told him,
"*Kitaki* [Okay], across there . . ."
She took a piece of wood and said,
"Make a target.
Stick this piece in the ground across there
and this other one over there."
She let her grandson stand right here and said,
"Take aim and shoot the arrow like this,
Shoot and try to hit the target across there."
He watched her.
His grandmother shot the arrow.
When he retrieved the arrow she said,
"Okay, your turn to shoot."
He tried to hold the arrow,
but it fell to the ground.
He kept trying and soon was able to hold it.
As he drew the bow string his grandmother said,

"Kita'ak ikna nalkengnaqluku pitgarru."
Pitgaraa uniurrluku.
Kiituan elitengaa una pillni.
"Tua-i tutgarrluk tua-i,
tuani piuraqina."
Tua-i pirraarluk' iterluni.
Tutgara'urlua im' tayima.
Tutgara'urlua imna,
kiituani-gguq una pitegcautni kiarqurluku piyaurtuq.
Taukuk-llu yuq'ugni nall'arquranglukek.

Iterluni tua-i.
Itran tua neqliurluku.
Neru'uraũrlulria,
qavaq'aqili tua-i
iqmiaqluk' im' tua-i neqni.
Aling,
tupak'artuq cungaqerrluni.
Ak'a tua egalret cungagiaralliut.
Tutgara'urluq taun,
anngami-am tua-i pitgaquuq.
Tua-i pilnguami tua-i pillia,
"Tutgarrluk,
takuilalriaten negamegnek.
Kiani-qaa kiatemegni imkunek tumyararpagnek tanglanrituten?
Tamakut tamaani pulayararpiit,
anguq'apiar iteryaqunaki."
Inerquraa.
Tua-i niisngaluku maurluni.
[Cukaluku piciqaqa.]

Tua-i cat iliitni piuq ayagngami,
"Ciin-kiq maurluma makutgun pulayaratgun pisqessuitanga?"
Tua issratni imingluku.
Itengluni-ll' tamaavet iterluni.
Atmani tua imirluku.
Cevv'artuq-gguq maaten pulayara'arpall'er man' ak'akika.
Kanani-gguq taũgken qukaani,
penguqucugaq kan'a.
Matarrlun',

"Okay, now shoot and try to hit the target across there."
He shot the arrow and missed.
He slowly began learning the principle.
"Now, *tutgarrluk,*
you keep practicing," [she said].
Then she went back into the house.
Her grandson didn't come in for a long time.
Her grandson
would look for his arrow after he shot it sometimes.
And he began hitting his targets.

He finally came into the house.
She prepared food for him.
While he was eating
he fell asleep,
with food still in his mouth.
Aling [Oh my].
He woke up startled, chagrined because he almost overslept.
Dawn's light already filtered in through the skylight.
He went out again
and started shooting his bow and arrow.
Grandmother noticed him and said,
"*Tutgarrluk,*
you have been going out to check our snares.
Haven't you seen a trail up above our place?
Never go in
that long and deep path."
She cautioned him.
He followed his grandmother's advice.
[I'm telling you the shorter version of the story.]

One day as he was checking the snares he said to himself,
"I wonder why grandmother told me not to go in this path?"
He began to fill up his bag with ptarmigan.
As he continued along he began to enter the path.
He had filled up his pack.
As he walked he merged onto a long wide path.
He looked and noticed a little mound
in the middle of an open area.
Becoming curious about the knoll,

paqnakngamiu tauna,
atmani yuuluki
tauna-llu pitegcautni naparrluki
atrarluni.
Tekitaa-gguq maaten neng'ulliniluni.
Uivurqiliu-gguq.
Uivuraraa-gguq maaten amingqelliniluni.
Tuaggun tua itliniluni.
Pug'uq-gguq maaten
nukalpialler kiugna palurngal'
amini taũgaam uavet tangvagluku.
Ngeñgaarlun' aqumlliniluni.
Mayurngami tua-i taum' amiigem caniqerranun
aqumqalliniluni.
Eniin ilua man'a cataunani.
Kiugna-wa-gguq quliini,
cauyaq kiugna.
Cauyacuar.

Tua-ll' ngeñgaarlun' taun' makcami cauyani tegua.
Nuagtaallia qeciraqluku.
Mumni-ll' tauna nuagtaarluku.
Aqumenqegcarluni kia aturtuq,

> *Qa-kem-yuu-raa-nga.*
> *Qa-kem-yuu-raa-nga.*
> *A-lla-ne-qa pa-yu-gey-gu.*
> *A-yaa-yaa-quu-rra-yaa.*

> *Qa-kem-yuu-raa-nga.*
> *Qa-kem-yuu-raa-nga.*
> *A-lla-ne-qa pa-yu-gey-gu.*
> *A-yaa-yaa-quu-rra-yaa.*

Taqngami kaputellia tuavet cauyani.
Tua-i palurrluni palurtuq kiugna.
Tayim imna.
Tua-m' ngeñgaartuq.
Aqumuq.
"Qakumi-llu tanem imna piqatarta."

he removed
his backpack,
placed his bow and arrows beside it
and began walking down.
The knoll, he discovered, was a house.
Then he slowly walked all the way around it.
As he circled around he saw an entryway.
Then he began crawling through the doorway.
When he emerged up through the floor hole
he found a hideous looking *nukalpiaq* lying on his belly
looking right at him.
He grunted and sat up.
After coming up the floor hole he moved to the side
and sat down.
The inside of the house was bare.
On the back wall, above the man,
hung a drum.
It was a small drum.

When the man sat up he grunted and took his drum.
He spat on the drum head and rubbed it.
He also moistened his drumstick.
After securing his seat he began to sing,

> *He has called me from inside.*
> *He has called me from inside.*
> *Bring food for my guest.*
> *A-yaa-yaa-quu-rra-yaa.*

> *He has called me from inside.*
> *He has called me from inside.*
> *Bring food for my guest.*
> *A-yaa-yaa-quu-rra-yaa.*

He stopped and shoved the drum handle into the floor.
Then he rolled back on his belly.
Everything was quiet for a moment.
He grunted again.
He sat down.
"Heck, when is she going to respond!"

Tua-m' cauyani tegungamiu nuagtaa.
Tua-m' aturtuq,

> *Qa-kem-yuu-raa-nga.*
> *Qa-kem-yuu-raa-nga.*
> *A-lla-ne-qa pa-yu-gey-gu.*
> *A-yaa-yaa-quu-rra-yaa.*

> *Qa-kem-yuu-raa-nga.*
> *Qa-kem-yuu-raa-nga.*
> *A-lla-ne-qa pa-yu-gey-gu.*
> *A-yaa-yaa-quu-rra-yaa.*

Tua-m' taqngami cauyani kaputellia.
Ataam palurrluni.
Uitaqanrakun yugtanguq cakemna.
Pugyarturtuq negiliq kan'a.
Arnaulliniluni.
Tumnaq-gga qantaq tegumiara.
Tua-llu ciutminek niituq tutgarrluk,
"Qantaq tauna akurturyuguaqerluku pilgutacirpetun
anqerreskina."
Tungminun cautaa mikelngurmek imarluni.
Aqsiik ullingqalutek.
Tuluryagglainarnek kegguterluni. [*Temciyukartuq*]

Yagucaku akurturuarluku amigmun qecelliniluni.
Anqercami kingutmun.
Eglerquraqerlun yiirtuq pamna,
"Yii-i-i-i.
Usvitutaaqtallraa.
Unguvarpeni tuani taqciqamken pii."
Kingyaartuq
kenerpall'er tamana.
Tekicamiki imkut atmani atemkallii.
Pitegcautni-llu teguqerluk' aq'velliniluni.
Kingyartuq anguniarallia tamaa-i pulayarat iluatni.
Aqesgimek ataucimek igcilliniluni.
Tautnaurturlun' tua-i
kiituani nem'ek tungiignun ayanguq

He took his drum and moistened it again.
He sang again,

> *He has called me from inside.*
> *He has called me from inside.*
> *Bring food for my guest.*
> *A-yaa-yaa-quu-rra-yaa.*
>
> *He has called me from inside.*
> *He has called me from inside.*
> *Bring food for my guest.*
> *A-yaa-yaa-quu-rra-yaa.*

Then he thrust his drum into the ground again
and rolled back on his belly.
After a moment they heard someone entering.
A parka ruff emerged up through the entrance hole.
It was a woman.
She held a wooden bowl.
Immediately the grandson heard a voice inside his ears,
"When she begins to give you the bowl
jump up and leave at once."
When she turned around he saw a baby in the dish.
The baby's stomach was slashed open.
It had only canine teeth. [*Chuckle*]

As she handed him the bowl he leapt towards the doorway.
Once outside he began running home.
After he ran a while he heard someone behind yelling,
"Yii-i-i-i-i.
You try to behave shrewdly and outsmart me.
I'll never stop badgering you as long as you live."
He swung his head back
and saw a huge ball of fire coming.
When he came to his backpack he swung it onto his back
and grabbed his bow and arrow and ran on.
He looked back and saw that it was gaining on him
so he dropped one ptarmigan on the pathway.
He continued doing that along the way
and began heading

tuatnaurlun'.
Waniwa-ll' nangneq ellirluni,
tamaa-i-am agiituq.
Ataam egvikaa.
Tua atmairulluni.
Tua-ll' aqvaqurlun' ayagtuq.
Kingyartur-am ak'a-m' tua-i im' agiirtellria.
Utaqallia pakiulluku.
Maaten-gguq kenrem taum iluani tangertuq
tunguuralriartangqelliniluni.
Tauna tua piyuciaraulluku
waniwa tekitniaraan pitpallia.
Nipqerreskili-gguq im' keneq.
Atakulliniluni.
Ullagluku maaten pillia
mikelnguum tauna nat'rallruaraa qukarturluk' tua-i
pitgallia.

Tua-i ak'a yurarngan tutgarrluk
maurluan pillia,
"Qanrut'laryaaqamken-ggem.
Mikelnguullerpeni tauna nat'rallruaraqan."
Iquklituq. [*temciyukartuq*]

Ellam Irniara
Mary Mike, May 1993

Tua-i-wa atsiyarluteng tamakut, tua-i-w' atsiyalrianun maligullua. Taukut angyapigmek angyalget maligteqatarluki wangkuk anglicarteka-llu. Yugyagluteng arnat.

Nasaurlullraulua, aunraryugnaunii-llu. Tua-i-llu ayagluta. Tamana Qip'ngayagmek pitularaat camani. Qip'ngayagmiullret nunat wani akuliitni kuik kelutmun nunapigmun pulamaluni. Tamaaggun cav'urluteng ayagluteng, cav'urluteng-w' ayaglaameng. Cav'uranritaqameng-llu ukamarluteng ilu'uvkaamek piluku angyaq atsiyat tamakut ayagaqluteng. Ayak'aqustengqerrluni yaaggun ciumikun kingumikun-llu caqiagaqan. Ukamalriik paūgkuk malruulaamek.

towards their house.
Soon there was only one ptarmigan left
while it continued to pursue him.
He threw the last ptarmigan.
With his backpack empty
he continued running.
He looked back again and saw that it still came,
so he stopped, loaded his bow, aimed and waited.
As he aimed at the fireball, he saw in the center
a small black hole.
He aimed at that spot
and as it grew near he released his arrow.
The flame immediately went out.
By then the sun had already set.
When he examined the path of the fire
he saw that his arrow had pierced
a child's old boot sole.

When the grandson entered his house
she said,
"I kept telling you again and again.
That was your old boot sole when you were little."
End of story. [*chuckle*]

Child of Ella

Mary Mike, May 1993

People were out harvesting salmonberries, and I went with a group to gather some. My stepmother and I went out with these people that had an *angyapik* [lit., "real skin boat"]. There were many women traveling together in the boat.

I was still a young girl, long before I had my first menstruation. We left. They call the river down there Qip'ngayak [Black River]. It was a river going up through the tundra starting from the middle of the old Qip'ngayagmiut site. They rowed up that river, their usual way of getting to places. And sometimes they tied a rope to the boat and pulled it forward from the shore. One person would be in front and another at the back to guide the boat. There would be two people on shore pulling the boat.

Tua-i atsiyarluta. Taukut-llu Nunallerpagmiunek, Qulirat-gguq nunakaat taun' Nunallerpak Qip'ngayagaam iluani, kiturluku kiatmun. Avtellragnun-am, Qip'ngayagaq maani, man'a-w', man'a-am cali allamek atengqertuq, tuavet arulairluteng. Atsat-gguq nautukiitnun. Pelatekiurluteng arnat tua-i. Kuuliarkanek-ll' imkunek ciamruulkunek ayaulluteng, kelleqluteng pilaameng. Equgtaitelartuq tamatum atsiyarviit tungiit.

Unuaquan-ll' tuan pilliukut, tuani-w' tekiyutemteñi ayagyaaqellriit qaill' pia. Unuaquan-ll' ikik pilliukut. Tua-i iqvaryarluta tagluta. Angli-ll' tagnarqenrilami, pelatekarput tua-i wani yaaqsigpek'naku kana-i iqvarluteng ukut. Wiinga-llu-w' tua-i iqvaqlua. Canek kangiralegnek, kangiralget nurnaitellratni atmagluteng pilaameng naivuurluk'muirqan atmagaqluku.

Tua-ll'-am tua-i iqvalnguqercama-am, taukuk arnak piagka, anaanairutka, anglicarteka, ilaput-llu-w' ava-i yaatiigni iqvarluteng, avatemteñi. Tamaani-am tua-i nunapigmi wangkun, aqumlua-llu nunapik taman' naanguaqluku. Cali-ll' taklayungaqama taklarrlua piaqlua. Calnguama, mernuilliama-w' pilrianga, nangerrlua ayakacilua maaggun ururrlugmek tekiskilii. Uruarauluni. Nunapiim ilii marami uruaraulartuq atsat-ll' nauluku. Arumayunqeggluteng tamakut urumi naumalriit atsat. Tamaani-am tua-i urukun tuaggun pekcama piqertua maaten, ingna-kiq cauga? Qaterluni ingna ullagpailemni mecikvailemku. Maaten ullagluku piaqa wangni una uuteki'inraq peksuq. Uuteki'inrartun tua-i angtaluni. Ecuirpak tanqigpak. Kan'a-ll' im' kavirliq esiq, tua-i-w' waniw' tuar tungaunaku tuar tangvakeka ugaan ecuitem man'a qeltii.

Tegulerluku-am tua-i peksucuklua, makunun yaqulegnun uutekanun-llu peksuksukluku. Agqerruskilaku taukugnun. Tekicamkek tua-i tuqluralukek manikilaku peksutnilua. Atakiirakili, "Ataki. Calinrauga?" Ullaucamku tua-i waten tumemnun piluku. Ukuk tuaten irr'iqaqilik imkulutek ciin-ggur-una atsam nalliini, tukellriit-wa tamakut yaqulkussiit irniarit. Una-gguq ciin waten ecuunani, kukumyarinrauyuk'ngermegen'gu-llu mikenruniluku kukumyarinrarmi. Cali anagulluni ecuunani caarrluunani man'a qainga.

We began our berry-picking journey. And the old site of Nunallerpagmiut, they say, the old site of Nunallerpak on the Qip'ngayak river, was where the Qulirat [the Ancients] had once lived. We went past that old site. At the place where they divided, Qip'ngayak was here and the other river here [*gesturing*]. The other river has a name, too. They stopped at that place. They say it was a place where salmonberries [actually cloudberries] grew in abundance. The women began putting up the tent. They had brought some wood pieces for tent stakes as they were accustomed to bringing whatever they would need out there. The area where they went to harvest salmonberries usually didn't have any trees.

Perhaps we began picking the next day, or maybe the first day we arrived. I don't remember. Perhaps we went out the next day. We went back to pick berries. Since the berries grew fairly close to the river, they began picking not far from the tent. I was picking also. They used five-gallon metal cans for picking berries, and when they were full they packed them on their backs.

When I got tired of picking, I looked and saw my late aunt and my stepmother picking over here, and the others were picking beyond them. I began playing on the tundra, and I sat and looked at the foliage, entertaining myself. And whenever I felt like it I would lie down on it. After awhile, perhaps it was when I felt rested, I stood up and walked and came upon a mossy area. It was all moss. On the tundra, down in the flat lands, some of the land is usually moss, and salmonberries grow on it. The berries on the moss are always ripe. As I was walking on the moss, I noticed something up ahead. Before I got close enough to see well, it looked white to me, and I wondered what it was. Then I approached and found what appeared to be the egg of a mallard. It was as big as a mallard egg. It was quite transparent and very bright. The shell was so transparent it was as if I were looking straight through to the red yolk inside.

I quickly picked it up, thinking I had found an egg, assuming it belonged to one of the ducks flying around there, and excitedly ran over to those two. When I reached them I addressed them and held out my hand and told them that I had found an egg. Curious, my aunt said, "Let me see. What kind of bird egg is it?" The egg was in my outstretched hand. Then they were both astonished and asked why such an egg would appear during the salmonberry season. Many kinds of birds' eggs had already hatched. Although they thought it might be a common

Kitek-gguq maurlumnun nasvakarlaku. Aglua tua-i tangercecamku naken pillrullranek aplua. Apqaqlua-am tua-i naken pillrullranek. Yaaken tua-i uruaraam qainganek piniluki, imum menuitqapigtellriim uruaraam qainganek. Tailuni. Tauna-ll'-am tumekluku arnarkaūrluullgutni taumek tua-i tangercelluku. Ak'a taum arnarkaūrluunran pikiliu, Ellam-gguq una irniara. Igtaqngataa-gguq. Ellam-gguq irniaqngataa. Naken-llu-gguq pisia? Unglunek-llu piyukluku. Yaaken tua-i piniamku tailuteng. Tuavet ururrlugmun tailuteng. Tuaken tua-i nallunailan tangerrluku. Aren-gguq peksutenritua-gguq. Ellam-gguq igtaqngataa. Irniaqngataa-gguq. Tuavet nunakngalkiinun elliqaasqelluku. Wiinga-m' alingallaglua elliluku tua-i. Ellam irniara iillakluku igtellra, iciw' alingallaglua. Yuunrilngurnek cunaw' Ella irniangqerrlartuq. Umyuaqa-w' picimtun qanengssagluni.

Tua-i-ll' pianga taum, kitek-gguq waten iqelqugka nuagglukek qulmun elucira'arlakek. Aa, wiinga-m' qessalua alingallavsiarlua tua-i pingaitniluku, pisqengraanga-ll' anaanaūrlurma. Mayurciquq-gguq atam. Tauna mayunrilngermi-gguq atam eluciraram mayurrniaraa. Pingaitnilua-am alingama. Alingalliima tua-i Ellamun igtaqniluku, irniaqniluku piagnek. Pingaitelliniamku-am tua-i elliin taum arnarkaūrluum, elucilirluku ellian elliurluni. Uterrluta-llu.

Aren tua-i tayim nalluyagulluk' wii. Pelatekamtenun atraamta uitaluta. Tua-i uitavkenateng ukut arnat neq'liungnaqluteng tuaten. Kuvyamek-ll'-am kanavet, civciluteng qaurtuyagalillinian tauna kuicualler.

Qaillun-kiq pia Ella? Cellalliryullminek-wa cellalluirutlilria. Tamakucimek tang kinguakun tuaten ecuitetalriamek, menuitetalriamek tangerqaqsailngua. Peksutengssaglaryaaqua peksussalgullemni camani Black River-ami. Uutekaat, allgiarinraat-llu, kukumyaraat-llu piit wani ecuitlaryaaqut, taūgaam tuaten ayuqsuitut. Kan'a-ll' imaat im' kavirliq tangerrnaqsuitlartuq.

scoter egg, they said it was smaller, and they asked why such an egg would be transparent. It was absolutely transparent and unusually clean.

Then they told me to show it to my grandmother. When I brought it over, she asked me where I found it. I told her that I found it on the mossy ground and that it was on clean, undisturbed moss. She went over there. First she walked over to the other old woman to show it to her. The other old woman immediately said it was the child of *Ella*. She said it had probably been dropped. She said it was probably the child of *Ella*. She asked me where I had gotten it. And she wanted to know if it was in a nest. I pointed to the place where I had found it, and we all walked over. We came to that mossy ground. It was easy to see from where we were standing. Then I was told that I hadn't actually found an egg. She said *Ella* probably had dropped it. She said it may be its child. She told me to put it back where I had found it. I quickly put it there, because the idea that *Ella*'s child had fallen on the moss was awesome to me, and I became frightened. So I thought that *Ella* must have children that aren't actually people. Different thoughts were going through my mind.

Then she asked me to wet the tips of my little fingers [pinkies] and make sweeping movements up towards the sky. Gosh, I didn't want to, for I had gotten more frightened. I refused even though my poor old aunt encouraged me to do it. She said it would go up. She said if I did the hand motions it would go up, even though the naked eye would not see it actually happen. I told them I wasn't going to do it because I was scared. Since they said it was the child of *Ella* that had fallen, I had become scared. Once the egg was put back, the old woman, who was my late cousin's grandmother, made sweeping motions with her hands up toward the sky because I had refused to comply. Then we went home.

I soon forgot about it. We remained in our tent when we went down. The women were trying to catch some fish, too. They set a fish net since apparently there were a lot of little white fish in that slough.

I wonder what happened to *Ella* at that time? Perhaps it wanted to rain but decided against it. After that I didn't see a clean and transparent egg again. I used to go egg hunting down at Black River when I was still able to. The mallards and oldsquaw ducks eggs are opaque, and also those of the common scoter, but they aren't like the one I found. And the egg yolk cannot be seen through the shell in any of them.

Cellarrlituuq-gguq anuqliraluni. Cellarrlirturluni. Tua-i-gguq qialuni
Ella irniaminek igciaqami ellalluk aluvikluku. Anuqlirturluni. Tuaten-am
ayuqekutlalliniat.

Tuani-w' taukuk arnassaagaak qanaalutek tamatumek.
Mayureskan-gguq atam ellakeggirniartuq qianriqan. Aren,
piciunricaaqellria-w'. Tengssurviit-ll' pakmavet mayutuluteng,
irniangqellra nalluluku. [*Ngel'artuq*]

Ellalluk aluviklaraa-gguq, iciw' irniaminek igciaqami. Qaillun-w' pia,
cali-ll' pillrullian, peksutellrulliata tuaten qanelria taun' arnangiar.
Iqelqugni tua-i nuagglukek, tuar tang waten elucira'aralria qulmun.
Qavcirqunek-wa pia murilkenaurpakaryuilama. Qanruqu'urluku tauna,
kan'a-w' tua-i mayurrnguallni pillikii, aaniinun mayurteqatarniluku.
Canek-ll' allanek ilaluku. Aanii-llu-w' pillikii tua-i waniw' tuneniluku
ataam irniara igcillra.

Quinagnam-wa nuvevailganga tamaani agleryaurpailegma-ll' tauna
tuan' tekiartellrukeka. Quinagnamek assiilngurmek aturpailegma.
[*ngel'artuq*]

Aa-gguq. Tuaten-gguq pituuq. Tanqikekminun-wa tua-i ili waten
pivkarlartuq alairvikluku. Tua-i-w' tangerrluku tayim elliin
quinakenrilkeminun.

[When it fell] they say the weather would become bad and get windy. The weather would stay bad for a long time. They say that *Ella* would be weeping since it had dropped its child. The rain was its tears. It would stay windy for a long time. That was what they would say.

At that time the old women were talking about that. They said that it would stop crying when the child was sent back up again, and the weather would be good again. *Aren* [expression], it's not actually the truth, though. Big airplanes do rise up into the sky, not knowing that *Ella* has children there. [*Chuckle*]

Whenever its child falls, *Ella*'s tears come down in the form of rain. I can't really say, but perhaps the old woman was saying that because before the above incident occurred, someone else had found an egg like that. She wet her little fingers with her saliva, it seemed like she motioned up towards the sky. I don't remember how many times she did that because I didn't pay close attention then. She was talking to the one down there on the moss, the one she was sending up. She said she was sending it back to its mother. She was saying other things as well. Perhaps she was talking to its mother, saying that she was sending back the child of hers that had fallen.

I came upon [the egg] before knowledge of worldy things had permeated me and before I had started menstruating. It was before I had attained any carnal knowledge. [*chuckle*]

That's how *Ella* behaved. It could reveal itself to those who were pure. It could detect a person who was worthy and bright.

10. Kusquqvagmiut Qanemciit Qulirait-llu, Kusquqvagmiut-llu Kegginaqut

Ircenrraq Quliraq
Nickolai Berlin, Nunapicuaq, January 1994

Ikna qagatem ceñai, Iinrayaam qagatii ikna, ircenrraat ika-i. Ikegkut-llu, cali ikna qemirpall'er ceñaqvani—cameg-ima-tam' pilaqiit? [Cikiyakinraq]—tauna cali ircenrrauguq ika-i. Qainga pakemna kangra nanvarra'artangqertuq. Nanvarra'artangqerrnilaraat, egalrat-gguq tua-i.

Cupluralria-gguq tauna nukalpiaruuq, nangerrlun' tua-i aanaluni-llu. Tua-i pissuryaurrlun' ayagayaurrluni. Luumarvigmiunguluni. Ukaqvani-gguq tauna pillruuq ak'allauvkenani. Ukaqvallauluni, taũgaam ciuqvaaraulun' tua-i nallumteni tayima.

Cupluralria, tua-i-gguq menuunani, caluni ellminek kencikluni. Angalkuuvkenani-ll' tua-i cauvkenani, taũgaam maligtaqulluni qanruyutminun tamalkuitnun, maligtaqutengnaqluni yuuluni. Tua-i-llu-gguq ircenrraat agaani ayagayaurcami tua-i tangaagaqluki. Ircen'errnek tangaagaqluni tua-i maa-i tua-i. Taũgaam mallguuqsaunaki.

Tua-i-llu-gguq allamek-am maligluni-am qagatem ceñiikun ceñirrlutek anguarturlutek pillermegni yaqulegcurlutek, ircenrraat makut paircarturakek upalriit—calriit angualriit. Uivellilriit-wa qagatekun angyakun. Paũgkuk-wa-gguq neviarcak merkun maaggun, nunam ngeliikun, mer'em qaingakun piyuaguralriik. Umcigimalutek naquggluarlutek nacarrluteqlutek-llu. Arillugnek-llu—arillugnek pilaqait aũgkut mecungniurcuutek'lalput avani, makut dog salmon amiit. Amiitnek tamakut ulap'angqellruukut imumi. Wiinga-ll' angullruanka. Wiinga-ll' aturaqluki.

Kuskokwim Stories, Kuskokwim Masks

Ircenrraq Story
Nickolai Berlin, Nunapichuk, January 1994

At the *qagan* [lake from which a river flows] of the Iinrayaq River live *ircenrraat*. And at that broad-ridged hill located close to the [Kuskokwim River]—what was its name? [Cikiyakinraq]—it is also populated by *ircenrraat*. There is a little lake up on top of it. They say that little lake serves as their window.

They say Cupluralria was a *nukalpiaq*, having grown to be a hunter living with his family. He was already a skilled hunter. He lived in Luumarvik. They say he lived during relatively recent times, but this occurred before I was born.

Cupluralria was well-groomed and had good self-esteem, and he was a decent and honorable man. He was not an *angalkuq*, but he lived according to the traditional teachings of the ancients. He was a law-abiding citizen. When he started to hunt, he would see the *ircenrraat* across there. He saw them frequently nearby as they moved around going about their business. However, he didn't try get close to them.

One time when he and another person were paddling along the shore of the *qagan* hunting birds, they saw a group of *ircenrraat* coming up ahead. They were moving, going around the lake in a boat. Up on the lake shore there were two girls walking along on the water. They were fully clothed with hoods pulled over their heads and belts around their waists. They wore fishskin mittens—*arilluut* were waterproof garments we used to wear made out of dog salmon skins. We used those fishskins instead of rubber for our waterproof boots. They were in use when I was born, and I used to wear them, too.

A. H. Twitchell-aam qugyuguaq pillra Napaskiarnek 1900-aam nalliini. Twitchell-aaq-llu igamini qanlliniluni uum-gguq qugyuguam ungularai cetuat pissulrianun up'nerkami. Qugyuguam-llu-gguq aipaan pillran [wani tarenrami cataunani] cetuat ungularai pissulrianun uksumi.

One of two swan masks A. H. Twitchell collected at Napaskiak in the early 1900s. Twitchell wrote that the mask represents a swan that drives white whales to hunters in the spring, while its partner drove whales to hunters in the winter.

Tamakunek-ll' aturlutek, arilluarlutek amiragtuumalutek-llu tamakunek naquggluarlutek-llu. Nacarrlugteqluteqlutek-llu. Maaggun ngeliikun nunam merkun piyuaguralriik. Unkut-wa-gguq angualriit unani angyakun ircenrraat.

Tua-llu-gguq Cupluralriim tauna aipani keluminun pivkarluku ceñamun culu'urrlutek. Tua-i maa-i teguarkauluku. Maa-i tua-i maaggun piarkaulutek. Cupluralriim-gguq pia, "Mat'um tang aipaa naspaaqerlaku teguyugngakumku, tegukumku nuliqniarqa; tangaavkarpakalartut." Tua-i-llu-gguq keluqliqluku waten culu'urrlutek, Cupluralria-ll' kelliuluni utaqalukek. Maa-i tua-i piyuagurlutek tass'uqu'urlutek. Tua-i-gguq tamaa-i aglenrraraungamek nunakuarlutek. Nunakuartellukek. Unkut anguarluteng unaggun ilakek.

•

Tua-i-llu-gguq waniw' tua-i tekillukek, maa-i tua-i tekiteqatarlukek tauna aipaa irr'illermini—nutaan-llu tangrrami pillilria—irirtellni nallulliniluku. Ir'iqercan—[ngelaq'ertuq] kall'allagluni taman' assigtaak, agtuusngallrak man'a. Kall'alliin-gguq arulairtuk. Arulairrlutek-gguq qanqertuk, "Kaaka. Niuget." Kelutmun-llu-gguq tua-i caqiqaniqerlutek. Aren tua-i yagtengraani tua-i nurturlukek. Tua-i kiturlutek. Tauna tua-i aipaa naspaayugyaaqluk' teguyugyaaqluk' tangaavkarpakalaata nulirqenaluku. Nulirtuqsaunani-gguq tamaani. Tua-i-gguq tangaagaqlun' tamaa-i tua-i. Tua-i taun' pelluglun' tuani.

Tua-i-ll'-am qagatem ceñiini kiirrarmi waten pillermini pilliniuq qagatem tua-i ag' akia ikingqaluni. Agaa-i-gguq nunat tua-i nunarrluut, ircenrraat nuniit. Keluat-gguq tua-i tuar-gguq taicilria canek irnerrlugnek iniaritnek. Tua-i-llu-gguq piqerluteng akma tua-i quaquarluteng quugaarpak pugniluku. Tua-i-gguq una-i atraqraluteng qayatgun maliqluteng. Malirqelluteng tua-i una-i narulkaquluku. Narulkaquyaaqluku-gguq un'a cayagaq. Kanaqlayagartun-gguq un'a angtaluni qak'arrnaurtuq quugaarpak.

They both wore garments out of fishskin. They were wearing fishskin mittens and fishskin boots and belts around their waists. Their hoods were pulled over their heads, too. They were walking on the water along the lake shore. Down from them were the *ircenrraat* paddling along in a boat.

Then Cupluralria and his companion landed their kayaks along the shore. They were close enough so they would be able to grab one of them. They were coming right up to them. Then Cupluralria said, "I'll see if I can take one of the girls, and if I can, I'll marry her; they've allowed me to see them for many, many times." They came up on shore, and with their kayaks next to each other and Cupluralria closer to the water, they waited for them as they approached. The girls were walking, holding hands. They were walking on shoreland for they were girls referred to as *aglenrraraak* [two who have reached puberty]. The others had made them travel on land. Their families were traveling in the boat down from them.

As they got closer to them, Cupuralria's companion looked with fascination—perhaps he saw *ircenrraat* for the first time—and as he watched them, he didn't realize that his whole body had tilted to the side. When his kayak suddenly tipped to one side [*chuckle*] their kayaks banged against each other loudly. At the sound, the two girls halted and said, "Listen. Listen to the sounds of the *niuget* [dead]." Then they moved further to the side, away from them. Cupluralria reached out an arm to try to grab one, but the girls were both out of reach as they passed by. He was going to see if he could take one of them for a wife since they always had allowed him to see them. At that time he was still single. He would always see them out there. Then that incident passed.

Another time when [Cupluralria] was alone hunting along the lakeshore, he looked and saw the other side of the lake and there was Nunarrluut across there. It was an *ircenrraat* village. Behind the village there was a legion of translucent seal guts hanging like fog. Then suddenly he heard people in the village yelling, "*Quaq, quaq, quaq.*" It was a signal they gave when a *quugaarpak* [legendary creature said to live underground] began surfacing in the water. He watched them quickly launch their kayaks and begin to hunt for it. They threw their harpoons at it while hunting. They were attempting to harpoon some little thing down there that appeared to be as big as a muskrat as it surfaced and dove back in the water, that *quugaarpak*.

Elliin-gguq tua-i Cupluralriim qayani tag'arrluku-w' tua-i iiqerluk' tangvaurluki palurngaluni. Tangvaurluki tua-i una-i. Qalarrluteng-gguq, "Aling aren. Amci at' tua-i, caskuyangnaqiciu ata. Nayukatallngiim Atiin-am tua-i atraquni una-i tua-i, maa-i tua-i pitaqerkaugaa. Ciullengnaqeqerciu." Narulkaqungermegteggu nall'arteksaunaku. Tua-i-llu-gguq piqerluni ikna, agna, yug-agna tanqigcetqapiarlun tua-i ika-i, tanqigcetqapiarlun' tua-i, qayamek atrarciluni. Maaten-llu-gguq pia qayaan-ll' enri alaunateng amirtuumangraan. Qantaa-llu-gguq wani qayaan iluani alaunani. Tua-i-llu-gguq atraami narulkaamiu egmian nall'arrluku. Tamakut tua-i ilain nutaan narulkaqungarrluku nall'arqaq'ngarrluku. Tagutenga'arcatgu tua-i ukatmurucatgu, yaani pisqelluku taum piluki, pilaasqelluki. Qayani tua-i tagkanirluku yaatiitnek tua-i palu'urrluni tangvauralliniluki pilallratni.

Tagtaat-gguq tua-i taunarpall'er-gguq tua-i angluni. Ang'urluni imna kanaqlayagartun angtangatelleq. Pilagluku-gguq tua-i avenqegquraraat-gguq tua-i tauna-llu pitaqestii amllenruvkenani. Amllertatkurluteng tua-i pikaugurluku avenqegquraraat tamarmeng tua-i. Tua-i-llu-gguq qaqiucameng ayagluteng tua-i ikavet tua-i kingunermeggnun uterqaqluteng. Tauna-gguq Nayukatallngiim Atii, pavani tua-i ilani ayangraata tarrilluni caksuggnguarturluni. Kiituani-gguq kiimellirtuq. Tangvaurluku tua-i. Kiimi-gguq elliami ukatmun takuyartuq. Takuyarluku ullagluku tuaten pia, "Aling. Nalluyuklukuten-w'-am tua-i iirumayaaqellriaten wangnun. Nallunrilkemken tua-i. Tuanlucin atrarpailegma-ll' nallunrillrukeka. Nallunrillrukeka wanlucin. Kitek nernaurtukuk." Qantani piluku qayaminek. Akutamek-gguq imarlun' qantaa. Elliin-llu-gguq qantaa, taquiquratuani taum' aanami, qantaa akutamek imarluni. "Kitak nernaurtukuk qantan piluku. Nerellgutekqernaurtukuk tua-i." Caugarullutek nerciqiarlutek. Qantatek tua-i waten piqerluk.

Taum-gguq ircen'ertaan tangertaarturagak kankuk qantak. Tangertaarturarraarlukek-gguq pia, "Aren, tauna tang tua-i akutan wiinga neresciigalkeka nerngailkeka. Nualilria tang. Nualirtuq. Qantarpet imirtek'lallra qanruskiu, pikiu, alerquqiu uum kinguani tamualuki tunut itumtesqevkenaki." Tamaani-gguq tamualuki itumlluki egcetaaqata'arqamegteki pitullruut caskunek pingqenritlermeggni. "Atam tangvakarru qantarpet taun imaa akutan." Tua-i-llu-gguq teguarrlun' qukaanek nalugluku. Akutaq-gguq taun nengluni tua-i agarcan-llu-gguq peg'arcani ayuqucimitun mec'arpak qantaanun ek'arrluni. Tua-i

Hidden from the shore with his kayak drawn up, Cupluralria watched them. He just sat there and watched them. Then one of them said, "*Aling aren!* [expression] Come on, would one of you strike it with your weapon? Nayukatallngiiq's father will certainly get it when he comes down. Would one of you get it before he does?" One of the men threw his harpoon at it but missed. As Cupluralria watched, he saw a very shiny person coming down from the village. He was very bright. As he brought his kayak down, its frame was visible behind the skin covering. Cupluralria could see a wooden bowl inside the kayak. As soon as he came down, he harpooned the animal and killed it instantly. As the men pulled the animal toward land, the bright one pointed to the other side of the lake where Cupluralria was hidden and told them to skin and cut up the animal there. Then Cupluralria pulled his kayak further back, went down on his belly and watched as the men worked on the animal.

As they hauled up their catch from the lake, he noticed that it was actually a huge animal. The animal that appeared to be as big as a muskrat was quite large. They began cutting it up and divided it evenly among themselves. The one who caught it got the same amount as the others. When they were done, they started to go back across to the village. As everyone left, Nayukatallngiiq's father stayed behind, walking around back there doing something. Soon he was the only one left there. Cupluralria kept watching him. When everyone had gone, the bright one turned toward him. He walked forward and said, "*Aling.* You probably hid yourself there thinking that I didn't know about it. I knew you were here. I knew you were here before I left the village. Now first, let's eat." He got the bowl from his kayak. The bowl was full of *akutaq*. Cupluralria's own bowl was also filled with *akutaq*, for his mother always filled it before he went out to hunt. "Get your bowl and we'll eat. Let's finally eat together." They sat down facing each other ready to eat, placing their bowls between them.

The *ircenrraq* sat for a moment and viewed the contents of the bowls. After he examined them he said, "Oh no! I can't eat the *akutaq* in your bowl. I won't eat it. You see, it has too much saliva in it. It has too much saliva. Tell the maker of your *akutaq* never to chew the caribou fat when she makes it." They say back in those days when they didn't have the appropriate tool, they would chew the fat to melt it. "Look what happens to the *akutaq* in your bowl." Then he lifted a piece from the middle of it. The *akutaq* stretched as he lifted it, and when he let go it slapped back into the bowl. He said he wouldn't eat it because it had too

nualirniluku nerngaitniluku. Qantaminek tua-i tuaken nerluni nutaan. Nerlutek tuaken qantaanek.

Nererraarlutek-llu-gguq tua-i uqurrarmek cikirluku, taum avganek pimi. Avganek cikirluku, taumek tua-i pisqelluku. Uterrlutek-llu tua-i avvullutek. Aren tauna-gguq tang ikarpaurtellria tua- i, cikiutii anglirillinilria qayaan iluani.

Tua-i-am tuaten tua-i tayima tua-i. Tua-i tangaagaqluni ircen'ernek yuilqumi, agaaken Luumarvigmek ikaken ayagaqami. Taum Luumarvigmiut ciuliaqellikai.

Allanek Nunanek Kelgiluteng Kalukalallrat Akulmi
Nickolai Berlin, Nunapicuaq, January 1994

Kiarte'urluq-wa tuaten tauҧaam tua-i kalukpagalallrulria. Qauҧna-ll' amirkanek tus'arrluku teveqvik'lallrukii qasgim egkua. Kan'a Anguyaluk' imna arnaq, tauna yuraqata'arqan, nangertaqan nutegnek-llu akiqliqellriignek ayakatarautengqerraqluni. Tua-i-w' picuami pillilria.

Unaken [amirkanek] kipuqluni, pikaminek kipuqluni allamiaqan. Allamiaqan amirkar-tamaavet tevtaqluk' tauna yura'arqan. Lumarrat tuaten saggluki.

Tauna yuarun kiingan elicungcarluk' elpet. Tua-i allam-llu cali yuarun alla cali elicungcarluku cali. Angutem yuaruciaqestiin yagirayarai elitnaurulluki taumun. Tua-i ellilluk' egmian. Eliteng'ermeng tua-i atakuaqan yuraraqluteng tamaaken Maatessaam ayagnillranek ayagluteng. Tamarmeng makut Paingarmiut, Nanvarrlagmiut, Nunacuarmiut-llu tuatnaluteng tamarmeng tua-i tamaaken elitnaurluteng.

Tua-i-ll' kelegyungami iliit, Nunacuarmiut-llu kelgameng ukut Nunapicuarmiut, Paingarmiut, Nanvarnarrlagmiut-llu tamalkuita kelegluki, neqkanek upqaarluteng neqkaitnek. Tua-i allaneqluki qimugtait tuaten nerqelluki. Tua-i allaneqluki. Arnartuumarmeng-llu pilriit arnalgirluteng pilriit—segganqellriit arnartuumarmeng pilartut, ak'allaurtenrilnguut. Tua-i tuani qasgimi unugpak yurarluteng.

much saliva. He told Cupluralria to tell his mother not to melt tallow like that anymore. Then he ate the *akutaq* from his own bowl. They both ate from his bowl.

After they ate, the *ircenrraq* gave him a little bit of oil. He gave him half of what he had. He told Cupluralria to take it home. Then they separated. Oh my, while he was returning home the amount of oil he had in his kayak increased.

And then that incident passed. Whenever he went hunting from Luumarvik, he continued to see *ircenrraat*. The people in Luumarvik were probably his ancestors.

Invitational Food and Gift-giving Festivals in the Tundra Villages
Nickolai Berlin, Nunapichuk, January 1994

A man named Kiarte'urluq used to give away lots of food and gifts. He hung bearded seal skins across the [inside] back of the *qasgiq*. Whenever Anguyaluk [his daughter] stood up to dance, she held new rifles at her sides as she began to *ayakata'ar* [start out]. He had arranged that because he was a good hunter.

He bought lots of them [bearded seal skins] from the coast. He bought them for the celebration every year. He hung [at the back inside wall of the *qasgiq*] many bearded seal skins when Anguyaluk danced. He also brought rolls of cloth to give away.

A woman would practice dancing to only one song at the celebration. And another woman would practice for a different song. The man who composed any song would teach the appropriate motions to the dancer. She would learn it right away. Village people would dance every night, starting at the beginning of March. All the villages of Paingarmiut, Nanvarnarrlagmiut, and Nunacuarmiut did that. They would begin practicing their songs.

And when they were ready to invite guests from the other villages— for instance, if people of Nunacuarmiut were ready—they would invite guests from Nunapicuarmiut, Paingarmiut, and Nanvarnarrlagmiut when all the food was ready. They would feed both the guests and their dogs. Some men brought their wives—the younger men usually brought their wives with them. They would dance all night in the *qasgiq*. They began

Tuluq qasgiruaq kia imum piliara Kusquqvagmek pillrat 1890-t nalliitni. Cetaumauluteng yuguat cauyalriit talliman-wa yuralriit. Yuralriit iliit enirarautmek tegumiarluni enirarautiin nuuga yaquleguartarluni. Pikani-wa qasgim qilii qilaamruyaak malruk agalriik tuluq-wa cali yaquleguaq *Ellanguarluteng* yura'arqata pilaucillracetun. Alaska State Museum, Juneau

Ivory *qasgiq* model, probably collected on the Kuskokwim in the 1890s. Four ivory drummers beat time while five men dance. One of the dancers holds an *eniraraun* (dance stick) with a bird at its tip. Suspended from the *qasgiq* roof are two global lamp frames and a small ivory bird like those hung from the *qasgiq* ceiling during the presentation of the *ellanguaq*. Alaska State Museum, Juneau, IIA5350 (28.3 cm high)

Atakuklagmek ayagluteng tua-i erteqatarluk' iliini tua taq'aqluteng, qaqiutaqluteng. Qasqercirluteng-gguq aklunek, lumarrarnek, kapkaanarnek, tuntut-ll' amiitnek, nutegnek tuaten. Qasgimun quyurciluteng nunat taukut, itrulluteng taukut kelelteng cikiutekaitnek, avenqegtarkaitnek, pitarkaitnek. Tua-i-gguq pitarluteng. Tua-i-gguq qasqercirluteng. Tuaten.

Qasqercirluteng-gguq tua-i apeqmeggnek. Wall' yuralria-llu yura'arqan imna-llu tua-i lumarraq tua-i imuaq, imgumalria tamalkuq, nangertaqan yuraqatalria kiugna, nasaurluugaqan-wa tua-i pilalriit angayuqaak, aatii pilalria, qasgikun uivevkarluku taman' lumarraq yuut tegumiaqluku nenglluk', ilii-wa tua-i, ilarrii. Wall'u qaũgna ilavkugmek piluku amirkat-llu maklaaret amirkat, qavcin-llu tayima amlleret iliini, tamaavet teveqluki. Yuraqatalria-gguq tua-i nangrucirluku. Wall'u-llu iliini nutegmek-llu atuumaksailngurmek tegumiarrarluni meng'aqan ayakatararaqluni yuraqatalria. Ilii-llu amirkam makliim qainganun nangerrluni tuss'araqluku yuraqatararaqluni.

Cikiutekauluteng tamarmeng pitarkauluteng tamakut, allanret imkut pitarkaqluki. Kalukalria-llu—ava-i iciw' ata'urlurput kalukaryartularniluku malrurqugnek takumni qanrutkekeka.

Qunun'aq piluku ciumek pitqarraallrani yaquleyagarmek, pitegkengqarraallrani. Taũgken aũgna alqairutvut pillrani, Yuuguralria aglenrraraullrani, tuaten ũgayarcetqatarluku pillrani, nutaan murilkepiarluk' pillruagka. Canek tua-i imkunek-llu kuusqutnek ulligtaruarutnek, tamalkuan tua-i qasgilluku. Qasgilluki cat avenqegtarkait allanret. Akutarugaat-llu qantarugaat akutanek imirluki qasgimun agulluki.

Tua-i tamarmeng pituut tuaten. Kalukartuurluteng tua-i makut. Tuaten tua-i kalukarqameng carrarmek piyuitut.

dancing in the early evening and sometimes finished just before daybreak. People in the host village would bring gifts such as cloth, traps,
caribou skins, and guns to the *qasgiq* for their guests. The items they
brought their guests were *pitarkait* [lit., "things they are to catch"].
Traditionally, the gathering of the gifts and food in the *qasgiq* was also
called *qasqercirluteng.*

Qasqercirluteng was the name they gave the process. Or when someone stood up to begin dancing, especially if the dancer was a girl, her
father would bring in a bolt of cloth and have the assembled begin
unrolling the cloth making a big cloth circle in the *qasgiq.* They would
make a circle with just a portion of the cloth. And one of the men from
the host village would put up a line at the back of the room and hang
bearded seal skins there one after the other. They did those things when
a young dancer stood up to dance and called it *nangrucirluku* [lit.,
"providing one something to stand with"]. Or sometimes a dancer
would hold a brand new rifle in one hand and do the *ayakata'ar* as a
singer began to slowly sing and softly drum the song preliminary to the
beginning of the dance. And sometimes young dancers would do the
ayakata'ar standing on a bearded sealskin.

Every single thing they brought into the *qasgiq* was to be given to
their guests. They were things the guests were going to "catch." And
then there was the person who would present the gifts—you know
earlier I mentioned our poor father going over to Nunapicuaq to give a
kalukaq.

The first *kalukaq* he gave was to celebrate Qunun'aq's [Nick Chris's]
first catch, honoring the first little bird he caught with a bow and arrow.
But when he gave one for our older sister Yuuguralria, at her first
menstruation, I remember the occasion quite clearly. The ritual called
uɡayarcelluku [stripping her of childhood possessions] was done for her.
He brought a woven grass basket filled with dried whitefish into the
qasgiq. He brought things to be divided among the guests. He brought
many bowls of *akutaq* as well.

That's what everyone did in all the villages. Families held *kalukat*
[celebrations] for their children. When they had *kalukat,* they always
brought plenty of things to give away.

11. Ceñarmiut Qanemciit Qulirait-llu, Ceñarmiut-llu Kegginaqut

Arnaq Kegginaqurluni Maklaguanek
Paul John, Nunakauyaq, April 1994

Tua-i-llu maani maa-i Kusquqvagmi qanemciq. Tamaani alangaarpallrat, unkumiut imarpigmiut angutet tamarmeng alangaarpallratnek-am qanemcitangqertuq.

Atam unani imarpigmi maklagnek pitukait, wagg'uq qialuteng nepliatuut anglluumaluteng mermi. Waten-llu taũgaam qaneryarartarluni, pugkuni-gguq tangerrnarqerkaukuni waten ciutegnegun niitnarquq. Niitenrilngermi taũgken cali iliini murak kalevvluku ciutmun tugruciiquq, qalriq taũgaam. Tua-i-gguq tauna ciutegnegun niitevkenaku waten muragkun taũgaam niitnarqelria iignegun tangerrnaituq taũgaam nuuqiignegun pugngermi pugciquq. Tuaten-am kangingqerrnilaraat.

Una waniw' qanemcikqeryuutma aũgna qalriryaraat, tua-i tauna qalrillrani arnaq alangaallratnek angutet unkumiut. Kiagmi urenkutmek-am tailliut unkut ceñarmiut Kusquqvagmi maani kevgirarkauluteng apeqmeggnek.

Tua-i kiugkut tua-i kiani Kuigglugmi mumigarutelliniluteng tamakut kuigmiuqliit ceñarmiuqliteng katurtelluki. Maaten-gguq tang ceñarmiut tua-i katurrluteng kiavet Kuigglugmun piut, tua-i tuaten kegginaqumeggnek qalriuciliriqatalriatangqellinilria apqiitnek. Maaten-gguq tang piut arnamek ilaluteng. Arnauluni tua-i ciungani-ll' imarpigteksailnguuluni tua-i.

Tua-i angutet tamakut nalqigqelluki kegginaqumeng kangiit, umyuartait. Arnaq tua-i taun' tekicatni tauna manillinia kegginaquni maklaguaq, tua-i im' unkumiutaq. Arnauluni tua-i. Qanlliuq, ellii-gguq

Coastal Stories,
Coastal Masks

Woman Presenting a Bearded-seal Mask
Paul John, Toksook Bay, April 1994

There is a story that comes from the Kuskokwim area. It is a story about how all the coastal men were struck with astonishment.

Out in the ocean bearded seals cry out underwater. There is a saying that if a hunter was to see the seal when it comes up, he should be able to hear the cry. And sometimes, even though he couldn't hear anything, if he dipped wood forward in the water he would be able to hear the cry of the seal. They say the one you couldn't hear with your naked ears, but only through that wood, could not be seen but would come up. I've heard that from people.

I wanted to mention something about *qalriryaraq* [way to mimic animal sounds, specifically a large male bearded seal's mating call]. This is an account of a woman who used this method and surprised the coastal men. One summer the coastal people arrived at a village on the Kuskokwim for a ceremony.

The river people and the coastal people gathered in the village of Kuiggluk [Kwethluk] for a ceremony. When the coastal people arrived at Kuiggluk, they learned that their hosts were going to present masks using the *qalriryaraq* method. They also realized that one of the presenters was a woman, a woman who had never gone hunting out in the ocean.

The men began presenting their masks and explaining the meanings behind them. When the woman's turn came she revealed a bearded seal mask. This was a woman doing this. She said that since she was so

Inglukellriik kangirilutek yaassiigcetun kegginaquk pitarkaruagnek kegginarlutek qanragnegun taqukaruak uyangqalutek. Avapailitarlutek muragayagarnek elucqeggianateng ukinrunateng-llu. Nallunaunatek nutaraullermegni tamarmek qaqimalutek qirussingqellruyaaqlutek, aipaan kangrani qirussillra tayim cataunani, aipaan-llu cali avatiini qirussillrit tayim cataunateng. Thomas Burke Memorial Museum, Seattle

A pair of rectangular animal face masks from the mouths of which seal faces emerge. The rings on both are rough and broken on the corners, without holes for attachments. When new, the masks' similarity was more apparent, as one retained its flipper and fish appendages but lost the image attached to the top of the head, whereas the other has a wooden hunter in a kayak on its top but has lost its four side appendages. Thomas Burke Memorial Museum, Seattle, 1.2E642 (36.8 cm) and 1.2E643 (29.5 cm)

waniwa unaken ceñamek tekitellriit unkumiutarmek cikiraqatni quyarpalaami cakneq, tua-i quyalallni pitekluku uumek waniwa imarpigmiutarmek pilivkallruuq ellimerriluni angutmek piliyugngalriamek. Quyalallni pitekluku cingumatekluku elliin, tua-i waten pissurnariaqata pissulriit unani unangqaqulallerkaat pitekluku.

Tua-llu-gguq tua-i qalriuciliriqatarniluku. Qasgit anguqallrenka aũgkut ukinerngalngurnek wagg'uq kalvagyaranek amingqelallruut. Tamakucianun tua-i tayima nallimeqertelluku, tauna tua-i kegginaquq arnam all'uku nallimeqertelluku tayima, tuarpiaq-gguq maklakapik unani mer'em akuliini qialiciryaraacetun, tuarpiaq- gguq nep'ngumaarallermini qalril' tua-i ayuqeqapiarluku.

Tamakut-gguq angutet kinguani qalrirraartelluku qanaaluteng, ugaani-gguq-wa tua-i ayuqessiyaagpakaaku makliim qalriuciryaraa, ava-i-gguq imumek tua-i nep'ngumaarallrani tuarpiaq-llu-gguq angutet ilaita maaggun kevkarrluni una qakmallegtellriit cunguit. Tua-i tuaten ilait qanemciluteng. Tua-i-w' ayuqessiyaagpakaakut makliim qalriuciryaraa. Tauna tua-i arnaq pipiggluku pillrulriamek ap'laraat qanemcikaqamegteggu.

Kegginaqum tua-i atuucian ilii. Tua-i cingumaluki imarpigmiut arnam taum tuatnalliniluni ayayuileng'ermi. Tua-i-llu amiigmun kalvaggluni, nallimluni tayima, nepliruarcetlermini tauna maklak ayuqeqapiarluku-gguq tua-i. Maklagtun nepii ayuqeqapiarluni.

Tutgara'urluq Avelngaam Yuurutellra
Dick Andrew, August 1992

Tua-i-lli-wa-gguq anuurluqellriik uitalinilriik kuigem ceñiini. Tua-i-gguq yuulliniaqellriik tua-i mallurarnek taũgaam tua-i ner'aqlutek. Ilait-gguq nutaraunaurtut mallut. Tua-i tuaten yuulliniaquk. Tutgara'urlua tua-i tauna ayagyuaruluni angevkenani.

Tua-i angturringluni tutgarii tauna, tan'gaurluulliniami. Tua-i ayagataqekii maurluan taum tua-i. Waten-ll' iqvaquaqlutek atsat piurtaqata. Anglinglun' tua-i piyugngaringengluni anuurluan taum tangvallrani. Cakuni tua-i piarkaurrluni.

thankful for the seafood she received from the coastal people when they came, she asked a carver to make a seal mask for her. She was grateful for their gifts and was presenting the mask so their good fortune would continue when they went out hunting.

She told them she was ready to make the mask call out. The *qasgit* I've seen had underground entrances they called *kalvagyaraq* [from *kalvag-*, "to go down, usually into the ground"]. As soon as the woman put on the mask, she exited through the floor opening and disappeared down into the underground entranceway and began to cry out. She cried out exactly like the bearded seal.

After the presentation, the men said she sounded so much like a seal that they felt their foreheads open up and pull back from the experience. Some of them said that was how they felt since she sounded so much like a bearded seal. When people talked about her, they believed she was truly representing the animal.

That was one dimension of the use of the mask. The woman did that to ensure more good fortune for the coastal hunters, even though she didn't go out on the ocean herself. And when she disappeared down through the floor opening into the underground entranceway and cried out, she sounded exactly like the bearded seal.

A Boy Seeing a Tiny Vole-Man
Dick Andrew, August 1992

There was a grandmother and grandchild who lived along a river. They remained there and survived on *mallut* [beached carcasses]. Some of the dead animals they found were still fresh. That was the way they lived. Her grandchild was very young.

Soon her grandchild, a boy, grew bigger. As he grew, his grandmother always took him out into the wilderness. They picked berries when they ripened. He continued to grow until his grandmother considered him old enough to hunt. She knew when he would successfully pursue game.

Caqerluni atam maurluan pillinikii enrilngurmek qagken napamek aqvatesqelluku. Aqvalluni tua-i, naspaaluk' tak'urangraan qaill' pitaluku. Itrucaku enrilnguaq tamana qeltairturalliniluk'. Qeltairluk tua-i. Qeltairraarluk taqngamiu yaateliurluni ancilliniuq qip'armek. Qelulliniluk' iquug-ingkuk piqerluk' urluvercetun piluku, qelulliniluk' tamatumek.

Tua-ll' tutgaraminun tunllinia naspaasqelluk' waten pakiurluku. Pakiurluk' tua-i qelumiin pikni tua-i pakiurluku. Aqvatesqellinia tua-i enrilnguarmek amilnguarmek. Aqvalluni. Tua-i iqua-am terirluku waten piyarirluku, yaateliurluni camek enrrarmek cingiliqerluku, cingilirluku nemrulluku yaavet. Taqngamiu pillinia anluku qagaani cetaarnek yaqulecuarnek napani naspaasqelluk' pitgaquluk'. Anluni tua-i pitgaqulun' yaqulecuar piluk' pitgaraqluni. Iliit caqerlun' nall'arrlug-iggluni. Itrucaaku tua-i maurlurluan taum meqtaqcaaralliniluk' tua-i meqtanqegcaarluku, kenirluku kenicuarluku maurluan taum nerrliniluku.

Aren quyalliniuq taqngami, nangengamiu tauna yaqulecuar. Pilliniuq, "Aren quyanaqvaa-ll' tua-i cavailegma tua-i nuta'arturcetarpenga. Nutaramek tua-i neryaqlirpaa-ll' tua-i." Quyaluni tua-i cakneq.

Tua-ll' kuicuar un'a entaqan tua-i amlliqerlun' ikavet qer'aqertaqluni. Pilliniuq tutgarii agaavet pissuryugluni. Tua-i-ll' maurluan tua-i pillinia kingunra nalluyagutenrilkurrluku yaaqvanun ayaasqevkenaku. Tua-i napani pulaarturluni ayallinilun' egtuugmek tangllinilun'. Tua-i tangrrami pitgaqiini igtelliniluni. Aren anglaningelliniuq tamakunek, anglaniluni pitgaquurluki.

Tua-i-ll' mat'umun carr'ilqamun anlliniuq. Anngami akianun egmian cali ikavet qerarluni, tua-i pitgaquurluni anglanipiangluni tua-i. Anglaniluni. Maaten-am ellangelliniuq murilkenritlerminek unullinilria man'a. Imkut-llu tamaani ellangvailegmi anglaningellermini nekevraartum acianun pitani unilluki. Tua-i nallunairturluki unicaaqluki.

Tua-i ellangelliniuq unillinilria man'. Tan'geriyaurrlun' waten uksuarmi. Qakurnaryaurrluni-llu. Tua-i utertelliniuq atauciq egtuuk tegumiaqurluku. Ellangami utertelliniluni anglanillerminek.

Utertenglliniuq tua-i kinguneqsukmi tungiinun. Imkut-llu tayima unitellni egtuugugaat pitarugani nalluyagulluki tua-i nalliit tayima. Atam

One day his grandmother asked him to fetch a willow branch from outside. He went out and got one, though it was rather long. When he returned with the willow branch, she began to peel off its bark. She removed its skin. When she was finished, she reached to the side and pulled out a twisted thread. Then she strung the stick, lashing both ends to form a bow.

She handed it to her grandchild and asked him to try the string. He drew the bowstring, and it worked. Then she asked him to go fetch a thin willow branch. He went out to get one. Then she carved a little notch at the end and, reaching over again, she pulled out a small bone point which she secured to the tip. When she finished, she told him to go outside and test it on the little birds in the trees. He went out and started shooting at a bird. He hit it and it fell down. When he brought it in, his grandmother plucked it very clean. And after she cooked it she ate it.

Oh my, she was so grateful when she had finished eating the little bird. She said, "Oh, I'm so thankful you have provided me with fresh meat before something happened to me. Oh! it's been so long since I've eaten fresh meat." She was very thankful.

Then, whenever the tide went out in the little river down there, he jumped over to the other side. Her grandchild said he wanted to hunt across there. His grandmother told him not to go far and to watch the direction of his home very closely. Then, when he walked inside the trees, he saw a grouse. You know, the grouse which are dark like ptarmigan. When he shot it, it fell to the ground. Oh my, he began to have fun shooting at them.

Then he came out to a clearing. When he came out he kept going across to the other side, shooting his bow and having a great time. He was having so much fun. When he came to his senses, he noticed it had gotten dark. Along the way he was having so much fun he left his catch under a spruce tree. He left them so he could find them again.

It already had gotten dark when he became aware of what he was doing. It was in the fall, like now. And it was starting to frost, too. He started going home holding one grouse in his hand. Once he was aware of his surroundings, he started going home.

He started going towards what he thought was his home. He couldn't remember where he had left all the grouse he had caught. Then he came

imumun anlleqngalkeminun carr'ilqerpagmun anllinilria. Anngami, tan'geraarmi, ikavet anellmi tunglirneqngalkiikun ukatmun ayagturalliniuq. Ayainanermini necuarmek imumek tekicartulliniluni, tua-i tanqigceñani. Tanqigmek tua-i piluni qamaken kenurramek, kenurrarluni. Tekicamiu qinqalliniuq necuaqegtaar man'a, nerr'ayagaq man'a kenurrarluni. Ikani-wa ingluani acicuar ikna, acirraq ikna. Maaten-gguq tang kiugna egkuq pillinia ipuuksuaraak kiugkuk agauralriik egkumi ingluani-wa qerrullillracuayagaak. Arenqialami mernuami tua tuavet taklartelliniluni acicuarmun. Qavaryartuaraqalliniuq mernuami tua-i piyualnguluni urugarcami. Tamana-ll' enem ilua kiirceterpayagiimi. Qavaryartuaraqanrakun cakemna.

> *Kia kia kia kia kia*
> *Qa-a-lu-raag-ka tai-yar-kek*
> *Uk-suaq-lii-qa-qa*
> *Ca-mek pi-yu-kam-ken*
> *Uk-suaq-li,*
> *Ma-nuu-ka-ma-a*
> *A-nga-a-ngaar i-ngi-i-ngii*
> *Aa-rruu-rra-ya-a-a*

Tupakalliniuq ca qakemna. Ca qakem' qaill' pia? Tuamtell' tua-i nepaircan qavaryartuaraqalliniuq. Tua-ll' qakemna-am imutun,

> *Kia kia kia kia kia*
> *Qa-a-lu-raag-ka tai-yar-kek*
> *Uk-suaq-lii-qa-qa*
> *Ca-mek pi-yu-kam-ken*
> *Uk-suaq-li*
> *Ma-nuu-ka-ma-a*
> *A-nga-a-ngaar i-ngi-i-ngii*
> *Aa-rruu-rra-ya-a-a*

Tua-ll' tupakaami pilliniuq, "Aling ca tam' qakem' pilarta?" Maaten tang piqalliniuq imkuk kiugkuk, "Aren kiugkuk pilalliak cak'mun." Ullagarrlukek qerrullillrayagaak taukuk, "Tua-i qaaluraagken tua-i. Qaaluraagken tua-i. Neplirpiiqnak, qavarnilrianga tang." Egglukek piqalriim tua-i qavaryartuaraqanrakun,

out to a clearing that looked like the one he had seen before. When he came out in the dark, he began going towards where he thought he came out earlier. As he was going, he came upon a little bright house. Light was coming out from a lamp inside. When he reached it, he peeked into it and saw that the inside looked very nice and all lit up. There was a little bed on the side across there. He looked toward the back and saw two little ladles hanging on the wall and tiny little underwear on the side. And since he was so exhausted, he lay down on the little bed. As he was tired from hiking, he began to fall asleep. It was warm inside the little house, and when he warmed up and began to fall asleep, someone out there began to sing,

> *Who who who who who*
> *Would give me my two spoons*
> *Uksuaqli*
> *What do you want*
> *Uksuaqli*
> *My ?manuukaq*
> *A-nga-a-ngaar i-ngi-i-ngii*
> *Aa-rruu-rra-ya-a-a*

He suddenly woke up and heard something out there. He could not tell what it was. When it got quiet, he began to fall asleep again. Then someone out there started to sing again,

> *Who who who who who*
> *Would give me my two spoons*
> *Uksuaqli*
> *What do you want*
> *Uksuaqli*
> *My ?manuukaq*
> *A-nga-a-ngaar i-ngi-i-ngii*
> *Aa-rruu-rra-ya-a-a*

Then when he woke up, he said, "*Aling,* what the heck does he want out there?" Then he suddenly noticed those two back there, "Oh my, perhaps someone out there is asking for those two back there." He ran up and grabbed the little underwear, "Here's your *qaaluraagken* [two spoons]. Here, take your *qaaluraagken.* Would you be quiet, I'm sleepy."

Kia kia kia kia kia
Qa-a-lu-raag-ka tai-yar-kek
Uk-suaq-lii-qa-qa
Ca-mek pi-yu-kam-ken
Uk-suaq-li
Ma-nuu-ka-ma-a
A-nga-a-ngaar i-ngi-i-ngii
Aa-rruu-rra-ya-a-a

Tua-i kiugkuk kiigkenka umyuaqertak, kiugkuk ipuuksuaraak. Ullagarrlukek egtellinilukek qanerlun', "Tua-i qaaluraagken tua- i." Tua-i-ll' qava'urlulliniluni. Nutaan nepaiteqerluni pinqigtevkenani. Taukuk ipuuksuaraak nangengagnek qerrullillrayagaak-llu taukuk nutaan qavalliniluni.

Maaten tang tupagyartulliniuq qerrulluku cakneq. Qerrutqapiarluku. Uilluni maaten piuq ellami maani. Maaten-gguq tang acini tangrraa avelngaam cangluin qaingitni qavallinilria. Avelngaam yuuruyulluku.

Tupalliniuq tuan' maktelliniuq erqaarallinilria, akerta yaa-i pug'qatarallinil'. Tua-i makcami maaten kiarrluni pilliniuq imna man' anvillra im' carr'ilqaq. Tua-i kinguneni tua-i nallunriqerrluku. Tamaaggun ceñirquraqerlun', pitani ataucirraq tegumiaqluku, kuigtek tekicamiu uyangtellinia tua-i eningaluni. Qerarluni. Tua-i uterrluni qerarluni maurluminun. Maurluan pillinia, "Aling tua-i peng'garrluten. Tua-i tekituten cavkenak." Tua-i pitani ketiinun eg'arrluku.

Nutaan taum kinguani tua-i tamakussu'urqelria. Tua-i nutaan tuaten pinqigtevkenani egtuugnek pitgaqulallinilria tua-i. Tua-i tuaten man'a qulriaq taktalriaruuq.

After he tossed them and started to doze off again, someone out there started to sing,

> *Who who who who who*
> *Would give me my two spoons*
> *Uksuaqli*
> *What do you want*
> *Uksuaqli*
> *My ?manuukaq*
> *A-nga-a-ngaar i-ngi-i-ngii*
> *Aa-rruu-rra-ya-a-a*

Then he remembered those two in there. He remembered the two little ladles back there. He ran up and grabbed them and tossed them out saying, "Here's your *qaaluraagken.*" Then it got quiet, and he fell asleep. When the two little ladles and the tiny underwear were gone, he finally fell asleep.

He was very cold when he woke up. He was extremely cold. When he was fully awake, he noticed he was outside on the ground. When he looked at the place where he was lying, he discovered he had slept in a vole's nest. A vole had transformed into a person in order to save him.

When he woke up, he was still holding the grouse he had caught. He woke up in the early dawn, and the sun was just beginning to appear in the horizon. He got up and looked around and found himself in the clearing he had left before. Then he instantly knew where his home was. He walked along for a while, and when he came to where he had come out he looked down to their river and saw that the water was low. He went across. He walked across and returned to his grandmother. His grandmother said to him, "Oh my, I was worried about you. Now you are home safely." Then he tossed his catch down in front of her.

After that he continued to hunt them. What happened to him before didn't repeat itself as he continued to hunt grouse. That is how long this *quliraq* is.

Aanakalliiq
Dick Andrew, January 1994

Tua-i-w' tauna makumiutaukuni tayim—Kuigmiutaulliuq-llu tauna. Nallunrilkait-wa tayima qanemcikestekait. Kuigmiutaungatuq taun'. Kuigmi taman' qanemciullrungatuq. Aanakalliim tuar taun' kegginaqkii tauna. Niitelallruaqa Aanakalliiq. Aanakalliiq ciutegni tekiarrlukek qanerluni.

Aanakalliiq tuaten ayuqellrungatuq yuk mikelnguq tauna. Wall'u-q' cauga taun' kegginaquq taun' avayalirluni. Napanguanek-qaa pingqertuq? Maani tauna Kuigmi kiani yuurtellruyaaqngatuq. Taunguyaaqngatuq tauna Aanakalliiq.

Irniangyuunani tauna arnaq nasaurluq angayuqerluni-llu. Tua-i-llu-gguq irniangyuilan angalkum irniangecetaarluku, irniangevkangnaqluku. Tua-i-llu-gguq an'uq maaten ciutegni tekiarrlukek qanerluni. Tua-ll' inerqullinia aanii talluqesqevkenaku, tua-i talluqesqevkenaku tua-i yugnun iirpegnaku irniaqesqelluku anglikan assiriciqniluku. Tua-i-ll' talluryuglun' cakneq irniayaaminek tauna ket'ni una canegnek tupiganek capluku. Tua-i-am' talluqluku inerqullrungraani taum angalkum talluqesqevkenaku watqapik.

Tua-i-llu caqerlutek angayuqaak unugmi tupagtuk cakemna mecartaqluni qiaryigtaqluni-llu. Maaten tua-i uyangulluk' aipaan naliagnek nulirran-llu pillinia ak'a aanami man'a evsiaran inglua ak'a nangllinikii. Tuqulluku tua-i nerluku. Taunguciqsugnarquq tua-i.

Tua-i-ll' nunat qakemkut elpengcarluki anluni maktesqelluki; ingna ak'a nangniluku irniacuariinun, tauna arnaq. Tua-i-ll' upluteng ayalliniluteng. Uksuarmi. Uksuarmi tua-i asvairluku qanikcangqertelluku-llu. Tua-i-ll' ayalliniluteng. Kuik-llu tua-i avtelliniluku waten negetmun qagaatmun. Tua-i-ll iliit angukaraat pilliniuq, "Imna tang canassuuteka caviggaqa calissuukar-im' nalluyagutellinikeka." Tan'gaurluut iliit uqilali cameg-akilirluku tua-i pinertutaciatun tua-i naspaasqelluk' aqvasqelluku. Aqvalliniluk' kingutmun aqvaqurluni.

Maaten-gguq tua-i tekicarturtuq auĝna mikelngucuar aurrluni tua-i mayurnauraa nepiaq tua-i-llu-gguq egaleq tekiskuniu tayim iggluni.

Aanakalliiq
Dick Andrew, January 1994

If that [mask] is from this area, maybe it is from Kuigmiut. The storytellers would know where it's from. That story may have come from Kuik. It looks like the face of Aanakalliiq. I used to hear of Aanakalliiq. Aanakalliiq's mouth extended to its ears.

Perhaps a child named Aanakalliiq had a face like that. What is that mask with so many appendages? Are those representations of trees? Perhaps it was one that was born up there in Kuik. I believe that's Aanakalliiq.

It is the story of a woman who could not bear children, and her parents were still alive. Using his powers, an *angalkuq* helped her so that she became pregnant. When the baby was born, they were astonished to see that its mouth was so large that the corners of his lips reached his ears. The *angalkuq* told the mother not to be ashamed of him and told her to let other people see him, and he said the baby would become normal when he grew up. However, the mother was very embarrassed, and she hung a woven grass mat in front of their bed. Although the *angalkuq* had cautioned her not to be ashamed, she couldn't help being embarrassed.

Once in the middle of the night her parents woke up to the sound of crunching and gnawing. Being curious, one of them got up and looked behind the mat and saw that the baby had already eaten one of his mother's breasts. He had killed her and was eating her. That mask must represent him.

They awakened and alerted all the people in the village, telling them that the baby had already eaten his mother. Then they all got ready, and everyone left the village. That was in the fall. During the fall the ice had become thick, and there was some snow on the ground. The people reached a fork in the river where one branch headed northward. Then one of the old men said, "Oh no! I forgot and left my carving knife!" He gave a little token to one of the most fleet-footed lads and asked him to run back for that tool. He ran back to get it.

As he approached the village, he saw the child crawling. He crawled to the top of the a house, and when he got to the skylight opening, he

Cuq'errluku tua-i kanaqauciatun aqvaqurluni. Egmian-llu tua-i itqercami caavtaaqerluni keluketukiinun angukaraam taum, nalaqluku. Tua-i anqerrluni aneksaitellinian tua-i aqvaqurluni pulayaratgun ayagluni.

Tua-i-llu ilani tayim ayallruata, imna arulaingqallerteng tekilluku piqalliniuq aren tuntut makut tumait yaatmun ayagluteng. Tua-i-ll' amna kingunerminek piamiu angunayukluni—cukauq-gguq tauna mikelnguq waten aurrelaagaqluni—napamun nekevraartumun mayulliniluni. Mayurlun' tua-i amna kingunranek, "Aanakalliir ner'aqallii." Mayurluk, tua-i-ll' amna kingunranek, "Aanakalliir ner'aqallii." Aurrluni cukanrarluni.

Tua-i-ll' una-i imkut tuntut tumait tekicamiki piuraqerluni-am aturluki yaatmurrluni iqlutmun. Ayagngan tayim catairucan atrarluni imkut ilani maliggluki. Tua-i qagkumiut Aanakalliim kinguveqai. Makumiunguut ilait. Tua-i anagluteng taukut. Arenqiatuq alingnarquq tauna. Qagkumiungurrluteng tua-i taukut Aanakalliim kinguvri.

Angalkuq Ataucimek Iilek
Paul John, May 1994

Tamaani-wa ak'a waten angalkut ilait pinrilengraata-llu uum ilani tuquaqan kamakluku, "Ing'um tuqutellia." Tuaten-am tua-i pillermeggni angutem taum nuliani tuquan kamakluku tauna angalkuq tuqutelliniluku. Tuqucamiu-llu iik ikugglukek allam tuqullrem, kenurralleq tauna qikuq naparusngalriarani uitalria teguluku iik tuavet palurullukek kenurrallermun iirlukek.

Tua-i-ll'-am tauna unguiryuumalliniami ellarramini makcami unguirami yuaryaaqlukek tua-i iigni nalaqesciiganakek.

Tua-i-am ellamini cali, cikirtengqerrsugngiimi nallunrilkengaminek kaigalria iimek ataucirrarmek taum kaigavian cikiani wavet tua-i akuliraminun atauciungan elliluku. Iiluni ataucirrarmek taukugnun angutegnun malrugnun tuaken uksillmeggnek upaggaarluteng aqvailriignun tangercecami waten qanlliniuq, "Waniwa-gguq

fell in. He estimated the time the baby would stay in the house and as soon as the baby fell in through the window, he ran to the old man's house. As soon as he came in, he went directly to the old man's bed and started looking behind it for the knife and found it. Before he went back out, he checked to see if the baby had come out, and, seeing that he had not, he ran out along the path through the bushes.

In the meantime the rest of the people had continued on their flight. And when he returned to the place where they had stopped earlier, he noticed caribou tracks heading in the other direction. Being worried that the baby might catch up with him—they say the child crawled very, very quickly—he climbed a spruce tree. After he climbed up he heard from the trail behind, "Aanakalliiq, I've eaten her." The baby was crawling very quickly.

When the baby reached the caribou tracks, it began to follow them going in the wrong direction. When the baby left and could no longer be seen, he came down from the tree and followed the others. You see, the northern people are the descendants of Aanakalliiq. Some of them live in this area. Having escaped, they survived. That creature was very, very frightening and dangerous.

The One-Eyed Shaman
Paul John, May 1994

Back in those days when someone lost a relative they would blame the *angalkuq*, although the *angalkuq* was not at fault, saying, "He must be the one who killed him/her." There was a man who lost his wife, and, suspecting one particular *angalkuq*, he killed him. After killing him, he pried out his eyes and hid them under a lamp at another burial site.

And since he [the *angalkuq*] was able to come back to life in his own little world again, upon awakening he looked for his eyes but was unable to find them.

And, again in his own world, since he knew of someone who could grant him new eyes, he asked but was granted only one eye, which he put on his nose bridge. One-eyed, he allowed himself to be seen by two men who had come to get some food from a camp and said to them, "Even though I am one-eyed, I know I can become a member of your

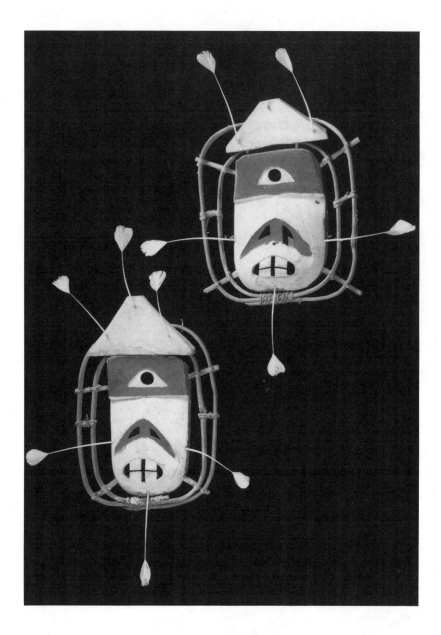

Inglukellriik kegginaquk at021 atauirrarnek iilutek pillrek Robert Gierke-m 1920s-aani. Ellanguarani canguat qirussilkek tayim cataunateng melqunek taugaam kapusvikumalutek. Thomas Burke Memorial Museum, Seattle

A pair of one-eyed masks collected by Robert Gierke in the 1920s. Wooden appendages rather than feathers probably originally projected from the masks' rims. Empty holes with broken feather shafts around the bentwood *ellanguat* indicate that appendages are missing. Thomas Burke Memorial Museum, Seattle, 1.2E632 (31 cm) and 1.2E633 (34 cm)

yuunqigcugngayaaquq iingqeng'ermi ataucirrarmek ilagarluki. Taũgaam-gguq mikelngurnun alikelarnayukluni waten iingqerkuni ataucirrarmek waniw' niugnun taũgaam ayakatartuq." Tamaani niuget aptuit, qilagmek aperyaraitellermeggni, tuqumalriit-gguq nuniitnek. Tuqumalriit niugnek pitullruit tamaani pitullrulliniit.

Tunutellgek
Elsie Tommy, Nuigtaq, May 1992

Cali taumek qanemcimek niitellrulrianga, ak'a avani. Tauna-gguq arnaq, waten up'nerkami makiraqataami uptelliniluni. Ivrucirluni tua-i naquggluni-llu, waten-ll' atmagluni ayaglun' tua-i. Kayangunek tekitaqami tua-i teguaqluk' issratminun ek'aqluki. Tua-i pivakarluni tunutellgem kayanguinek tekicami-am tua-i, malruulutek, tua-i teguqatarlukek tunutellek ciuqerranun mip'allalliniluni. Aarpagluk', "Aa-aa-aa, aa-aa-aa, irniagka atam taukuk uitatqaũrluqerkek! Elpecicetun tang irniamteñek qivrularyaaqelriakut allakaunrilngurmek elpecicetun ellangqerngamta."

Tua-i-ll' taum tangvakalliniluk, arnam taum. "Tegunrilkuvkek nunulirciqamken akwarpak unguvakarpenek irniarpenun kinguvarluni. Irniarpet-llu aturluku cali tamana cali kinguvarluni irniarkaitnun." Tua-i qanrutliniluku.

Tua-i-am taukuk teguyaaqellregni ellilukek tua-i qanerluni tua-i, "Tua-i kitaki tegunrillakek nunuliutekan tamana unguva uinga-llu quyakluku akurtuumaniarqa." Taum tunutellgem angraluku tua-i.

Tua-i-ll' tamakut imkut kayangut avurturallni tua-i enaitnun elliuralliniluk' qaqilluki tua-i. Uterrluni-ll' issratni imaunaku.

Tua-i-ll' tekican pillinia aaniin, "Qaillun pilriaten kayangutenricit? Kayangut-ggem amllertut."

Tua-ll' pilliniuq, "Tua-i-wa kayangucaaqelrianga kayangut ellilaqenka ikayuutekamnek tunutellgem qanrucanga, ilumun unguvamek cikirciullemnek, anelgutenka-llu unguvakaitnek cikiumallerkaitnek quyalua." Tua-i-gguq tauna tua-i tunutellgem taum qanrutellra tua-i ilakelriit-gguq tua-i kinguvallruut tua-i. Maa-i amna atauciq unguvauq, nangneqlikacaaq arnacuayaaq.

community. But I fear that if the children see me with one eye, they might be too frightened, so I am going to the land of the *niuget*." In those days they would talk about *niuget*, referring to the land of the dead, before they started using the term *qilak* [heaven]. The people that died were called *niuget* back in those days.

Two Arctic Loons
Elsie Tommy, Newtok, May 1992

I heard this story a long time ago. A woman was getting ready to go out to gather food in the spring. She put on her waterproof boots and a belt and left with a pack on her back. When she came upon any eggs, she would take them and put them away in her pack. She found two arctic loon eggs, and as she was about to take them, an arctic loon suddenly landed in front of her, yelling, "Aa-aa-aa, aa-aa-aa! Would you please leave my dear children alone. We do grieve over the loss of our children just as you do because we also have awareness and feelings."

Then the woman looked at the arctic loon for a moment [and was told], "If you don't take them, I will grant you a long life which will also be passed on to your children. And your children will also pass this down to their own children." The arctic loon told her that.

She placed the eggs back in the nest and said, "I will not take them for I have gratefully accepted the gift of long life you have granted me." The arctic loon agreed with her fully.

Then she turned back and returned all the eggs she had gathered back to their nests. She went home with an empty pack.

Then when she got home her mother said to her, "Why have you not found any eggs? I thought there were many eggs out there."

Then she said, "I did indeed find some eggs, but I returned them when the arctic loon offered me the gift of a long life, and I gratefully accepted the offer." They say there was a long line of generations that came from that person the arctic loon had spoken to. One is still alive over there now, the last one, a tiny woman.

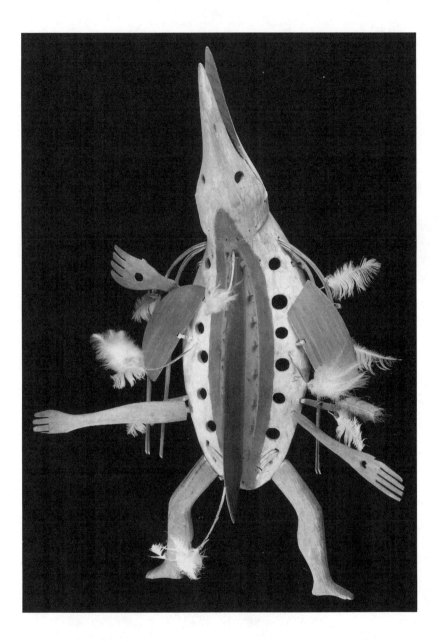

Tuulleguaq kegginaquq St. Micheal-aamek pillra Sheldon Jackson-aam 1892-aami. Tuulleguaq minguumaluni qatellriamek, tungulriamek kavirlimek-llu anipam-llu melquinek kapusvikumaluni. Yuan-wa iruk tallik-llu avategkeni tuulleguam. Tuulleguam-llu uyaqruan keluani muraggaq kapusngaluni yuum all'uku yuraquni tuaggun keggmiaqerkauluku. Sheldon Jackson Museum, Sitka

Common loon mask from St. Michael collected by Sheldon Jackson in 1892. The wooden loon is painted white, black, and red with snowy owl feathers attached. The loon's "person" (*yua*) is indicated by its human arms and legs. The mask has a horizontal bar behind the neck which the dancer held in his teeth, carrying the mask at a forty-five degree angle above his forehead. Sheldon Jackson Museum, Sitka, IIG11 (80 cm)

Qaleqcuuk Qatngutni-llu Kanaqlak
Dick Andrew, January 1994

Tuamtellu-gguq una qaleqcuuk imarpiim qukaani yuulliniaqelria. Waten-gguq tua-i irniangnariaqani imarpiim caarrlui quyurtaqluki. Nunamek-llu tangyuunani yuulliniaqel' qaleqcuuk.

Tua-i tuaten yuulliniluni. Tua-i-gguq irniyaaqnaurtuq kayangululiun' tuavet quyu'urqaarluk' ungluliluk', anuqengaqan-gguq tua-i unglui anuqem navgurluk'. Tua-i irniangesciiganani. Waten im' qanellrulria, "Aling wangi-lli kinguverraiteqatarpaa tua-i. Kinguverraunii wangtun ayuqelriamek kingunemni tangyuiciiqvaa yugni."

Tua-i-ll' waten qanlliniuq, cagmarivakaami tua-i irniaminek kayangumek, qanlliniuq, "Aling natetmun-kiq waniwa tengkuma, kanavatmun tengkuma nunamek tangerrnaciarciqsugnarqua. Cali-ll' negetmun tengkuma cali nunamek tangerrnaciarlua. Tua-ll' kiugkeñetmun tengkuma tangerciqsugnarqua nunamek."

Tua-i tenglliniluni. Teng'engami tua-i mayulliniluni pagaavet qulvanun. Tua-i mernullerkani piluku tua-i qulvani yaqiucuaqaqluni tengaurturalliniluni.

Tua-lli tua-i aūgna ciunra waten tapruagiriqetaarlun' tungulriamek tangengelliniuq. Maaten tang mecignarilliniut ingriullinilriit, ingrit. Ingrit tua-i nall'arrluki tekitelliniluki.

Tua-i-ll' imna tekitniaraami cilungelliniluni, cilungelliniluni. Ingrit-llu pellugluki kelutmun mararuaraq-llu man'a ingritairulluni nunaurrlun' tua-i manigiluni. Tua-i-ll' imna aciqsigiami waten qanertuq, pagaani im' ellurpailegmi qanelria, "Tua-i nunamek tangerpaaluglua yuullemni ketvani uitangaitua, keluqvani uitaciqua." Tua-i-ll' cilulliniluni cilurturalliniluni. Maaten tang aciqsigiami ciuneni tangerqeraa nanvak kankuk waten iqugteklutek akuliik qayikvayagnek imkunek canengqerrluni.

Tua-i-ll' imna mit'eqataami im' kana-i qanlliniuq, "Aling wangni-ll' mic'ara'arciqvaa." Nanvarra'armun tua-i mit'eqatarlun' nanvamun. Maaten tang avatii kiarquraqallinia ikiituut makut, ikiitullret ellangelriit napalriit. Imkut iciw' ikiituut qakimaluki naumatulriit. Ceñiini man' pilirlun' tamaa-i. Ikiituum kangranun mit'eqataaralliniuq mianiklun' tua-i mianiku'urluni aturluni,

Grebe and Muskrat Partners
Dick Andrew, January 1994

There was once a grebe who lived in the middle of the ocean. When it was time for her to lay her eggs, she would gather weeds and grasses in the ocean to build her nest. The grebe lived there, never seeing land.

There she remained. She would gather some grass and try to make a nest. She would gather some grass and weeds and make a nest to lay her eggs, but whenever the wind started to blow, it would destroy the nest. She couldn't have any children. She also said this, "Gosh! I may end up without any descendants. After I'm gone, the likes of me will never be seen by people."

Since she kept losing her eggs, she said this, "Gosh, if I fly away, which way now, for if I fly toward the west, I may not see land for a long time. And if I were to fly northward, I will not see land for quite a while. But if I fly eastward, I might see land right away."

Then she began to fly. As she flew she climbed way up into the sky. Once she was up there she soared, gliding and flapping her wings now and then so she wouldn't get tired right away.

While in flight she saw a dark line ahead of her on the horizon. She got closer and saw that they were mountains. So she went directly to them, arriving at the mountains.

When she got closer to land she began to descend, going lower and lower. She slowly came down and flew over the mountains and reached the lowland area. The land down below became flat and smooth. Nearing the land she said, "Seeing land for the first time in my life, I will not live close to the ocean, but will stay inland." Then she descended, coming down lower and lower and lower. When she got quite low, she saw two lakes separated by a strip of land where wheat grass was growing.

As she was about to land she said, "Gosh, I may be landing too soon." She was about to land on the lake. She looked around the lake and saw wild celery plants around it. They were dried up and pale. You know, when wild celery is not fresh anymore it dries up and turns white. There were many along the shore of the lake. Cautiously she began to land on a celery plant, singing:

Aa-yii-yaa-rra-ngaa ii-aa
A-yii-yaa-rra-ngaa ii-aa
Aa-nga-rraa-aa-ai
I-kii-tu-gaam qa-i-nga-nun
Tus-ku-ma
Mis-ku-ma
Ui-ta-yug-naa
Aa-ni-rraa-ii-aa-rra-nga-ii
Aa-nga-rraa-aa-ai!

Tua-i-ll' imna waten piurluni, tamana-ll' yuarutii iquklilluni, ikiitug-im' ayimtelliniluni nanvarraam tungiinun. Ayimcan aaryullagluni kanavet tua-i igpallallinilun', "Aa-aa, aa-ta-ta-ta-ta!" [*ngelartuq*] Tang tamaa-i qulirat.

Tua-ll' imna mic'ami kuimelliniuq yaavet tua-i qayikvayiit tungiitnun. Tamakucinun tua-i ayagngami nutaan tamaaken aūgauqlun' unglulillinilun' tamaaggun merkun, qayikvayiit maaggun akuliitgun. Nanvarraq taūgaam tamana tangvagluku, ceñeqvaanun tamaavet unglululuni. Nutaan atam unglululuni irniqertelluku, kayangungqertelluku kanaqlak un'a kuimelria ketiikun. Tua-ll' pillinia, "Aling unsuuq qatngutekluk' tang." Kanaqliim kiullinia, "Ii-i, qatngutekluk." [*ngelartuq*]

Ik'ikika-gguq waten piaqami, atrarqami tua-i anglanilalriik kanaqlak-llu. Kuimarlutek tua-i, ellaita tua-i qalriucimeggnek qalriagurluni, "Aa-ta-ta-ta-ta-ta." Tua-i anglaniaqluteng. Pilnguaqami tua-i ataam ungluminun piaqluni. Iciw' maa-i qaleqcuuget kanaqlagtaicuilnguq nuniit. Qatngutekngameng-gguq tua-i.

Paatnaqluteng. Tua-i ilumuuluni tuani qaleqcuuget ukut neplilriit tua-i-ll' ullalriani kanaqlagtaicuunani nuniit, pissutullemni tamaani. Ilumuluteng-am. Paatnaqngameng kanaqliit-llu.

Aa-yii-yaa-rra-ngaa ii-aa
A-yii-yaa-rra-ngaa ii-aa
Aa-nga-rraa-aa-ai
On the wild celery
When I set foot on it
When I land on it
I may stay
Aa-ni-rraa-ii-aa-rra-nga-ii
Aa-nga-rraa-aa-ai!

As her song ended, she landed on the wild celery plant, which snapped and fell toward the lake. When it broke, she got terrified and sang out, "Aa-aa, aa-ta-ta-ta-ta!" [*laughter*] See, these are some of the *qulirat*.

Then when she landed on the water, she swam toward the wheat grass. When she reached the grass, she gathered some and made a nest among the wheat grass. She made the nest close to the shore of the lake. Then, right after she laid her egg in the nest, she noticed a muskrat swimming by her. Then she said, "Gosh, you down there, you should be my *qatngun* [partner, a partnership based on granting each others requests that cannot be refused]." The muskrat answered, "Yes, let's be companions." [*laughter*]

Whenever she came down, she and the muskrat had fun playing together. While they were playing and swimming, she would sing, "Aa-ta-ta-ta-ta." They would have a great time together. When she got tired, she would return to her nest. You know, today where grebes are present, there's always a muskrat nearby. It is because of their special partnership.

They are partners. I found that to be true because when I'd hear grebes while I was hunting, I'd go over to the area where their songs came from and always found muskrats there. It's the truth. It's because they are partners.

Yugtun Igautellrit Mumigtellrit-llu:
Yup'ik Transcription and Translation

The Yup'ik people of southwestern Alaska speak the Central Alaska Yup'ik language, as distinguished from the Inuit/Iñupiaq language of the Arctic coast of northern Alaska, Canada, Labrador, and Greenland. Although structurally similar, Inuit/Iñupiaq and Yupik are not mutually intelligible. In the nineteenth century the Central Alaska Yup'ik language was one of five Yupik languages. The other four of historic times were three Siberian Yupik languages and Pacific Yup'ik (Alutiiq), which was spoken around Prince William Sound, the tip of the Kenai Peninsula, Kodiak Island, and part of the Alaska Peninsula. Together the two language groups—Inuit/Iñupiaq and Yupik—constitute the Eskimo branch of the Eskimo-Aleut family of languages.[1]

The Central Yup'ik language, of which there are four dialects in Alaska (Norton Sound, Hooper Bay / Chevak, Nunivak, and General Central Yup'ik), is spoken by Yup'ik Eskimos living on the Bering Sea coast from Norton Sound to the Alaska Peninsula as well as along the Yukon, Kuskokwim, and Nushagak rivers. The majority of Yup'ik speakers cited in this book speaks General Central Yup'ik, while a handful speak the Norton Sound dialect of Central Yup'ik and Cup'ig, the Nunivak dialect. All four dialects of the Central Yup'ik language are mutually intelligible with some phonological and vocabulary differences (Jacobson 1984:28–37; Woodbury 1984a:49–63).

The Central Yup'ik language remained unwritten until the end of the nineteenth century. At that time both missionaries and Native converts began developing a variety of orthographies. The orthography used consistently throughout this book is the standard developed by linguists

---

[1]Following the Alaska Native Language Center standard orthography, I have dropped the apostrophe when speaking of the Yupik family of languages and retained it when speaking of dialects within Yupik, including Cup'ig and General Central Yup'ik (Yup'ik).

in the 1970s and detailed in *Yup'ik Eskimo Grammar* by Irene Reed, Osahito Miyaoka, Steven Jacobson, Pascal Afcan, and Michael Krauss, *Yup'ik Eskimo Orthography* by Osahito Miyaoka and Elsie Mather, and most recently *A Practical Grammar of the Central Alaskan Yup'ik Eskimo Language* by Steven Jacobson.

The standard orthography for Central Yup'ik represents the language with letters and letter combinations, each corresponding to a distinct sound. The Yup'ik alphabet consists of: vowels *a, e, i, u;* stop consonants *p, t, c, k, q;* fricatives *v, l, s, g, r; vv, ll, ss, gg, rr; y, w, ug, ur;* nasals *m, n, ng.* Included in the standard orthography are three symbols: apostrophe ('), hyphen (-), and ligature or arch connecting two letters (⌒). The standard orthography never represents the same Yup'ik sound with different spellings nor is the same spelling ever pronounced in two different ways.

The following comparison in the new and old writing system will help those people familiar with the old system understand the new one. The example is a Bible translation of John 3:16–25 by the first Yup'ik converts and early Moravian missionaries taken from *Kanerearakgtar:*

> [16]Toiten Agaiutim tlamiut kinikkapigtshamíke kēngan Kitunrani tsikiutika, kina imna itlēnun ukfalra tamaskifkinako taugam nangiyuílingoramik unguvankriskluko. [17]Toi Agaiutim Kitunrak kanerstāriyagtorstinrita tlamiunik, taugam anertōmaskluke itlēkun. [18]Kina imna itlēnun ukfakuni kanerstarumangaitok, kinadlo itlēnun ukfanrílkune kanerstarumauk áka, toi Agaiutim kēngan Kituranun ukfánrilan. [19]Whanewhadlo una kanerstarun, toi tankik nunamun tutngeran yut tanigak kinkinruamigtgo tankigeme, tshaliating ashilata. [20]Ashilingortulrim tamarame nasivaganayukluke. [21]Taugam pitsiulramik atulrim tankik utlālára tshaliane nasivaganalúke toi Agaiutim piskute atuamigtgo.

Johnam angitlorstsistim natlonaitlga

> [22]Makutdlo kinguatugun Jesusak litnauranedlo Judeamun tikitut, toinedlo ilákluke wetauratlrok angitlorstsilunedlo. [23]Johnakdlo angitlorstsimiok Enoname, Salim yaksinritlkēne, merit ametlrata toine; yutdlo utlautut angitlorstifkaraluting. [24]Whanewha Johnak itersimaksaitok tsheli.

> [25]Toidlo Johnam litnaurai Jewsatdlo ilait kangingartut minuertsariarak pitikuko. [26]Johnamundlo ulautluting kanertut, "Ayokutsertorta tangerluko tauna Jordanam akiane ilaktlren natlonairutiktlgendlo angitlortsiok, yutdlo tamaraming itlē utlagat."

Here is the same passage written in the new orthography:

[16]Tuaten Agayutem ellamiut kenkeqapigcamiki kiingan Qetunrani cikiutekaa kina imna elliinun ukvelria tamaasqevkenaku taũgaam nangyuilngurmek unguvangqerresqelluku. [17]Tua-i Agayutem Qetunraq qanercetaariyarturcetenritaa ellamiunek, taũgaam anirtuumasqelluki elliikun. [18]Kina imna elliinun ukvequni qanercetaarumangaituq, kina-llu elliinun ukvenrilkuni qanercetaarumauq ak'a, tua-i Agayutem kiingan Qetunraanun ukvenrilan. [19]Waniwa-llu una qanercetaarun tua-i tanqik nunamun tut'engraan yuut tan'geq kenkenruamegteggu tanqigmi caliateng assiilata. [20]Assiilngurtulriim tamarmi tanqik uumik'laraa ullagyugpek'naku-llu caliani nasvagnayukluku. [21]Taũgaam piciulriamek atulriim tanqik ullalaraa caliani nasvagnaluku tua-i Agayutem pisqutii atuamegteggu.

John-aam angllurcecistem nallunaillra

[22]Makut-llu kinguatgun Jesus-aaq elitnaurani-llu Judea-mun tekitut, tuani-llu ilakluki uitaurallruuq angllurceciluni-llu. [23]John-aaq-llu angllurcecimiuq Enon-ami Sali-m yaaqsinrilkiini mer'it amllellrata tuani; yuut-llu ullautut angllurcetevkarnaluteng. [24]Waniwa John-aaq itercimaksaituq cali.

[25]Tua-i-llu John-aam elitnaurai Jews-aat-llu ilait kangingartut menuircaryaraq pitekluku. [26]John-aamun-llu ullaulluteng qanertut, "Ayuqucirturta tangerrluku tauna Jordan-aam akiani ilakellren nallunairutkellren-llu angllurceciuq, yuut-llu tamarmeng ullagaat."

The Yup'ik language, like all Eskimo languages, is a "suffixing language" made up of noun and verb bases to which one or more postbases and a final ending are added to denote such features as number, case, person, and position. For example, the word *Yup'ik* is derived from the noun base *yug-* (person) to which the postbase *-pik* (real or genuine) has been added, literally "a real person." Similarly, the word *yua,* "its/his/her person" is the same noun base *yug-* with the third person possessive ending.

Because of its reliance on the process of suffixing in the creation of words, Yup'ik and English often appear as mirror images of each other. For example, the English phrase "my little boat" would be written *angyacuarqa,* literally "boat little my" from *angyaq* boat, plus *-cuar(ar)* small, plus *-qa* first person possessive. The English sentence "I want to make him a big box" would translate *"Yaassiigpaliyugaqa,"* from *yaassiik* box, plus *-pak* big, *-li* make, *-yug* want, *-aqa* I-to-him, literally "Box big make want I-to-him." Translation is thus a continuous process of reordering.

As these examples indicate, Yup'ik words generally show a clear division between bases, postbases, and endings, which are "glued" rather than "fused" together, making them easy to identify. Yup'ik is also generally characterized by a one-to-one correspondence between the meaning and the sound shape of a base or postbase, albeit with regular sound changes. As a result, linguists designate Yup'ik an "agglutinative" language, a term derived from a word meaning "to glue" (Miyaoka, Mather, and Meade 1991:13–14).

Several grammatical features make for potential problems in the translation of Yup'ik accounts. First, relatively free word order characterizes the Yup'ik language. For example, the meaning of the English sentence "The man lost the dog" can only be conveyed by placing the words "man" "lost," and "dog" in this order. But a Yup'ik speaker can arrange the three words *angutem* (man), *tamallrua* (s/he lost it), and *qimugta* (dog) in any of six possible word orders with no significant change in meaning. However, it does not follow that word order is totally irrelevant to interpreting Yup'ik sentences. On the contrary, word order may be the sole key to appropriate interpretation where the ending alone would give two different interpretations. For example, the sentence *Arnam atra nallua* (lit., "woman / his name / s/he not knowing it") can mean either "The woman does not know his name" or "He does not know the woman's name." The same three words in a different word order, however, are less ambiguous. *Arnam nallua atra* is commonly taken to mean "The woman does not know his name." As contrasted with relatively free word order, the relative position of postbases inside a word is very rigid. Consequently, a word may have internally such syntactic problems as a sentence has in other languages.

Translation is also complicated by the fact that the Yup'ik language does not specify gender in third-person endings. When elders describe women performing *ingula* dances, we have translated the pronominal ending as "she," as that is the way an English speaker can best understand the Yup'ik orator's intent. Conversely, pronominal endings are translated as "he" when a male shaman performed with a *nepcetaq* mask. In general discussions, "s/he" is used.

The Yup'ik language also handles verb tense differently than the English language. Although some postbases place an action clearly in the future and others place action definitely in the past, a verb without one of these time-specifying postbases may refer to an action which is happening either in the past or present (Jacobson 1984:22). Accounts of events or customs that are no longer practiced in southwestern Alaska have been translated in the past tense. Where tense is specified, it is translated accordingly, for example, "In the past people celebrated the Bladder Festival." For a detailed discussion of Yup'ik grammar see Reed et. al. (1977), Miyaoka, Mather, and Meade (1991), and Jacobson (1995).

The way we refer to ceremonial processes is unlike some published sources. For example, the Bladder Festival has been referred to as *Nakaciuq* (Morrow 1984, Fienup-Riordan 1994). Although the Yup'ik language allows for such nominalizing, the verb *nakaciur-* (to be occupied with bladders) is usually followed by the postbase *+yaraq* (the way to be, do) to designate the ceremonial process, as in *nakaciuryaraq* (the way of doing something with bladders). Similarly, speakers refer to the Messenger Feast as *Kevgiryaraq*, not *Kevgiq*, and so on.

William Tyson (February 27, 1993) recalled, "That was what I observed. . . . I cannot imagine about things and speak, but I can talk about things I know." Indeed Yup'ik oral tradition pays close attention to detail. The line of descent from nineteenth-century Yup'ik traditions to the recollections of contemporary elders is clear. Yup'ik oral tradition is extremely conservative. Many contemporary elders were taught in their youth to carefully attend to the words of their parents and grandparents and never to repeat what they did not know from their own experience. Narrators claim only to speak for themselves. All stress that things were different in other places and that they can tell only about what they have observed or experienced (Morrow 1990). Yup'ik elders, for example, will not tell a story unless they know all its details, and their listeners pay close attention to insure that they make no mistakes.[2] Similarly, they are reluctant to describe past patterns of life, ceremonies, or subsistence pursuits in general. Instead, they consistently give information on the past in the form of first-person narrative in which they describe their own experiences.

Although the exact repetition of events that one has heard or observed is highly valued, Yup'ik storytelling allows orators considerable freedom in the phrasing they choose to elaborate these events. Yup'ik is

---

[2]This is the ideal, and loss through time does occur. Narratives recorded by Bethel students in the 1980s had significant gaps and inconsistencies compared to similar tales recorded prior to 1940.

a complex language in which the same noun and verb bases can be ordered differently or combined with different postbases to produce varying dramatic effects. Although an accomplished narrator does not have the freedom to change the sequence of events, he or she can embellish this sequence with considerable effect. Yup'ik narrative is far from rigid repetition, and no two accounts of the same story, even by the same narrator, are ever exactly alike.

This book would not have been possible without the years of work in bilingual education that preceded it. In the 1970s the bilingual education effort in southwestern Alaska incorporated a standard Yup'ik orthography established at the University of Alaska Fairbanks under the direction of Michael Krauss, making it possible to present accurate transcriptions and translations. Continuing their commitment to the Yup'ik language, Irene Reed and Anna Jacobson contributed dozens of hours to assist Marie Meade in refining her translations. A number of dedicated Yup'ik men and women with years of experience translating Yup'ik into English and vice versa continue to work with taped source material, including Oscar Alexie, Sophie Barnes, David Chanar, Anna Jacobson, Elsie Mather, Marie Meade, and Sophie Shield.

When I began work in southwestern Alaska in the early 1970s, tape recording of Yup'ik narrative was carried out only by linguists and other researchers. By the mid 1970s, however, both the Yup'ik Language Center in Bethel as well as Bethel Regional High School's Foxfire-inspired oral-history project had recorded hundreds of hours of interviews with Yup'ik elders. Although some tapes are technically flawed, many contain eloquent examples of Yup'ik oratory. Transcriptions and translations already have appeared in many publications, including Bethel Regional High School's *Kalikaq Yugnek* [Book from the People], *Yup'ik Lore: Oral Traditions of an Eskimo People* (Tennant and Bitar 1981), *Cev'armiut Qanemciit Qulirait-llu: Eskimo Narratives and Tales from Chevak* (Woodbury 1984b), and Elsie Mather's groundbreaking book on traditional Yup'ik ceremonies, *Cauyarnariuq* (1985).

Interest continues in interviewing Yup'ik men and women and translating their narratives for both Yup'ik and non-Yup'ik speaking audiences. Video recording by KYUK-TV in Bethel also captured the recollections of the last generation of Yup'ik elders to be raised in the *qasgiq*. The challenge facing the handful of Yup'ik men and women engaged in translation work today is to find ways both to preserve and to share this rich cultural resource.

Glossary

agayu/agayut. Religious representation/representations to which or through which prayers and supplications are offered; mask/masks (Nunivak Island); prayer/prayers or supplication/supplications

Agayu. Ceremony in which prayers are offered using masks.

agayu-. To beseech, to participate in a ceremony, to pray.

Agayuliyaraq. The way to make prayers, supplications.

Agayuyaraq. The way or process of praying or beseeching.

agenra. Chorus of a dance song, usually repeated during performance (lit., "its result of going from one place to another without crossing a barrier").

aglenrraraak. Two females who have reached puberty, two who have menstruated for the first time.

akutaq. Lit., "a mixture." Name given a food considered a delicacy which often includes berries, seal oil, shortening, boned fish, etc., and also sugar since its introduction.

aling. An exclamation used to indicate mild fear, surprise, or remorse, often translated as "Gosh!", "Oh!", or "Oh my!"

amikuk. A legendary creature, usually depicted as one difficult to capture, and often described as quite changeable.

angalkuq/angalkut. Shaman/shamans.

apallirturcuun. Dance stick (lit., "device for directing the singing of lyrics of dance songs").

apalluq/apallut. Song verse/verses and their lyrics.

aren. An expression indicating amazement or sometimes dissatisfaction when something goes wrong or when a mistake is made, often translated as "Oops!", "Gosh," or "Goodness."

arenqiapaa. An expression indicating astonishment, amazement, or excitement, often translated as "Oh my goodness."

arula/arulat. Motion dance/dances accompanied by songs with verses (*apallut*).

atam. An expression used to catch or direct a listener's attention to something.

avangcaq/avangcat. Mask/masks with appendages.

aviukaqsaraq. Ceremonial offering of food to spirits of the deceased.

ayakata'ar. A slow start at the beginning of a dance before the main movement (lit., "gradually about to go").

cangerlak. Bad luck, hard times, hardship, disease causing an epidemic.

Cauyarvik. "Place or time for the drum or drumming"; November.

caviggaq/caviggat. Man's carving knife with a curved blade, sometimes called a crooked knife (lit., "small piece of metal").

curukaq/curukat. Invited guest/guests to a *Kevgiryaraq* (Messenger Feast), from *curug-* "to challange, attack."

(c)ella agniluku. "(C)Ella crossing over," from *agni-* "to say or indicate that someone or something is going from one place to another without crossing an extended obstacle."

(c)ella. Weather, world, universe, awareness, sense.

(c)ellam iinga. Eye of *ella,* eye of the universe, eye of awareness.

(c)ella maligglugu. Following *ella.*

(c)ellam yua. Person or owner of the universe.

(c)ellange-. To become aware, to gain cognizance of one's surroundings.

(c)ellanguaq/ellanguat. Representation/representations of a given universe; a diorama (lit., "pretend or model world/worlds").

(c)ellanguaryaraq. The way to ensure *ella*'s benevolence [to the people]; the way to model *ella.*

ellugturyaraq. Symbolic brushing away of disease and afflictions during ceremonial dances (lit., "the way to repeatedly brush off things for some time").

Elriq. Ceremony for clothing the namesake of the deceased.

eniraraun/enirarautet. Dance stick/sticks, pointer/pointers (lit., "something/things to keep pointing with").

erenret. Days, dawning light.

evcugturyaraq. Brushing something away, brushing something off; dialect variation of *ellugturyaraq.*

eyagyarat. Ways to follow traditional practices, often abstinence, associated with birth, death, illness, puberty, and various other rites of passage.

Iicillra. A Yukon expression indicating amazement, astonishment.

iinruq/iinrut. Amulet/amulets; contemporary word for medicine.

iluraq. Male cross-cousin of a male, and by extension male friend of a male, especially one who is related.

imarnin/imarnitet. Seal-gut raincoat/raincoats.

ineqsuyugluteng. Celebration of an event marking a child's achievement of some kind, such as the first time the child completed a task or did something special (lit., "they are joyfully moved").

ingigun. Topographical indication of a natural feature usually seen from a distance, e.g. the edge of a lake, the ridge of a hill, rock formations on the beach, etc.

ingleq/ingleret. Wooden sleeping platform/platforms; bench/benches in the *qasgiq*.

ingula. Dance performed by women to *ingulaun/ingulautet*.

ingulaun/ingulautet. Slow, old-style song/songs to accompany an *ingula* dance.

ircenrraq/ircenrrat, ircir/ircit. Extraordinary person/persons that may appear in either animal or human form, often called "little people."

kalukaq. Celebratory feast.

kalukarluteng. They are celebrating, marking the event of a child's first catch or successful accomplishment.

kalvagyaraq. Underground passage in the *qasgiq* leading to the entrance from the floor, used as an exit during the winter (lit., "way to go down").

kass'aq/kass'at. White person/people, Caucasian.

kegginaquq/kegginaqut. Mask/masks (lit., "thing that is like a face").

kepun. Adze.

Kevgiryaraq. Traditional Messenger Feast.

kingullugqaqluki. They sang teasing or ridicule songs.

mellgar/mellgaraat. Man's carving knife/knives with a curved or bent blade, sometimes called a crooked knife.

merqelluki. Ceremonial anointing with water.

mimernar. Tree stump.

nangerceciyaraq. Way to make one stand up to present his/her first formal dance (from *nangerte-*, "to stand up"). See also *tukerceciyaraq*.

nangrucirluku. Providing him/her something to stand with.

negeqvaq. North, north wind.

nepcetaq/nepcetat. Shaman mask/masks (lit., "something that sticks," from *nepete-*, "to stick, cling, or adhere").

neqlicaraq. Ceremonial food offering to the namesake of the deceased.

niirarautet. See *enirarautet.*

nukalpiaq. A young adult male in the prime of life, usually a good hunter.

nukalpiartaq. A man more accomplished as a hunter than a *nukalpiaq.*

nunal'ircelluki. They made them feel welcome (from *nunalircete-,* "to provide someone with *nuna,* 'land' or 'ground'").

payugarciyaraq. The way to *payugarci-* (to take a snack over to a friend, relative, or neighbor).

pitarkait. Gifts the guests are going to receive (lit., "things they are to catch by hunting").

pualla. Fast-paced, northern-style standing dance performed by men.

putu. Standing dance performed by women while men perform *pualla.*

qagan. Lake from which a river flows.

qairvaaq. Huge, rolling movements of the ocean, huge waves, or water swells.

qalriryaraq. The way to call or cry out like an animal, specifically a large male bearded seal's mating call.

qamiqurnaq. Tree stump (from *qamiquq,* "head").

qasgiq/qasgit. Men's communal house with sweat bath, community center.

qaspeq/qasperet. Cloth parka cover/covers.

qasqercirluteng. They are gathering gifts and food in the *qasgiq* during a celebration/ceremony.

qatngun/qatngutet. Special friend/friends or cousin/cousins from whom one can request things and expect compliance.

qavaruaq. Lit. "pretend sleep"; the first hand motion in a *yurapiaq* dance.

qilaamruyaat/qilaunruyaat. A wooden piece with a light inside hung from the ceiling in the *qasgiq* while people danced.

qirussiq/qirussit. Wooden decoration/decorations or appendages around the mask.

quliraq/qulirat. Ancient time/times; story/stories from the time of the ancients; persona/personae from *qulirat* stories.

quugaarpak. Legendary creature said to live underground and emerge in bodies of water, revealing its relatively small head compared to its large body size.

taitnaurluteng. They are singing *taitnauq* songs to request something be brought into the *qasgiq* as a contribution or gift (from *taite-* "to bring over").

talircuutet. Songs for Iñupiaq-style line dancing.

talirluteng. Iñupiaq-style line dancing.

tarvaryaraq. Ritual cleansing or purifying with smoke from burning wild celery, wild parsnip, or tundra tea.

tekiqata'arcuun. Proper arrival or entrance dance (lit., "thing used to gradually arrive").

tukerceciyaraq. A debut, formal presentation in public, coming out ceremony (lit., "letting one hatch"). See also *nangerceciyaraq.*

tuluvkuyuggaq. Feather.

tunturyuaryuk. Rival of porcupine; a cariboulike character, also known from Bristol Bay, perhaps a traditional story character (also the name for the "Big Dipper").

tutgara'urluq. Grandchild, orphan child.

tuunraq/tuunrat. Animal/animals or extraodinary being/beings that help the *angalkuq.*

uiteraq/uiterat. Red ocher.

uǵayarcelluku. When a girl reaches puberty, a ritual done stripping her of childhood possessions (from *uǵayar-,* "to strip bare, to rob or pillage").

urasqaq/urasqat. White clay.

Usuuq. Vocative (calling) form used, instead of the personal name, to call the attention of a person near you when you want his or her attention.

uyangssuarluni. Rhythmic bobbing of the knees in dance by a woman, knees bent together.

yua/yuit. Its person / their people (possessed forms of *yuk,* "person"); its owner / their owners; his or her child / their children.

yuguaq. Effigy (lit., "imitation person").

yuk/yuut. Person/people, human being / human beings.

Yup'ik/Yupiit. Real or genuine person/people (from *yuk,* "person").

yurapiaq/yurapiat. Long story dances performed by women (lit., "real or genuine dance/dances").

yuraq/yurat. Generic term for Yup'ik dancing, also used to distinguish *arula* dances, consisting of both verses and a chorus.

yuarun/yuarutet. Dance song/songs.

Generally, unpossessed nouns ending in *q* are singular, *k* dual, and *t* plural.

References

Bethel Regional High School Students
  1975–76 *Kalikaq Yugnek* [Book from the People]. Bethel, Alaska: Lower Kuskokwim School District.

Jacobson, Steven A.
  1984 *Yup'ik Eskimo Dictionary.* Fairbanks: Alaska Native Language Center, University of Alaska.
  1995 *A Practical Grammar of the Central Alaskan Yup'ik Eskimo Language.* Fairbanks: Alaska Native Language Center, University of Alaska.

Mather, Elsie P.
  1985 *Cauyarnariuq* [A time for drumming]. Alaska Historical Commission Studies in History, no. 184. Bethel, Alaska: Lower Kuskokwim School District Bilingual/Bicultural Department.

Miyaoka, Osahito, and Elsie Mather
  1979 *Yup'ik Eskimo Orthography.* Bethel, Alaska: Kuskokwim Community College.

Miyaoka, Osahito, Elsie Mather, and Marie Meade
  1991 *Survey of Yup'ik Grammar.* Anchorage: University of Alaska, Anchorage.

Morrow, Phyllis
  1984 "It Is Time for Drumming: A Summary of Recent Research on Yup'ik Ceremonialism." In *The Central Yupik Eskimos,* edited by Ernest S. Burch, Jr. Supplementary issue of *Etudes/Inuit/Studies* 8:113–40.

Reed, Irene, Osahito Miyaoka, Steven Jacobson, Pascal Afcan, and Michael Krauss
  1977 *Yup'ik Eskimo Grammar.* Fairbanks: Alaska Native Language Center, University of Alaska.

Tennant, Edward A., and Joseph N. Bitar, ed.

1981   *Yupik Lore: Oral Traditions of an Eskimo People.* Bethel, Alaska: Lower Kuskokwim School District Bilingual/Bicultural Department.

Woodbury, Anthony C.

1984a   "Eskimo and Aleut Languages." In *Arctic,* vol. 5, *Handbook of North American Indians,* edited by David Damas. Pp. 49–63. Washington, D.C.: Smithsonian Institution Press.

1984b   *Cev'armiut Qanemciit Qulirait-llu: Eskimo Narratives and Tales from Chevak, Alaska.* Fairbanks: Alaska Native Language Center, University of Alaska.

1987   "Rhetorical Structure in a Central Alaskan Yup'ik Eskimo Traditional Narrative." In *Native American Discourse: Poetics and Rhetoric,* edited by Joel Sherzer and Anthony C. Woodbury. Pp. 177–239. Cambridge, England: Cambridge University Press.

This book is set in ITC Stone Serif and ITC Stone Sans from Adobe Systems Incorporated. Custom characters for Yup'ik were generated using Altsys Fontographer. Final editing and layout was done on an Apple Power Macintosh 6100 with a Radius Two Page Display/21gs using Adobe PageMaker.